Completing the Puzzle:

A Brain-Based Approach to Learning

Eric Jensen

Completing the Puzzle:

A Brain-Based Approach to Learning

©1996 Eric Jensen

ISBN # 0-9637832-5-4

Dedicated to the pioneers of Brain-based learning:
Renate & Geoffrey Caine, John Dewey, Leslie Hart,
Jean Houston and Susan Kovalik.

Additional copies may be ordered through the publisher listed below. For 25 or more copies, write, call or fax for volume pricing. Check, purchase order, Visa and Mastercard accepted. See money-saving video and workshop offer in appendix for details. Publisher contact:

Turning Point Publishing
Post Office Box 2551
Del Mar, CA 92014 USA
Phone (619) 546-7555
Fax (619) 546-7560

Preface

My personal interest in understanding the brain evolved slowly over many years. As a former reading and study skills teacher, I've always been interested in *how* we learn as much as what we learn. My first exposure to a brain-compatible course was a business workshop in June of 1980. It was based on the accelerated learning methods developed by Bulgarian pioneer Dr. George Lozanov. The impact on me was immediate. I asked myself, "How can we do this with teenagers?" Soon after, I envisioned an accelerated, brain-based, learn-to-learn program for teens. Based on this vision, myself and two partners formed an experimental, cutting-edge, academic immersion program.

The program was successful beyond our dreams. Graduates activated their intrinsic motivation, participated more in school and grades went up dramatically. The program became the subject of doctoral dissertations and was highlighted in the media internationally. From *Good Morning America* to *USA Today, The Wall Street Journal* and *CNN*, people took notice. Today, with nearly 20,000 successful graduates, attendees from all 50 states and many foreign countries, the proof is in: Brain-based learning approaches change lives. It turns discouraged learners into hungry-to-learn success stories. The evidence is not just anecdotal; over 10,000 pages of follow-up research on the students of brain-based learning corroborates this exciting phenomenon.

This book calls for the initiation of an educational paradigm change. The implications of these "brain-based" discoveries are going to be widespread and profound. We can make the essential changes needed in education if we collectively make it important enough to do so. Almost every change suggested in this book is either free or can be done simply at a surprisingly affordable cost. It's no longer a question of "Can we?" Let's admit we do have the resources needed to do the job now. The greatest fear of humanity is not that we are inadequate. Our greatest collective fear is that we are greater than we've ever given ourselves credit for. Can you step up to the challenge and accept the unique opportunity of transforming education? The world is waiting.

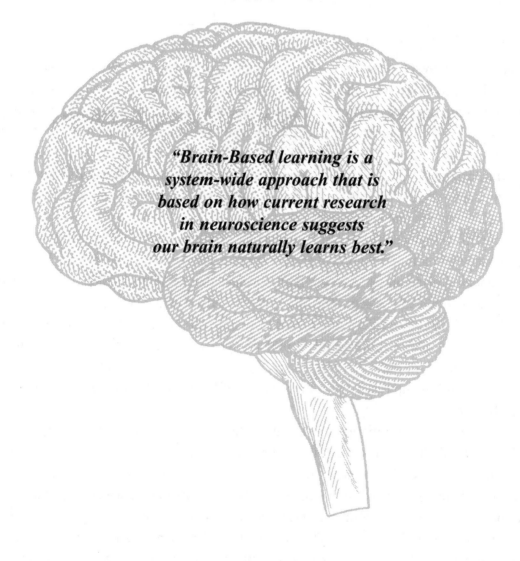

"Brain-Based learning is a system-wide approach that is based on how current research in neuroscience suggests our brain naturally learns best."

Table of Contents

Introduction

Upon hearing the phrase "brain research" some people may recoil as if a schoolmarm of yesteryear is scraping fingernails across a chalkboard. "What does THAT have to do with me, in my classroom?" It turns out that brain research has a great deal to do with your classroom. There's an explosion in brain research that is sending shock waves throughout learning, teaching and education. Stunning and dramatic discoveries may force all of us to look much closer at what we are doing in the classroom.

A common conclusion is, "I think and learn, therefore I know something about thinking and learning." But that's as crazy as saying, "I drive my car, therefore I understand how my engine works." Many now realize that we never had a coherent foundation for learning, it was merely a model for teaching and controlling the learners. Some educators and scientists now suggest we stop altogether and redesign what we do and how we do it.

The new paradigms of learning are emerging with spellbinding implications. They're a marriage of many powerful concepts in neuroscience including the role of emotions, patterns, gender differences, nutrition, environments, rhythms, biology, assessment, music, memory and enrichment. If these postulates hold true, many of our conventional educational models will be shattered like glass. Some would say, it's about time. The name for this new discipline is "Brain-Based Learning."

Predictions are this new field will continue to grow with the fervor of a windswept brush fire on a hot autumn day. But just as with anything, there ought to be a voice of caution. Brain research doesn't "prove" anything. Research merely suggests more "brain-appropriate" strategies. Will these strategies work all the time? No. They are not 100% foolproof because humans are different, humans make mistakes and humans cannot be caged and measured like rats. The discoveries and strategies implicated in this book are, however, all backed by strong evidence. As a result, this claim can be made: ***When we design learning around basic principles of how the brain learns, motivation, meaning and recall increase for all learners.***

Most schools are designed to be antagonistic to the natural and effortless way the brain can learn. That's because, over time, efficiency, economy, pleasing special interests and imposed agendas have created systems that have forgotten the main player, the human brain. These systems wear down an already over-burdened staff. They all miss the larger and more key issues. Schools ought to be designed to run around a simple concept: "How does the brain learn best?" and "How can our organization support that learning?"

The research on applied brain research is both compelling and comprehensive. We are all natural learners, so it's increasingly critical to understand how we, as human beings, learn best. Secondly, when students are provided with a learning environment that is optimal for learning, most learning difficulties disappear, most discipline problems are reduced by 90% and graduation rates go up. Students love learning, and with brain-based learning, most schools find that they can focus on the real issues, not the distracting peripheral ones.

The brain-based learning approach is no fad; it's neuroscience. It's tested and classroom-proven. Isn't how the brain learns fundamental to all that we do? In short, designing and organizing an organization around the way the brain learns best may be the simplest and most critical core reform to be initiated. Of all the changes that can be made and are being made, nothing will give you a better return on your time, effort and money as the developing "brain-based learning" paradigm. In the last 30 years, every single reform that came and went demonstrated examples of brain-antagonistic learning. If it's truly right for the brain of the learner, it sticks around. If it's not, it passes with the Edsels and other fads. *This is no "add-on" or passing notion...This is a genuine revolution in the way we learn...The paradigm shift is moving quickly.*

In its early stages, the brain-based movement was focused on isolated areas of research applications. Now, years after Hart's groundbreaking book, *Human Brain, Human Learning* and Caine and Caine's *Making Connections,* the pieces of the puzzle are coming together with great excitement. For the first time in recorded history, we can assemble a coherent biological framework of learning based on the way the brain is naturally designed to learn best. Far from any fad, it may be the most important educational breakthrough of the last hundred years.

At the same time, two of the frustrations of those who envision and articulate a new paradigm are the lack of empirical evidence and absence of social agreement. You'll find little mention of it in most books, journals and conferences. The staff at schools of education are routinely unaware of this revolution in neuroscience, one equivalent to the Renaissance. Most importantly, very few schools have leaders who either understand it or demonstrate the possibilities.

A common question I hear is, "If this new stuff is so great, where is it being used?" While perfectly understandable, the question is rhetorical; countless brilliant ideas have been slow to become a part of our lives. "If recycling is so great an idea, why isn't every school, business and home on this planet using it?" In time, more of us will. Right now, in learning organizations across the globe, determined individuals, cooperating teams and whole communities have successfully implemented brilliant, innovative, low-cost, brain-based solutions. We are slow to change habits; it's part of the brain's design. Plus, we have investments to protect and there is comfort and security in the known. In this climate, change takes time.

Fortunately, we live in a demanding world where many excited educators are willing to risk "the tried and true." Many have the courage to admit that twenty years of educational reforms have not produced the hoped-for results. In fact, in many areas, things are worse. Never before has there been so much at stake in education. Fortunately, never in our history have we gained so much insight about the function of the human brain. Never before have we linked so much brain research with educational practices so thoroughly. Never before have people been so ready to make the calculated leap to this new paradigm.

This book examines the initial stages of an entirely new paradigm in education. I am proposing a model in which we promote learning the way the brain is best and biologically designed to learn. In this crucial time in history, it seems that more of our future hangs in the balance than ever before. As a result, we must share what we know works, as quickly and as effectively as we can. Let's all pull together and make it happen. We have the knowledge, the resources and motivation. If not now, then when? If not you, then who?

While the early pioneers of the brain-based movement emphasized instructional practices, the larger picture has come together. In order to get optimal results, a complete approach, with all the parts, is needed. Start with an understanding of the brain. We'll do that in chapter one. Then learn the five areas that make up the brain-based approach. They are: instructional strategies, environments, curriculum, assessment and organizational structure. Unless all five areas are implemented, you'll get diluted results. This book reveals the keys from each of the five areas. It's a purposeful, orchestrated approach to learning and educational success. It's a journey which begins with the simple premise of understanding the brain. From that start, everything will fall into place. I promise.

Completing the Puzzle:

A Brain-Based Approach to Learning

Eric Jensen

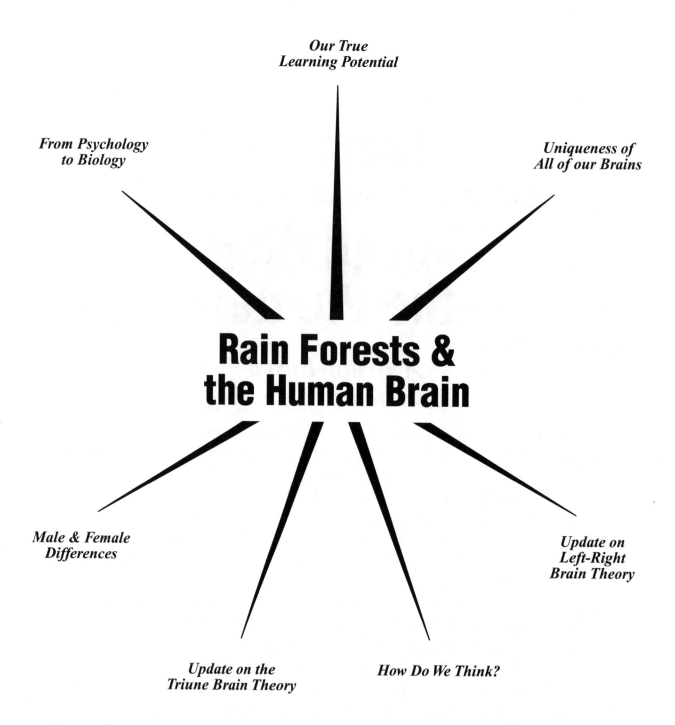

Our True
Learning Potential

From Psychology
to Biology

Uniqueness of
All of our Brains

Rain Forests &
the Human Brain

Male & Female
Differences

Update on
Left-Right
Brain Theory

Update on the
Triune Brain Theory

How Do We Think?

Chapter 1
Rain Forests and the Human Brain

Human Brain, Human Jungle

The history of technology has been a popular source of brain metaphors. Not coincidentally, the brain has been referred to in the 20th century as a telephone switchboard, a computer, a holograph and a massive city. The good thing about metaphors is that they can give you a framework for understanding. The bad thing about metaphors is that an inappropriate one can steer you in the wrong direction.

An orchestra could serve as a metaphor for understanding the brain; some neuroscientists prefer talking about the brain as a hormone-laden gland. Given what we now know about the brain, you may best appreciate the metaphor of it as a rain forest jungle. The jungle is active at times, quiet at times, but always teeming with life. The brain is similar. It is very active at times, much less at others, but always alive and busy. The jungle has its own zones, regions and sectors: the underground, the streams, the ground cover, the low plants and shrubs, the air, the taller plants, the trees, etc. The brain has its own sectors for: thinking, sexuality, memory, survival, emotions, breathing, creativity, etc. While the jungle changes over time, one constant remains true - the law of the jungle is survival *and no one's in charge!*

Just as no one runs the jungle, neuroscientist Michael Gazzaniga reminds us that no *single region in the human brain is equipped to run our brain.* It is well-connected, but there's no single "command center" for best efficiency. The author of the books *Brainstorms and Consciousness Explained*, Dr. Dennett calls our neurons, "armies of idiots...each working on its own draft of reality." Sound like a jungle? Everyone and everything participates to make the "jungle production" happen. A plant may not communicate with a bird or monkey, but it is used by them for housing, food or survival. Professor of physics at Syracuse University, Erich Harth says, "There is now a strong consensus that the putative unification of sensory perception and their elaboration...is nothing but a figment of our imagination." It's a wild concept, this brain of ours. Everything works towards "the big show" which is our life and its maintenance.

Keep that concept in mind; that the brain is best at learning what it needs to learn to survive – socially, economically, emotionally and physically. From your typical student brain's point of view, remember that "academic success" is often quite low on its list of to dos!

The analogy of the jungle is especially important when we consider classroom learning. A jungle has no "teacher" or "trainer." It is simply a rich, evolving system. The jungle has no short or long-term goals with one exception: the genetic goal is survival. It simply does everything it can to exist, both systematically and ecologically. In fact, it is messy, overlapping and inefficient in many ways. Our brain is similar. We have huge amounts of useless information stored, extinct programs running, and yet it still manages to help us survive. When we talk about the "real world" and say "it's a jungle out there," we mean it.

The brain is best at learning what it needs to learn to survive – socially, economically, emotionally and physically

From Psychology to Biology

In the 50's and 60's the dominant theory of human behavior (and resulting educational paradigm) came from the doctrines of behaviorists John Watson and B.F. Skinner. Their reductionist theories went something like this: "We may not know what goes on inside the brain, but we can certainly see what happens on the outside. Let's measure behaviors and learn to modify them with behavior-reinforcers. If we like it, reward it. If we don't, punish it." The educational system of the Western world "bought into" these theories on a grand scale. As a result, schools have continued to increase the measuring, defining and recording of behaviors.

You might protest and say, "That's the past. Haven't we also incorporated the work of Dewey, Piaget and Gardner into the system?" By and large, no. The most brain-based schools are those which utilize the multi-sensory, real-life approach, avoid rewards, are based on relationships and use thematic curriculum. Only a few schools including many of the Waldorf/Steiner Schools, Montessori and other isolated examples really "walk the talk." In general, most schools still run with an emphasis on content, control and imposed learning. Most schools separate and ration the arts, music, movement and creativity. Second languages are rarely taught in elementary years when the brain is best suited for it. They use rewards and punishments in everything from grades to discipline policies. The reality is that most kids go to school for only two reasons: it's the law, and their friends are there.

However, during the 1980's a whole new breed of science was quietly developing. By the 90's, it had exploded into dozens of mind-boggling sub-disciplines. Suddenly, seemingly unrelated disciplines were being mentioned in the same science journal articles. Readers found immunology, physics, genes, emotions and pharmacology seamlessly woven into articles on learning and brain theory. The new cutting-edge voices in the field of neuroscience featured names like Alkon, Gazzaniga, Crick, Rose, Damasio, Calvin, Squire, Herbert, and Edelman. Drawing from a wide multi-disciplinary body of technical knowledge about the brain, a new, paradigm-shaking proposition has developed. The importance of this paradigm to those who teach or train is stunning. It is no less than the destruction of our old behaviorist model of instruction.

Nobel-Prize laureate Gerald Edelman says our brain, biologically and functionally, does primarily whatever it has to in order to survive. He suggests much of our brain is neurologically pre-wired to learn. We have a predetermined genetic "menu" to select from, which we got from our parents. This includes the capacity to learn the 52 sounds of universal languages, their intonation and syntax. It also includes the ability to write, sing, create and play music, to think, plan, draw, problem-solve, sculpt, act, learn and a thousand other talents, each of which can be nurtured to varying degrees. Another Nobel Prize contender Michael Gazzaniga, says "...acquiring the capacity to speak French or English... or for that matter, any capacity – may reflect *little more than a specific environment guiding one of dozens of built-in systems to arrange and process information...."*

Our Biological Imperative

It may be that biologically, we are developing a better brain every generation by natural selection. *When we thought the environment (instruction) was teaching the organism, some feature of the organism may have, in fact, been merely stimulated to grow.* It's a sobering thought about the role of the teaching profession. San Diego bioanthropologist Willis asserts that "...(the new model)...demonstrates by cold and incontrovertible mathematics that most evolutionary change is not driven by natural selection at all. Instead it can be explained more simply, cleanly, and convincingly by random events–mere throws of genetic dice." In either case, through instruction or selection, the older behaviorist model is dead.

Neuroscientists today propose a stunning corollary to the earlier paradigm of the brain being designed to survive. Gazzaniga, author of *Nature's Mind* puts it best (you might like to read this next statement twice): *"Learning may be nothing more than the time needed for an organism to sort out its built-in systems in order to accomplish its*

The brain is poorly designed for formal instruction, it is not at all designed for efficiency or order... Rather, it develops best through selection for survival

13

goals." There's more: he also argues that from a biological perspective, *"...all we are doing in life is catching up with what our brain already knows."* Now, try and figure out implications for *that* in today's educational climate. You might have guessed that this book is only the start to a new way of thinking.

Joseph Pearce, author of *Evolution's End,* says we really can't teach the learner; we can only put them in environments which stimulate their pre-programmed learning. That's a strong imperative for providing the enriched "gifted" curriculum to *every learner.* No more tracking, no more low expectations. What Gazzaniga tells us is, you'll never know how intelligent a learner is *until you place the learner in an environment in which it makes sense for that ability, talent or intelligence to develop* (author's emphasis). The bottom line is, our brain is pre-wired to learn *what we need to learn to survive.* The brains that are "poorly-wired" (have considerable neurological damage) would, in the past, have had a lower chance, genetically, for survival. Theoretically, over time, they would disappear from the genetic pool.

Nature's biological imperative is simple: No intelligence or ability will unfold until or unless given the appropriate model environment

What we are talking about is simple: nature is evolving the best brains through natural selection. The "jungle of life" has no special programs for plants that need extra fertilizer or for birds that sing poorly. They survive or they don't. From a biological perspective, the fact that our brain, like our immune system, is designed solely for our survival, is important information. It implies dramatic changes in the way we organize formal education.

For starters, think of teaching as "learning to get out of the way of the learner." The brain is trying to learn, in order to survive. Design learning so that it is based more on learner needs in reaching social, economic and personal agendas. Many programs designed to incorporate this need to survive are in place already. They are usually community service, sports, apprenticeships, music, clubs and art. Perceived learner survival jump-starts learning on many levels.

In language areas, the message is clear. Get second and third languages in the curriculum for all students, not just those identified as capable, gifted or talented. Every student should get exposure to other languages while their brain is most capable of learning them. Later exposure often creates unnecessary frustration and lowered self-confidence.

Discovering Our Learning Potential

Learners are far more capable than ever imagined. Each successive study of the brain's potential has documented that the previous ones were often too modest. Estimates by neuroscientists

Huttenlocher and Edelman verify that the brain is the most complex organ known to humans. When all brain cells are linked together the number of connections our brain can make is variously estimated to be from 10^{14th} power (a hundred trillion), 10^{800th} power, to as much as ten followed by millions of zeroes (more than the estimated number of atoms in the known universe, which is estimated to be between $10^{80th-100th}$ power).

Professor Anokhin of Moscow University said, "We can show that each of the ten billion neurons in the human brain has a possibility of (establishing) connections with others *up to a figure with twenty-eight noughts (zeros) after it!* If a single neuron has this quality of potential, we can hardly imagine what the whole brain can do...."

> *Practical Application:* Maintain high learner expectations regardless of the evidence. Teach in many different learning styles and all seven intelligences so that the potential of every learner is tapped. Use alternative forms of assessment to provide avenues for those who learn differently. Provide a climate where every learner is respected and nourished. Avoid homogeneous ability grouping. Utilize multi-status and multi-age teamwork.

It is the biological and social imperative of schools to actively develop our learners' brains... not to assess and sort like apples

Brain Power

The adult brain, on average, weighs about three pounds. It has the consistency of a ripe avocado and is about the size of your two fists held next to each other, knuckle to knuckle. The most obvious feature of a human brain is the texture, the convoluted folds that seem to wrap around the upper brain. This area is called the cerebral cortex. It's about the size of a newspaper, wrapped around an organ the size of a cantaloupe—no wonder it's so wrinkled!

Fueling our brain's growth is an extraordinary network of cells called neurons. These cells number about 100 billion and have the capacity to make a nearly infinite number of connections. It's not the quantity of cells that count. Rats have more cells per cubic centimeter than humans. And whales and dolphins have bigger brains than we do. It's the connections between the cells that activate learning, consciousness, memory and intelligence.

The Brain's Timetables

Neurobiologist Lenneberg says we have three primary mental growth spurts: 1) age 18-36 months for walking and talking 2) age 5-7 for learning to read, write and do arithmetic and 3) age 11-15 for abstractions in reasoning, math and ethics. Harvard professor Kosslyn suggests the corpus callosum "May not be fully mature until age 12 or so; at six years of age only two-thirds of the callosal fibers are myelinated." He adds, "Frontal lobes of school-aged children are not fully mature; neurons in the frontal lobes are among the last to be myelinated." That's often known as "the math area." Many learners are not developmentally ready for the abstractions of algebra and geometry, yet it is a required subject for many 13 to 15-year-olds.

Neuroscientists and developmental specialists have found that in the early years, brain growth rates may vary dramatically. Differences range from as little as a few months to as much as three years in same-age children. Some four year-olds are ready to read, others are not. Epstein suggests that the brain has alternating stages of growth. The high growth stages may be particularly good for new learning. During the low growth stages, the brain may be doing a form of "consolidating," wherein the axons may be myelinating for maximum efficiency. It's almost like our brain itself may be biologically saying, "learn, debrief and consolidate, learn, debrief and consolidate." The impact of this may be tremendous. If a certain age (like middle school) is better for regrouping than offering new material, should we shift the emphasis away from academic skills to other skills like social and emotional literacy? Some successful schools already do this. He says 85% of all learners follow a similar growth schedule.

Researcher Dr. Pierce Howard says that our brain begins to lose cells starting at birth, about 100,000 a day. Others say cell deterioration begins about age twelve. The only discouraging news is that the brain does begin "pruning away" unneeded cells from about two years of age. It's not so significant how much we lose; we are born with so many cells, we can afford the loss of a few million. The good news is that we know the brain's plasticity and ability to grow, continues as one ages. But we must use it or lose it.

The human brain not only grows uniquely, it decays differently. We now know that the right brain of females has longer plasticity than that of males. This means it stays open to growth and change for more years in girls than in boys. Wree reports that the degeneration of nerve cells in the male brain precedes that of females by 20 years. Although the rate of loss by females is greater than that of males, it is still not enough to overtake them..

How Much of Our Brain Do We Use?

Although many say we use only two, five or ten percent of our brain, it's a moot issue. We "use" much of our brain on any given day. The real question is how much do we develop of our brain's capacity? In general, very little. If we measured potential merely by the possibilities for neural connections, we use far less than one percent. There is some evidence that we can see what is commonly called invisible (auras, electromagnetic fields, etc.), we can develop "photo-flash" reading skills, play any instrument, learn any language, stop our heartbeat at will, memorize phone books and live well past 120 years old. If we actively use our brain, it will grow and flourish, in spite of enormous handicaps. But to grow, it must be placed in the environment in which that type of growth is appropriate. And that's often not a traditional classroom. If we fail to offer the diversity and choice that the human brain requires for maximum growth, we can hardly point fingers at learners and say, "They're not motivated."

Each Brain is Unique

Teaching to the human brain means greater choice for learners and diversity in instruction. Why? Scientists have verified that just as with our fingerprints, no two brains are alike. In research by Edelman, the huge variability of retinotectal maps (thinking & perception) is emphasized. He says that not only are the maps not fixed, but in some brain areas, "there are major fluctuations in the borders of maps over time." Moreover, each individual map is unique. The variability of maps depends on your experience. "In the visual system alone there may be over 30 interconnected brain centers, each with its own map."

While some maintain that these studies validate the "holographic brain model" postulated by neuroscientist Pribram, there's more to it. Pribram said the brain operates through patches or neural networks. He never stated that the entire brain works as a single hologram, with every part of it functioning for any other part. He simply suggested a more interactive, less compartmentalized brain. Often each area of the brain "senses" what is needed and interacts on a rapid, but poorly understood, level of neural support.

Learning occurs when these "maps" all over the brain (not just in visual), talk to each other. They are often referred to as neural networks. The more connected they are to each other, the greater the "meaning" you derive from the learning. Each of these may have from 50-100,000 neurons in them. They represent life as you know it. In fact, if you don't have a representative neural network for something out there in the real world, it simply doesn't exist. That's why totally new concepts are so difficult to grasp at once; there are no networks to create the associations. It's almost as if all of your experiences are stored in a library (the cortex), full of books (stacked neurons) and the books with common bibliographies are all related (neural networks). The dynamics all result from your individualized life experiences and ever-changing body chemistry.

Because of the importance of neural networks and the brain's chemistry, neuroscientists today rarely talk of just networks. They talk of systems in the brain. The neurotransmitters in one area of the brain may affect the synaptic growth in another part of the brain. Our feelings

New concepts are difficult to grasp at once; there are no networks to create the associations

affect our thinking. As an example, your memory is not a location; it's a system. Your emotions are not in a specific location as much as in a system. Your thinking is not in a certain lobe of the brain as much as it's part of a larger system.

Physically, each brain, our "micro-universe" is quite different. As an example, brain size and weight among humans can vary as much as 50%. While Einstein had an average-sized brain, the writer Balzac's brain was almost 40% larger. Steven Kosslyn, a Harvard University psychologist, says that when it comes to physical size of the brain, "Bigger could be worse, because it impedes rapid communication between the neurons within the brain." Our brain's internal wiring is quite different, too. Two people are both at the scene of an accident. Each reports it in such a different way, it's hard to believe they are describing the same thing. Our perceptions, filters and biases are different from each other. Genetics and nature mold our brains into distinctly individual organs.

While each brain will have varying amounts of sexually specific characteristics, the generalizations about male-female differences still hold

Male and Female Brains

Finally, after years of persuasive research by Kimura and dozens of other eminent neuroscientists, including Butler, Levy, McGlone, Nyborg and Whitleson, the conclusions are profound: the male and female brain not only act differently, they are structurally different. There remains some dispute over the scope and magnitude of other physical differences. In their well researched book, *Left Brain, Right Brain,* Springer summarizes, "The frequency as well as the consistency of reports of sex differences in cerebral organization, ...lead us to accept their reality...." Males and females have entirely different chemical resolutions and they process and use various locations in the brain differently. These verifiable physical differences may explain vastly different behaviors by male and female learners.

The male brain, on the average, weighs 49 ounces and the female brain, 44 ounces. A larger brain size may exist as simply relative to a larger body size.

Yet, researchers Levy in Chicago, Diamond at Berkeley, Stewart of Concordia in Montreal, Kolb of the University of Lethbridge in Alberta, Canada and LaCoste all report clear-cut, male-female brain differences. Kimura says, "Taken altogether, the evidence suggests that men's and women's brains are organized along different lines from very early in life." Variances within the same sex do exist, but certainly not to the same extent as those differences found in opposite sexes.

The list below of sexually determined differences makes a strong statement. It seems that prenatal hormonal influences are the primary difference-maker. Not all women are 5'5" tall and not all men are 5'9" tall. On the average, men are taller than women. Because you find a woman 5'11" tall, it doesn't invalidate the norms. In that same spirit of averages, the range of the differences listed below is more like a continuum. In the same spirit of averages, neuroscientists have found many physical differences. Examples of sexually determined differences include:

- *length of the nerve cell connectors*
- *thickness and weight of the corpus callosum*
- *nucleus volume in hypothalamus*
- *pathways that the neurotransmitters follow*
- *density of nerve cell strands*
- *shape of the nucleus in the hypothalamus*
- *thickness of the left and right side of the cortex control centers*
- *location of control centers for language, emotions & spatial skills*

Hormone levels are the single greatest indicator of gender-related behavior, thinking and problem-solving

With hormones as a critical determinant, PMT (premenstrual tension) has it's male equivalent: ETL (excess testosterone levels). Kimura reports that hormone levels (testosterone in the male and estrogen and progesterone in the female) are the single greatest indicator of gender-related behavior, thinking and problem-solving. Springer says, "High levels of prenatal testosterone slow neuronal growth in the left hemisphere, allowing relatively greater development in the right hemisphere." Translated means "Boys start off more right-brained than girls."

Correspondingly, female scores depend strongly on their menstrual cycle. Dr. Howard confirms they perform higher on verbal and fine-motor skills when their hormones peak, and score 50-100% higher on spatial when their hormone levels are their lowest. A whopping fifty percent of all psychiatric and emergency medical hospital admissions occur during the five days before their menstrual period. Males score higher on math and spatial tasks when their testosterone levels are higher (but not if they are too high). Testosterone production soars in males between ages 12-25; not coincidentally, that's the age bracket with the highest crime levels.

Here's where the research gets particularly interesting. Moir and Jessel report testosterone tends to preserve automated, ritualized behaviors. That means *males, once they learn a behavior, are more likely to be able to preserve that behavior, good or bad.* Hence, you'll find more hardened criminals and more single-minded, ladder-climbing corporate or athletic successes among males. In females, the estrogen suppresses automated behaviors. Hence females tend to excel in occupations where this is an advantage: communications, relationships, sales, management, marketing, training, analysis and negotiations.

The Senses & Gender

Males and females almost live in a different world created by the processing of very different sensory information. Researchers Garai and Scheinfield, McGee, McGuiness, and Bracha say that the female brain is very different from the male brain with regard to sensory perception. Women often report having experiences that men don't understand, such as intuition, food cravings or social interaction clues. Nature or nurture? It's both! Here is a summary of some differences between males and females:

Hearing: The female ear is better able to pick up nuances of voice, music and other sounds. In addition, females retain better hearing longer, throughout life. Females have superior hearing, and at 85 decibels, they perceive the volume twice as loud as males. Females have greater vocal clarity and are one-sixth as likely as a male to be a monotone. They learn to speak earlier and learn languages more quickly. Women excel at verbal memory and process language faster and more accurately. Infant girls are more comforted by singing and speech than males. In contrast to this summary of research, however, German researcher Klutky says females showed no significant auditory advantage in his own studies.

Vision: Males have better distance vision and depth perception than females. Women excel at peripheral vision. Males see better in brighter light; female eyesight is superior at night. Females are more sensitive to the red end of the spectrum. They excel at visual memory, facial clues and context. Females have a better ability to recognize faces and remember names. In repeated studies, women can store more random and irrelevant visual information than men.

Touch: Females have a more diffused and sensitive sense of touch. They react faster and more acutely to pain, yet can withstand pain over a longer duration than males. Males react more to extremes of temperature. Females have greater sensitivity in fingers and hands. They are superior in performing new motor combinations and in fine motor dexterity.

Activity: Male infants play more with objects, more often, than females. Females are more responsive to playmates. The directional choice called "circling behavior" is opposite for men and women. In other words, when right-handed males walk over to a table to pick up

The female brain is very different from the male brain when it comes to processing sensory perception

an object, they are more likely to return by turning to their right. Right-handed females are more likely to return by circling around to their left.

Smell and Taste: Women have a stronger sense of smell and are much more responsive to aromas, odors and subtle changes in smell. They are more sensitive to bitter flavors and prefer sweet flavors. A "significant advantage" in olfactory memory was found by Klutky. Differences in the brain also relate to the effects of contaminants from beauty products. By using neuroradiological imaging to assess brain shrinkage, Harper and Kril authors of Alcohol and Alcoholism, found that women are "more susceptible to the damaging effects of alcohol than males."

Summary of Common Gender Differences

Males: Testosterone levels correlate with the following five behaviors: aggression, competition, self-assertion, self-confidence and self-reliance. Boys show a much earlier specialization of the right brain than girls do. Boys often have trouble, because of right brain specialization, in learning to read early in life. Adolescent boys are more physical than adolescent girls. Boys are better at problem-solving individually. Moir reports the problem-solving tasks that favor men are: 1) target-directed motor skills (archery, football, baseball, cricket, darts, etc.), 2) mentally rotating objects, disembedding tests (locating objects, patterns from within another), 3) mathematical reasoning, word problems and 4) use of spatial cues of distance and direction in route-finding.

Females: Since reading is both verbal and linguistic, it makes sense that girls generally learn to read earlier than boys. Females do better than men in the following areas: 1) mathematical calculation, 2) precision, 3) fine-motor coordination, 4) ideational fluency, 5) finding, matching or locating missing objects and 6) use of landmarks to recall locations in context. Females excel better at solving problems by talking them through. Dr. Howard reports that when female hormonal levels (progesterone and estrogen) are higher, their math and spatial skills are lower. When their hormones are lower, they score higher on spatial and the mental rotation tests.

Biologically, the female left hemisphere develops sooner than the male one. If most 4-5 year old boys are not ready to read as soon as 4-5 year old girls, we should stop labeling boys as "developmentally delayed" or "hyperactive" because they are more developed spatially and kinesthetically (right brained and often a discipline problem).

Boys are better at individual problem solving, girls are better at talking problems through

The brain is a built-in electrochemical "power plant"

> **Practical Application:** Educators may want to offer more flexibility in the scheduling of tests. Ideally, girls would be able to take math tests during the first two weeks of the menstrual cycle and take verbal or written tests during the last two weeks. If you must take a test with both, schedule the test according to your greatest priority for success. Schedule male testing (for math and spatial) early in the day when their hormone levels are highest. Save verbal, writing and interactive work (discussion and sharing) later in the afternoon when their testosterone levels are lower. Allow boys to have more desk and play space around them. Allow females to work together more.

How far should we go with this information? Even if you don't want to change things now, be flexible. Gender equality would say we treat both sexes the same. But the sexes are not equal. If females need more bathrooms because they use them differently than males, we should build more of them. That's not equality, that's fairness.

Energy Flow and the Brain

What runs the brain? The fuel is primarily oxygen, glucose and nutrients from blood flow. Our brain runs on about 20 watts of power, generated from our brain's own electrochemical "power plant." At rest, if the brain's energy level was a 100%, it's only 97% while sleeping and 103% while doing intense problem-solving. It's the reaction of sodium and potassium ions which create the electrical energy. The levels of a typical individual neuron typically range from +50 to -70 millivolts, depending on the charged state of the cell.

The energy flow in our brain seems to move up and down on a **vertical axis**, from the brain stem to the cortex and back down again. Our brain is designed to process spatially, from small particles to larger spatial relationships, from **left-to right** hemisphere. It gets even more interesting. We seem to process time differently in different areas our brains, from the **back to the front**, from our past to future. Our amazing brain is processing time, as well as thoughts, feelings and actions.

Update On the Triune Brain

Education, like other fields, can often get caught up in trends. During the 70's, a common topic was the right and left brain. Needing something more complete, educators in the 1980s became intrigued with a 1949 model proposed by Dr. Paul MacLean. He is the former Director of the Laboratory of Brain and Behavior at the United States Institute of Mental Health. MacLean proposed that our "triune brain" acts as if we actually have three brains in one: 1) the so-called R-complex, the "oldest" or reptilian area including the brain stem and cerebellum, 2) the mid-brain (limbic area: amygdala, hippocampus, hypothalamus, pineal gland, thalamus, nucleus accumbens) and 3) the neomammalian (cerebrum & neocortex). The functions of the three areas are quite different, he says.

To understand MacLean's model of the brain, think of an office building. Let's say the lower level has maintenance and custodial workers. They make sure the building has heat, electricity, air and is structurally safe. On the middle level we have the employees who provide the daily needs, the "what's real" - the feelings, the energy, the motivation and the life-blood of the business. On the top level is executive management who understands trends, forecasts, creativity and does the long-term planning. The brain itself is quite similar, he said, in its functions.

It sounds good, but is the triune brain model accurate? Today's research is changing our opinion. Ask a large number of neuroscientists, and, surprisingly, many *will not have even heard* of the triune brain theory. It's not widely accepted as compatible with today's brain research. It's a model; and like most models, it breaks down under a more exacting scrutiny.

Recent research has confirmed that *nearly every part of the brain is involved in nearly every activity*. Cytowick says the lower brainstem discriminates and decides between sensory signals. Vision is distributed to several areas of the brain. Virtually every area of the brain is involved in language. Calvin says language processing is so fragmented, *we have different places* for nouns, verbs and syntax. In fact, he says, second and third languages are located in overlapping and different areas of the brain. Our emotions, say Damasio and Restak are widely distributed in areas including, the cerebellum, the top of the brain stem, the limbic area and prefrontal cortices. We have two visual system locations, one dedicated to object vision and one dedicated to spatial locations, says James Haxby of the National Institute of Health. Movement and balance are controlled both by the frontal lobes and the cerebellum. UC Davis neuroscientist Springer says, "...most psychological functions should be associated with the activity changes in *multiple areas* or defined pathways in the cerebrum." (author's emphasis)

Is the upper brain truly the sole bastion of higher order thinking skills? Is the neocortex "what makes us most human," as triune brain theorists have postulated? British neuroscientist Lorber found 150 adults with virtually NO neocortex (they had 5% or less because of childhood hydrocephalic disease). They had normal basal and limbic structures, but the neocortex area was 80% water. Now, here's the shocker: these "brainless" people had IQ's ranging up to 120. Many held advanced professional degrees, got along well with others, and had normal lives. What Lorber's studies tell us is that the brain is quite remarkable, even when just 5% of the neocortex is used. Additionally, more functions than we earlier thought are handled by the subcortical regions. That should tell you something about the importance of the neocortex compared to the limbic and lower brain areas!

Dr. Paul Churchland, author of *Engine of Reason: Seat of the Soul*, says that our thinking is much more complex and overlapping than earlier thought. He says our entire mid- and upper- brain are part of our thinking, connected by recurrent networks which loop over and over on top of one another. We form far-reaching neural networks that cross most of our brain's boundaries. He says our thinking is very "whole brained" and not an isolated feature. In parallel, neuroscientist Karl Lashley revealed that removal of up to one fifth of the cortex caused no appreciable loss of memory. The intriguing thing was that it didn't matter which part of the cortex! At the 1995 International Conference on Neuroscience, a symposia chaired by Dr. W.T. Thatch of Washington University School of Medicine, explored the subject of "Specific roles *of the cerebellum* in cognition." (author's emphasis) That area was previously thought to only deal with balance, posture and coordination.

Is the brain stem the oldest part? New biological evidence reported by Dr. Christopher Willis author of *The Runaway Brain,* suggests that the forebrain *may be the oldest, not the newest* part of our brain. This is contrary to MacLean's earlier theory that the reptilian brain area was evolutionarily first.

Having said that, there are still some useful generalizations that can be made. MacLean did make an important contribution to our understanding of the brain. The lower brain, which includes the area just above your spinal cord, monitors and acts as a switching station for the physical world. The behaviors of this part of the brain are instinctive, fast-acting and survival-oriented. It is the part of the brain that's responsible for learner behavior such as:

- *social conformity...common habits, grooming, clothes, etc.*
- *territoriality...defending "my stuff, my desk, my room"*
- *mating rituals...flirting, touching, attracting another*
- *deception...often forms of subverted aggression*
- *ritualistic display...trying to get the social attention of peers*
- *hierarchies...the dominance of leaders, "top dog" behaviors*
- *social rituals...the repetitive & predictable daily behaviors*

Our mid-brain area contains the amygdala, hippocampus, thalamus, hypothalamus, pineal gland and some scientists believe, several other key parts. It is the part of the brain most widely know to affect:

Brain-based learning is not a recipe or formula... Earlier understanding may be found incomplete as our understanding of the brain improves

24

- *social bonding and attachments from parental bonding*
- *hormones, feelings of sexuality*
- *emotions, both positive and negative*
- *what is true, valid and what we feel strongly about*
- *contextual memories*
- *immediate expressiveness*
- *long-term memory*

The cerebrum and the neocortex covering it, are the upper 80% of the brain. It includes the frontal, occipital, parietal and temporal lobes and provides us with these abilities:

- *thinking, reflection, consciousness*
- *problem-solving, computations*
- *language, writing and drawing*
- *long-range planning, forecasting*
- *visualizing, envisioning*
- *reading, translating and composing*
- *creativity in art, music and theater*

The lower brain will always override the other two brains' tendencies when it comes to survival

Each of the three areas of the brain influences the other. The part of the brain with the highest priority for survival behavior seems to be the mid- and lower brain. If a brick is thrown at your head, the cortex asks the size, color, origin and weight. It also is curious about why it is being thrown at you. The mid-brain feels afraid or angry, but the lower brain (stem) *will always override the other two brains' tendencies when it comes to survival.* It simply says to your body, "Duck, now!" That's quite a useful survival response!

What Causes Us To Think?

There are plenty of theories on this topic, but no one seems to know for sure. Biologist and philosopher Paul Churchland says our thinking is the result of countless micro-networks that stretch across the brain and feed back on top of themselves. To him and to many other scientists, including physicist Eric Harth, our thinking is, "A composite of armies of neural connections." But what makes those connections happen?

One of the key parts of the brain is the reticular activating system or RF (reticular formation). It is centrally located and straddles the major sensory pathways which allow it to get top quality information first. It helps us make our moment-to-moment decisions, particularly on where to give our attention and when to switch our primary reaction strategy to: 1) a more **proactive** area (the cortex) or 2) the more **reactive** (the limbic and lower brain area).

This simple decision, made thousands of times per day, determines to a great deal, the quality of your life. Specifically, it is located near the junction of the mid-brain and brain stem. Nobel laureate Crick and physicist Herbert believe that while other parts of the brain contribute towards consciousness, the reticular formation (RF) is essential for it. While the thalamus is the gateway to the cortex, the RF is the "guardian of the gateway." This area is also a prime site where drugs modify consciousness.

Some have described the RF structure as a "stack of fuzzy poker chips" along the spinal column. This may be the closest thing your brain has to a central processing center. Its primary job is to commit you to any one of about 16 gross motor modes of behavior (sleeping, running, speaking, grabbing, etc.) based on the latest split-second nerve impulses. What it does that is critical to organizing your perception of the world, is isolate which parts of sensory information flowing through will be enhanced and which will be suppressed. That function is critical to your sanity and survival. In Springer's work, Nobel laureate Eccles says that the right hemisphere cannot truly think at all and that there are not separate minds. This system, they both say, creates the process of thinking, but has no particular location.

Three primary processes in the brain are of particular interest to educators. First, **the reticular activating system** seems to be a primary switching system for attention, how we filter our senses and react to incoming data. It's located at the top of the brain stem, next to the mid-brain area. Second, the **synapse** is critical because that's the way cells communicate and how we learn. Third, the **chemistry** of brain, the hormones and other reactions are what either make learning happen, or not. They can get us high or bring us down, make us forget or remember and make us violent or civil. In much of the rest of the book we'll continually refer to these three processes. They are, as best as can be understood today, at the heart of learning.

Our Lopsided Brain

It's reassuring to know that much of the original work of Nobel Prize Laureate, Dr. Roger Sperry, who discovered the functioning differences between left and right brain hemispheres, remains valid. The controversy since then has been created by overly zealous enthusiasts who insist on creating a "them vs. us," bad-good, "super-logical vs. intu-

The bottom line is this...even the best of the neuroscientists still have a tough time understanding how the human brain can think

ition" war. Books have appeared which draw up the battle lines over the "old left-brain way" and the "updated right-brain approach."

However, updated research by Levy has confirmed that *both sides of the brain are involved in nearly every human activity.* It's all a matter of timing and degree of involvement. Gazzaniga says that "...events occurring in one hemisphere can influence developmental events occurring at the same time at very remote parts of the other hemisphere." It is best to leave the hemispheric puzzle as simple and unbiased as possible. Use the two sides more as a metaphor for understanding how we process instead of pigeon-holing all behaviors into either left or right brain as a blueprint for a reductionist model.

There's a greater number of motor fibers in the nerve pathways from the left hemisphere to the right side of the body. This may indicate a biological preference to right-handedness. The right hemisphere's frontal and central regions are wider, as are the left brain co-occipital lobes. The major lateral groove, the sylvian fissure, is longer on the left side. The left temporal planum is also larger than the right, as is the parietal operculum. In the prefrontal area, the left areas are smaller then the right side, but more hemispheric "folding" may compensate. Blood flow is unequally distributed; it often depends on which appendages are in use.

The corpus callosum, the largest of the hemisphere's interconnecting nerve fibers, develops at a slow rate, causing the two hemispheres to develop unequally. While some researchers, such as Levy, believe the corpus callosum copies the messages from one side to another. Neuroscientist Pribram says the brain operates through patches or pocket holograms called neural fields. Cook describes the role more as topological inhibition. That means that an excited neuron *on one side* sends a generalized, contextual message *to the other.* The message simply calls on related programs to prompt further understanding. It's like a politician in a helicopter dropping leaflets onto a nearby neighborhood to spark interest. This model explains how we "turn on" our ideas, like a sparkler throws out sparks on New Year's Eve. In the learning context, both left and right brain learners can have their advantages.

Originally it was thought that the left brain controlled the right 50% of the body and the right brain controlled the other 50%. Researchers now know that our brain is asymmetrical. Iaccino asserts that *the left brain is in charge "in a majority of cases, regardless of body side."* Considering how much else in the body is asymmetrical, that's no surprise. Humans have functional preferences for handedness, eyedness and earedness. Robin & Shortridge report breast, kidney, ovary, nasal and testes tumors occur more on the left-side of the body.

While our brain works as a whole, it's still true that the left side processes "parts" (sequentially) and the right side processes "wholes" (randomly)

How function-specific is each side of the brain? It varies a great deal. Using PET scans, blood flow activity can be measured on hemisphere-specific tasks. Listening to another speak may seem like a left hemisphere activity, since it is the side that processes words, definitions and language. In fact, the female brain processes both language and feelings at the same time far more efficiently than the male brain. In *Trends in Neuroscience,* Ross' evidence suggests the right hemisphere processes the inflection, tonality, tempo and volume – which are actually more critical to the *meaning* of the conversation.

Current research is shattering most of our old notions about what is left or right brain

Left Brain	Right Brain
prefers things in sequence	comfortable with randomness
learns from part to whole	learns whole first, then parts
stimulated by function	stimulated by appearance
phonetic reading system	whole language reader
likes words, symbols, letters	wants pictures, graphs, charts
rather read about it first	rather see it or experience it
unrelated factual information	relationships in learning
generates optimism & hope	deals with the moment's emotions
detailed orderly instructions	spontaneous, go with the flow
prefers internal focus	more likely external focus
wants structure, predictability	open-endedness, surprises

Is music a right brain experience? Think again. Researchers discovered that musicians process music more in the left hemisphere and non-musicians process it more in the right one. So much for the old adage that music is a right brain activity! Musicians, it seems, tend to analyze music more than the novice. Right hemisphere flow was greater on more demanding tasks than the left. There's a "...very general role for the right hemisphere in attention or vigilance" says Springer.

This may also be a function of chemistry (as many other brain functions clearly are). Research by Pribram found that norepinephrine, a neurotransmitter linked with attention, novelty and arousal, is found in greater concentrations in the right hemisphere. Dopamine, a neurotransmitter linked with fine motor and the initiation of action sequences is found more in the left hemisphere.

James Iaccino claims that although each hemisphere does have some clear-cut specialization, each side "still requires the other to complement its overall functioning." Geffen says students will recognize faces in their left visual field faster than in their right. We recall better the location of objects when the material is initially presented to the right hemisphere (left field). But in one study, picture stimuli got a faster reaction when presented to the left hemisphere, and letters more quickly when presented to the right. Why? *The task to be performed is as or more important than the nature of the stimuli,* researchers found. In other words, use matters as much as category type, for hemispheric arousal.

Creativity and Logic

The notion that one side of the brain is logical and the other side is creative, is outdated. We can become very creative by following and using logical options, patterns, variations and sequences. The work of Edward DeBono on lateral thinking reminds us that one can use "left-brain systems" to be creative. For years he has articulated processes to arrive at creative solutions through sequential methods.

PET (positron emission tomography) scans give specific locations for brain activity, telling us which part of the brain is used during specific activities. In *Care and Feeding of the Brain,* Maguire reports that in studies by Yale researchers Ahern and Schwartz, it was found that the *right side of the brain* was the most activated when the learner was *feeling depressed, negative, or stressed.* When the learner was feeling a healthy optimism about life and the future, most activity was found on the left hemisphere. However, an excessively "Pollyanna" view of reality is linked to right hemisphere activity, as is those who overestimate good feelings and deny negative ones says Mandell in *Psychology of Consciousness.*

Learners may be much more effective if taught how to process negative moods or events which could impact their learning. Make sure that the skills needed for thinking things through, and learning optimism, are part of the learning. Learning optimism comes from conflict-resolution skills, goal-setting skills, a sense of belonging and acceptance, visioning activities, developing a sense of value and purpose in life, and physical vitality.

Recapturing the Whole Brain

The right side of the brain can intuit many logical things. Drawing, composing and painting may seem like a right hemisphere activity, yet artists show bilateral activity. In the planning of artwork, they follow their own logic and rules about shapes, colors and sounds. An artist can express anything on canvas, clay, glass, metal or paper. However, for the art to be acceptable to the masses, it needs to follow very specific, certain (though unwritten) rules of proportionality, color scheme, balance and order. The right brain, it seems, does prefer its own kind of holistic order.

Learners may be much more effective if taught how to process negative moods or events which could impact their learning

In the 70's and 80's, there was an emphasis on teaching more to the "right-brained learner." Current brain research tells us that we generally use both sides of the brain, most of the time. The right brain emphasis was simply an important "pendulum swing" to create awareness in an area that was under-represented.

That means relatively speaking, there is more activity in one hemisphere than another. It's time for us to insure that *both* types of learning and teaching are represented. We can now focus our efforts on "whole-brained" learning and drop the "left vs. right" argument.

The prevailing research in neuroscience avoids the definitive left-right brain labels. They now use the term "relative lateralization"

 Practical Application: Both parts and wholes are important to learning. Neither should be emphasized at the cost of the other. Some of those who are promoting "right-brain thinking" might do more good by promoting "whole-brain thinking." Provide learners with global overviews. Provide them with a sequence of steps that will be followed. If you use an overhead transparency, first show all of it, or all of your overheads for the day or for the whole course. Then you can sequence them, one idea at a time. Alternate between the "big picture" and the details. Validate that we are "whole-brain learners."

It's still a good idea to encourage parents to encourage their children to use more of their right hand. While you already know that it's a socially and culturally biased right-handed world, you may also be interested to know some other consequences. Left handers are five to ten times more likely to develop learning disorders, have immune deficiencies and to live a shorter life. The question is, "Is that genetically determined, or is it because the left hand was used more?"

It's become increasingly clear the brain works as a system. While there are parts of the brain that specialize, when it comes to most of your everyday operations, it's more useful to think in terms of process, not location. Learning a new task activates several parts of the brain. Memory activates several parts of the brain. Thinking activates several areas of the brain, although the more you know about a subject, the less work your brain has to do to think about it. Presumably, more neural networks, with more traveled pathways, makes your brain more efficient.

One of the most interesting areas of research lately has been the discovery that the brain is very much a feed-back and feed-forward system. The old model of the brain was that information flowed through it from one part to another. Today's research confirms that a huge amount of information moves backwards from even our senses! Authors of *Wet Mind,* Kosslyn and Koenig say that our visual system is in fact helping create images as much as it is reporting data from the outside world. This works in parallel with the fact that every area of the visual sense that sends information to another area, also receives fibers from that area. This process assists us in forming images, visualizing and as a safety buffer for short-term storage. It's been common knowledge that the right hemisphere is more active during visualization and mental task rotations. But since our brain operates as a system, it may be no surprise that there is evidence that the left hemisphere also plays a role in mental image transformations. Even reading single words is a complex activity which activates several areas of the brain say Kosslyn and Koenig. Thus, with all the research about left and right brain, it serves us better to think of the brain as a highly interdependent system, not modules.

Now, with this background about the physical brain, let's turn to instructional strategies and the implications of a more brain-based approach.

Reflection and Analysis

- ❖ In what ways can you translate the key three or four theories and discoveries presented here into practical everyday useful ideas?
- ❖ What information in this chapter do you already apply?
- ❖ Did you think of any questions about this material? What were they?
- ❖ Did you have an emotional reaction to any of this information?
- ❖ Specify what was different and new to you? What was familiar and what was review?
- ❖ How did you react intellectually? Do you agree or disagree with any ideas explored in this chapter? Which ones and why?
- ❖ Let's say these things are, in fact, true about the brain, what should we do differently? What resources of time, people and money could be redirected? In what ways do you suggest we start doing it?
- ❖ Generate the most interesting or valuable insight(s) you got from this chapter.
- ❖ Make a plan for your next step, a realistic, practical application of what you've learned, and outline it.
- ❖ Can you foresee any obstacles you might encounter? How can you realistically deal with them?

Author's note: Typically questions at the end of a chapter are designed to elicit recall. These questions were created to trigger discussions, not right answers. Since the processes are identical for developing reflective meaning, the questions are the same at the end of each chapter. Obviously, the content of each chapter is different, so your responses will change.

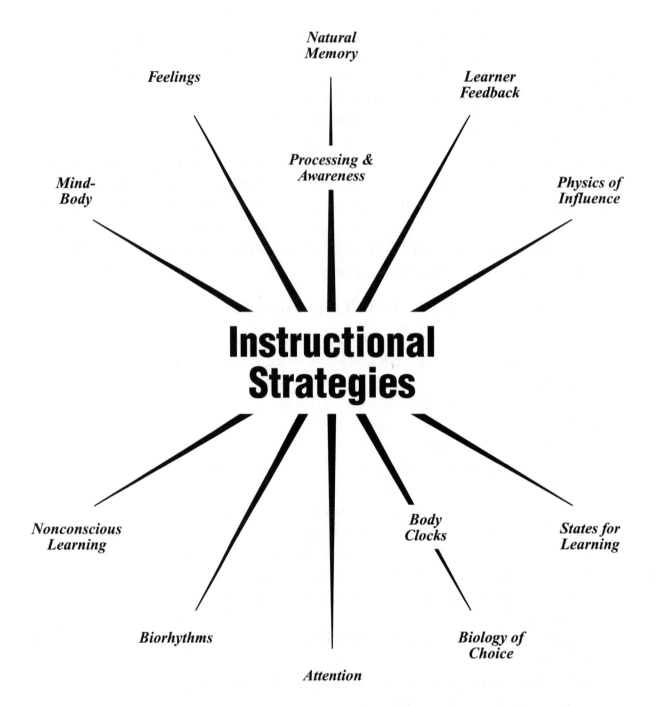

Chapter 2
Instructional Strategies

The Marriage of Mind and Body

For years, we've treated the mind and the body as if they were two different entities. Physically, by location, they are. But in other ways, they're not separated. In fact, to your brain, the rest of the body *is more like an extension of itself.* New research has confirmed there are similar chemicals found throughout the body that are present in the brain. And the chemicals are the primary determinant of your behavior. For example, the "gut feelings" you experience in your stomach are from the same identical peptides present in your brain. The sensory data input from the body gives the brain more than its eyes, ears, taste and smell. The body acts like a huge antenna. Stand next to a television set with rabbit ears and notice the difference in reception! Endless streams of information about pain, pleasure, temperature, touch, vibrations and movement are processed by the brain *as if those things are happening to the brain itself.* We are, indeed, an integrated system for sensing and learning.

Many scientists have gathered data that support the mind-feelings-body connection. There's extensive information about the role that enrichment, nutrition, exercise, attitude, lifestyle, posture and emotions play in learning. There are studies by Damasio, McGaugh, Pert and LeDeoux on the role of emotions in learning. There is research on the role of exercise and stimulation by Diamond and Greenough. Learning is linked to our hormones and biochemical rhythms, say Armitage and Klein. Connors, Wurtman and Healy remind us about the role of nutrition. The compilation of that research is persuasive and compelling: ***All learning involves our body, our emotions, and our attitudes...brain-based approaches address those variables more comprehensively.***

Our entire brain system works together, as one. It's chemically and electrically fueled to produce the illusion of one brain. Each of these is run by the brain's chemicals and is working for the overall survival of the "system." Our body and brain are a miraculous electrochemical concert that plays 24 hours a day. While the old academic model addressed primarily the intellectual part of learners, the prevailing model says we learn with our minds,

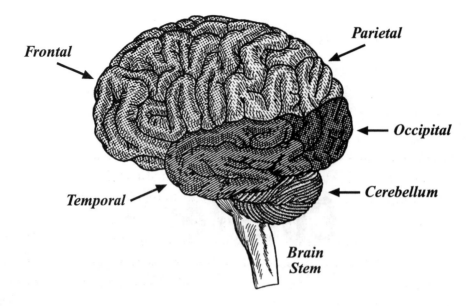

Frontal

Parietal

Occipital

Cerebellum

Temporal

Brain Stem

heart and body. It also says that the better we deal with all of the learner's issues, the more effective we'll be in teaching and learning.

The brain illustration above illuminates several key areas of interest to our discussion. The frontal lobes are related to long-term planning, creativity and thinking skills. As with all areas of the brain, there is tremendous overlap in function and process of the brain. The cerebellum, at the back of the brain, was thought to be responsible for balance, coordination, gross motor movement and posture. New evidence suggests it may have a role in cognition. The brain stem is the primary processing area for our body's signals. The hippocampus, which is in the mid-brain area, is known to be responsible for intense and long-term memory. Knowing a bit about the brain and its key areas, leads us to some important conclusions. One of them is that when we better understand what is influencing our learners, we might be more empowered to affect those things.

Practical Application: Develop a greater awareness of all the factors influencing your learners. Then, take the time to influence as many of the variables as you can. Think of all learning as mind-body. Deal with the feelings and the physical body as well as the cognitive side. Teach emotional health, physical well-being and you'll get better results. You can set a good example and role model the benefits of exercise, nutrition and stress management. You can send home handouts and suggestions for your students on how to better manage their bodies and mind-sets. You can teach relaxation, offer more stretch breaks and better manage your students' states.

Attention for Learning

To learn in a structured environment often requires our attention. The human brain has a built-in attentional bias for certain types of stimuli. Since our brain isn't designed to consciously attend to *all* types of incoming stimuli, *it sorts out that which is less critical to our survival.* The **reticular formation** is at the top of the brain stem and the base of the limbic system. This is the part of our brain that integrates incoming sensory information. Using peptide receptors, it regulates our general level of attention. It also regulates our focus-diffusion cycle and internal-external shifts in awareness. Although the brain is very good at immediate change and contrasts, it's poor at discerning slow trends. Thus, the design seems to be for the short-term. That's why extended classroom attention is rarely appropriate.

When you do need attention, the brain researcher Cloniger says three neural systems run our lives. They are: 1) the cortex's **quest for novelty,** 2) the midbrain's **hunt for pleasure** and 3) the lower brain's **desire to avoid harm.** That's a perfect summary of our daily lives. Try new things, seek pleasure and avoid getting hurt. In the classroom, a teacher uses those rules of the brain to get attention when it's appropriate. Novelty gets our attention and challenge maintains it. You can't do much better than that in a learning context. Good teachers have always used these states to create an "attentional state" or as Madeline Hunter referred to them, "an anticipatory set." The novelty is basically anything that is a contrast from the existing situation. Often it means the arousal of emotional states like:

- *suspicion, intrigue, surprise, curiosity, suspense or confusion*
OR
- *anticipation, hope, security, fun, acceptance or self-confidence*

"How to Get Rid of Wrinkles Without Surgery," the tabloid headlines blurt. "The One Lawsuit That Will Affect Everybody's Pocketbook"–news at eleven, the television teases. What gets your attention on television is the change, the novelty, the "shock effect." Television constantly uses commercials that play into our brain's bias for high contrast, emotions and novelty. They keep trying to outdo one another to get our attention.

Yet, your learners can become "TV numb," jaded and "overshocked" by television and tabloid-type constant high contrast stimuli. As a result, in a typical learning environment, they may become bored,

Any stimuli introduced into our immediate environment which is either new (novel) or of sufficiently strong emotional intensity (contrasting) will immediately get our attention

35

listless and detached. But teachers who capitalize and use appropriately our brain's principles can get and keep attention more effectively. This is only useful for the short term, however.

All use of novelty in an educational context must be balanced with ritual and predictability. In fact, the more predictable the learning, the more room there is for novelty. You can use ritual and routine for your openings, processes and closings. Then use novelty in the presentation of the content. Or, use ritual in the presentation and novelty in the process. As long as there is a balance. Too much novelty and your learners experience chaos and stress. Too much routine and your learners experience boredom and apathy.

You can either have your learner's attention OR...they can be making meaning for themselves but never both at the same time

 Practical Application: Use the brain's bias for novelty and high contrast. Be outrageous and different, but also *focus more on designing learner-generated projects* so that you don't have to be a "shock-show" to run a class. Then the novelty and variation of other learners provides much of the attentional bias needed.

Getting Attention But Not Keeping It

The old paradigm was "get the learner's attention and keep it." That's outdated and brain-antagonistic. We don't want the brain's attention all the time, or even a majority of the time. If your attention is "external" because something has your attention, you can't be "internal" and making any meaning out of it. Learners need time for acquisition, practice, reflection, making meaning and building recall. Attention is a useful precursor to some kinds of learning, but not all. Remember, learning is a very different process than attention. Television shows can keep your full attention for hours and you still might learn virtually nothing. You not only can have attention without meaning, you simply *can't* have both at the same time.

The value of attention in the classroom is so that the content of the learning and meaning can be influenced. The old way was to try to get and keep student's attention for most of the time. That's not a model of learning. It's a model of control. *You would never want to have the learner's attention all the time.* They would learn very little. In fact, it's appropriate to have your learner's attention, in most cases, for most types of learning, only for a small minority of the total time.

Quality learning may begin by attracting the learner's attention with novelty, emotions, relevance or curiosity. Then, once the learner has had time to learn the material in the way they do it best, it's time for integration, meaning and memory. The notion of continuously "keeping the learner's attention" is biologically and psychologically outdated.

It makes more sense for the teacher to be less of the "show." Capturing the learners' attention then becomes less of an issue. Giving the learners more control and allowing them to choose complex, interesting life-like projects will focus their attention on their learning instead of on their daydreams. Good teachers have used these concepts for years.

The best teachers have learner's attention less than 20% of the total class time

---

Practical Application: We can take advantage of the brain's quest for novelty by eliciting states of curiosity, oddity-interest, suspense, awe, confusion, surprise and the ah-ha! We can take advantage of the brain's hunt for pleasure by creating states of anticipation, hope, security, fun, self-confidence, acceptance, success and satisfaction. The third category, avoiding harm is a bit trickier. We must never threaten with harm, of course. But we can get attention by offering ways for learners to avoid embarrassment, hurt, anxiety, fear or ridicule. Remember, as a teacher, there's no meaning in what you say. Start with getting attention. Then make plenty of class time for understanding, processing, elaboration and verification. Meaning has to get constructed between the learner's ears. Then, end with celebration.

Learning With Feelings

The mid-brain area is not one, but actually is composed of several related structures: the amygdala, hippocampus, thalamus, hypothalamus and the pineal gland. On the borderline between the limbic area and the brain stem lies the top of the critical reticular formation. Combined, these regulate our attention, immunity, hormones, sleep cycles, appetite, sexuality, emotions and more. Our mid-brain area may be the glue that holds our whole system together. The carriers of our emotions are peptide molecules which are composed of a chain of amino acids (one short of protein). There is a far greater number of neural fibers extending FROM the mid-brain into the neocortex than there are going from the neocortex INTO the mid-brain. From a survival viewpoint, this makes sense–when you feel strong fear, the brain places a priority on that emotion over any other information. This is important evidence that emotions are more important and powerful to the brain than higher-order thinking skills.

On one level, this brain area is the seat of all emotional bonds, healing capacity, intuition and the immune system. This area ties all three parts of our brain together, directing attention where it is needed. The **amygdala** is a small almond-shaped structure and is critical to linking memories and emotion. It processes the emotional content of information and memory. It's made up of two nut-sized structures which are highly connected to most other brain areas. It regulates breathing, circulation and other automatic body functions. Like the reticular formation, it is most concerned with our survival and the emotional flavoring or interpretation of feelings in a situation.

Emotions are more important and powerful to the brain than higher-order thinking skills

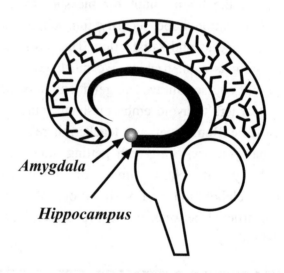

Amygdala

Hippocampus

The **hippocampus** has been described by O'Keefe and Nadel in *The Hippocampus as a Cognitive Map* as critical to the use of episodic memory. The content of our experiences are processed by the hippocampus while the emotional flavor of our experiences are processed by the amygdala. Calvin says that "The overlap of frontal lobe sites for emotion and visceral function is particularly promising because of the link to higher cognitive processes - spinning all those "what if" scenarios that contribute to anxiety, worry and suffering."

Neuroscientist LeDeoux suggests that this part of our brain is responsible for suppressed memories. He says that the thalamo-amygdala circuits may be critical because they mature early and operate before the neocortex and hippocampus is fully functional. This means early intense emotional experiences, especially fear, are always going to be operational in our lives because they happened to the immature "emotional" brain before our "thinking" brain, has a chance to sort out the meaning.

Maybe the most amazing thing about this part of the brain is that while all of us can be presented with evidence that something is true, it is not verified in our own world until we *feel* that it is true. In spite of all we have learned from reason, science, logic or common sense, we do not feel that anything is true until our mid-brain, the limbic portion, which deals with emotions, says that it is true.

In *Descartes' Error; Emotion, Reason and the Human Brain,* Damasio argues that the brain, mind, body and emotions form a linked system. He criticizes the typical neurologist's narrow-mindedness regarding the role of emotions: "...while uncontrolled or misdirected emotion can be a major source of irrational behavior, ...a reduction in emotion *may constitute an equally important source of irrational behavior"* (my emphasis). He adds, "...certain aspects of the process of emotion and feeling are indispensable for rationality." Emotions, he says, are not separate, but rather enmeshed in the neural network of reason. They help us shortcut our decision-making process and allow us to include our values in thinking. The implications for this in classroom learning are tremendous.

Many other researchers including McGaugh, Pert, MacLean, O'Keefe and Nadel have written about the critical role of emotions in learning and the link between cognitive data and emotions. Dr. Paul MacLean, pioneer in brain research, says that the most disturbing thing about the way the brain is "wired up," is the limbic system which insists that ultimately the learner must *feel that something is true before it is believed.* MacLean says with puzzlement, "The limbic system, this primitive brain that can neither read nor write, provides us with the feeling of what is real, true and important."

Learning and meaning are driven by feelings; The brain is virtually a box of emotions

❖

I feel, therefore, I am

We are more driven by emotions than logic

Why It Has To "Feel Right"

The mid-brain area may be critical to how we make meaning of the world. Calvin suggests that since wide areas of the cortex interact with the limbic system, your personality is as much in your hypothalamus and limbic area as it is in the cortex. The **thalamus** and **hypothalamus** (walnut and pea-sized respectively), also help regulate our emotions and safety. The thalamus regulates external processes and the hypothalamus monitors internal information.

Researchers Campbell & Grossberg discuss how the structure and function of hippocampal and infero-temporal processing may be linked. Learning areas such as categorization, attention, memory, novelty recognition and memory search, all work together at different stages of development.

But while researchers have known that the infero-temporal cortex can recognize both specialized and abstract information, Campbell proposed a link that may verify the relationship between how we feel and how we learn. Dr. Candace Pert, former chief of brain biochemistry at the National Institute of Mental Health, says, "The emotions are not just in the brain, they're in the body... this may explain why some people talk about gut feelings." We are more driven by emotions than logic. University of Oregon professor Robert Sylwester says that because the limbic portion of the brain tells our cortex how to feel about things, *it is actually implying what you might want to do in the future.* In that sense, each part of our brain has input into our decision-making. The more we understand about how our brain distributes and values feelings, the greater the implication there seems to be for classroom learning.

Practical Application: The emotional state of your learners is at least as important as the intellectual-cognitive content of your presentation. Never avoid emotions; deal with them. Allow negatives ones to be processed out and positive ones to be utilized. Make sure you put your learners in a good emotional state before you present the material. Allow your learners time to de-stress first, then make the learning enjoyable with amusing activities so that the emotions are positively engaged.

Nothing is true until you feel it is true

Earlier research suggested that the limbic area is the source of our emotions. But that's only partly true. The old model of the limbic brain as the sole domain of our emotions is in jeopardy, like a ship "taking on water." Both Damasio and Restak suggest that our feelings are processed in other areas of the brain such as the prefrontal cortices and the cerebellum. New research suggests that our feelings *are not restricted to our brain.* In fact, they may be throughout our body. Bergland, in *The Fabric of Mind,* suggests that our brain is more like a gland. He says that the hormones that our brain produces are dispersed throughout our body. These long-distance chemical messengers can give us the reaction called "gut feelings." We are deeply feeling creatures with checks and balances in every area, including something as simple (or is it?) as "knowing what we know."

Richard Bandler co-discoverer of neurolinguistic programming, suggests that our brain has three criteria which must be filled in order for it to "know what it knows." These criteria give the brain its "self-convincers," and they vary from person to person. Learning is one thing; the brain must get verification of it to truly believe it. The three criteria the brain requires are 1) Reinforcing the learning in your preferred modality; visual, auditory or kinesthetic, 2) Reinforcing it for the right number of times; for some it's once, for others it may be 3-20 times, and 3) Reinforcing it for sufficient length of time; for some it's a couple of seconds, for others it may be minutes or even hours.

Once we have reinforcement about what we have learned in our preferred modality, (the right number of times and for the right length of time), we will feel that it is true. We believe it and have a gut feeling for it. Until then, it's data, but not a "felt meaning."

When each of these three things occur, in your preferred combination, you have a feeling that *what* you know, you *really* know. As an example, we've all heard someone say, "I'll believe it when I see it." That's a case of a visual learner who HAS to see it. Another might say, "I saw it, but I just don't believe it." They call their neighbor first and find out whether they get agreement, then they decide. And a third might say, "If I can touch it, hold it or be there first hand, I'll believe it." These three examples represent modality variables: visual, auditory and kinesthetic. In addition, a frequency variable defines how much repetition, ranging from one to ten times, each learner requires before believing something. A duration variable indicates the length of time learners need for affirming information, ranging from as few as a couple of seconds to an entire minute.

Learners not only need to learn but also need to know that they know

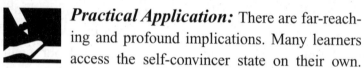 ***Practical Application:*** There are far-reaching and profound implications. Many learners access the self-convincer state on their own. They simply know how to convince themselves of what they know. They tend to be more self-confident, often even arrogant. However, many learners simply do not know what they have learned. A learner must "know what he knows," or he'll leave the room thinking he has learned nothing. He goes home and his parents ask, "What did you learn today?" He says, "Nuthin," although he actually did learn a lot. Brain-based approaches ask us to elicit this state. It can be done through activities which engage all three criteria - pair-share with three others, for example.

Self-convincers are especially critical when it comes to changing beliefs. If a student *already believes* that he or she is going to succeed, it takes only "maintenance reinforcement" to preserve that belief. If a student believes that he is a failure and you want him to convince himself that he is a success, all three of his criteria must be met. Otherwise, *the belief stays the same.* Emotions, beliefs, fears, worry, they are all intermingled.

In general, "at-risk," slow, discouraged, or low-level learners have inappropriate self-convincer strategies. They often don't know what they know and have little self-confidence. Or, they may self-convince too easily, meaning they give up on learning at the more in-depth levels. On the other hand, the so-called "gifted" learners are often more accurate at self-convincing. As a result, they tend to have more self-confidence.

Multiply that scenario over a thousand times and you have learners with little or no self-confidence, motivation or love of learning. If you are too easily self-convinced, you are gullible. If you are too hard to self-convince, you're a skeptic.

In a learning context, the engagement of emotions at the end of an activity can help the brain to "know what it knows," to give the needed stamp of approval. Listen for expressions that let you know that others are processing the veracity of an experience. Someone says, "It just doesn't feel right." Another says, "I'll believe it when I see it." A third says, "Wait 'til he hears about this." These phrases indicate an attempt to feel convinced about something. Only then will there be actual belief. Believe you have learned something and you start to enjoy learning.

This is why the "constructivist" devotees are right on the money. The brain has to construct meaning. *You can't give meaning to another, you can only give information and allow the learner to create meaning.* Those who emphasize "covering the content" are outdated. Provide learners with the resources to construct their own way of understanding the material. This in turn, gives the learner time to have positive feelings about it and to succeed. Increased learner self-confidence follows, along with intrinsic motivation for future learning.

Many rituals that celebrate the learning can do more than just make the learning fun, they can also seal the information and experiences in the brain as real and worth remembering. To make sure that all your students leave your class in a state of "knowing what they know," provide activities that give them a chance to validate their learning. It's actually quite easy. The activities should use all three modalities, last for several minutes, ideally with several persons or for several times. They might teach a peer, put on a role play, write in their journal, do self-assessment or teamwork. Do these activities at the end of the learning, so that students can discover what they know and if what they know is "on track."

Practical Application: There are many ways to include the emotional side of our learners. Social activities can help. Provide opportunities for students to engage emotionally after a learning experience. It could be learner enthusiasm, "high five's," acknowledging their partner, balloons, fairs, singing, student-made gifts, displays, cheers, drama, role-plays, dance, a round of applause, noisemakers, a chance to show off, quiz shows, party poppers, gestures, debates, chants, festivals, rituals and simple celebrations. It could even be as simple as an enthusiastic student conversation about the topic. The key is simple, but critical: engagement of emotions leads to learners "knowing that they know it." This leads to self-confidence and motivation to learn more.

Cultivating Emotional Intelligence

We now know emotions are essential to learning, meaning, intelligence and thinking. For example, one of the key locations for our emotions is the amygdala. It matures earlier than the cortex, letting it store early traumas before we have the capacity to sort them out. As a result, the amygdala gets the emotions before the message is even relayed to the cortex... not good. In most situations, we can be in a state of rage before the cortex realizes it. Early emotional memories occur before we even have the vocabulary to understand or process them, says LeDeoux. Is it any wonder the enormous sales of programs, seminars, books and tapes that deal with emotional issues? It's half of the bestseller list!

Cultivate the ability to deal constructively with emotions

What are some implications of our brain's emotional design? We must first acknowledge the importance of brain emotions, and give them the credence as an addition to the seven intelligences. In *Emotional Intelligence,* Dr. Goleman describes the profound and diverse impact that emotions have on our lifestyle. But our culture has to take them out of the closet of the "mysterious" and put them out on the table for discussion. Once emotions are safe enough for people to talk about, we can gain better insights and tools to work with them. While our emotional illiteracy can ruin our family, finances and health, our ability to deal constructively with our emotions can lead to a rich, happy and satisfying life. Schools will have to strengthen the way they deal with learner emotions. There is no way around it. This means dealing with these issues more as an on-going reality, not an anomaly. Offer skill-building in:

- *How to handle distress. This is critical to the learning process.*
- *Managing attention/feelings. Otherwise, discipline problems go up.*
- *How to develop rapport. Friendships can help learning.*
- *Decision-making. This can help build life skills.*
- *Self talk. Teach to make it positive not negative.*
- *Dealing with loss & grief. Learners are impacted by relationships.*
- *Self awareness. Learn when, how and why we emote.*
- *Communication skills. Learn to ask, share and listen.*
- *Conflict resolution. How to deal with upsets, fights & arguments.*
- *Relationship skills. How to form, enhance or alter relationships.*

Until we acknowledge that we are, in fact, emotional beings and learn to deal constructively with that reality, we'll continue to have more and more problems. Our emotional literacy is related to discipline problems, dropout rates, low self-esteem and dozens of other learning and life skill problems.

Processing and Awareness

Learning can take place both consciously and nonconsciously. When we say consciously, we mean that we are aware of what we are learning, while we are learning it. Nonconscious learning means acquisition–we are taking it in, but there is no attention or awareness of it. Most classroom learning happens without the knowledge of the teacher. In fact, Donchin insists, *in excess of 99% of all learning is nonconscious*. Other research goes even further. Physicist Nick Herbert says, "Consciousness represents much less than one part per hundred billion of the processing power of the brain." Consciously, Herbert explains, we process only 15-50 bits of data per second. That's just a small part of the whole.

Visually, we process about 100 million bits of data per second. In fact, the most frequent decision we make is where to shift our eyes for attention (over 100,000 times per day). From our auditory channels we transmit about 30,000 bits per second. Kinesthetically, our tactile stream of data can exceed 10 million bits per second. In short, our brain is processing an enormous amount of sensory input, and it relays very little of it to our conscious attention. There's good reason for this; it prevents being overwhelmed with useless information.

Domains of Learning
How does our brain learn?

Non-Conscious Learning

We are not aware of 99% of what we learn. We're designed to pay attention to just one sensory input at a time. For example, we might not consciously notice another's non-verbal body language, but we respond to it.

Survival Learning

We learn what we perceive we need to learn for survival. It can be physical, intellectual, emotional or cultural survival. For example, we learned to eat, dress ourselves and speak–it was pure need.

Choice Learning

This is something we don't have to learn, but would like to learn. Includes hobbies, avocations, electives, anything for fun. For example, learning a new recipe, how to use a new software or reading a novel.

Imposed Learning

Anything that removes choice; it is forced upon us by another. Can be formal instruction, lectures, required classes or subjects. For example, it might be a class that you have to take to graduate.

How the Brain Constructs Meaning

Meaning is a critical part of the whole learning process. Unfortunately, most school students are drowning in information and starved for meaning. Yet for years, educators have assumed that what they were offering was automatically meaningful. It's not. What's especially interesting is how meaning mediates our representations of things. *How we feel about what we learn, changes how we perceive it.* Cytowic says we use the "Osgood" subjective scale of differentiation. It weights the initial way we filter concepts in three ways. It is first evaluated on a good-bad continuum. Then it's weighted in terms of potency (impact, size, power) and finally, the activity criteria (movement, warmth, excitement). If a student thinks a political leader is fairly good, low power and boring, meaning may be low.

The search for meaning is innate. All learners are trying to make sense out of what is happening at all times. Learners need time to "go internal" and create individual meaning for everything they learn. Yet, what creates meaning? Most teachers don't know! Recent brain research suggests that three factors are critical to learner-created meaning:

1. Relevance. On a cellular level, it's the activation of existing connections in neural networks. It relates to something the learner already knows some information about. The more relevance this has to the learner, the greater the meaning. This could be in an abstract form such as a geographic connection ("This city is just like yours in its weather, culture and size") or it could be a concrete connection ("My morning walks have meaning and are important to me. Why? I don't know; they just are.")

2. Emotion. When the learner's emotions are engaged, the brain "codes" the content by triggering the release of chemicals that single out and "mark" the experience as important and meaningful. Emotions activate many areas in the body and the brain, including the prefrontal cortices, amygdala, hippocampus and often the stomach. This may give meaning to something without you having any understanding of it.

3. Pattern. The context helps make it part of an overall pattern. Context can be social, intellectual, physical, economic, geographic, political, or any other pattern that provides the pieces of the puzzle, which make meaning. It's like the difference between: 1) picking up a random jigsaw puzzle piece and trying to understand it, versus 2) holding the piece and seeing the cover of the puzzle solution and locating where the piece fits in. This can come in the form of the grand "a-ha!" experience or simply over quiet reflection.

Our brain craves meaning and the quest for it causes us to derive any pattern we can from information. The brain craves meaning so much, that when information is lacking, it creates or makes it up. Let's say you go out to a restaurant. Another couple enters the restaurant, waiting to be seated. You know them; they are married, but not to each other. Suddenly, in the absence of information, your brain immediately begins constructing reasons, scenarios and models of understanding. You ask yourself, "Didn't I see those two together last week at a meeting? Didn't they both volunteer to work on the same organizing committee?" What the brain isn't given, it makes up.

Here are some common illusions. We know that some people see things that others do not. Why? The meaning is not in the graphics. The meaning, or interpretation of the graphics, is of course, in the mind of you, the reader. Do you see (in order of the graphics) a triangle, a dog and Napoleon? If so, remember that's what your mind brings to the illustration. What the artist drew was three circles, an afternoon of fallen leaves and a scenic view near a lake.

All Learning Requires the Appropriate "State"

A state is a distinct body-mind moment composed of a specific chemical balance in the body. The presence or absence of norepinephrine, vasopressin, ACTH, testosterone, serotonin, progesterone, dopamine and dozens of other chemicals, dramatically alter your frame of mind and body. Our states are affected by: 1) our thoughts; mental pictures, sounds and feelings and 2) our physiology; posture, breathing, gestures, eye patterns, digestion, temperature.

We can be in a state of joy, a state of despair or a state of suspicion. For learners to learn, they must first be in the appropriate state for learning. Each physiological state has a corresponding set of behaviors, says Maguire. That means a student who is sitting in the back of the room, with his arms folded, leaning back in his chair, has little chance of learning. His state called "this is stupid," has a corresponding library of behaviors, and learning is not one of them. The student who sits up front, nods his head while you talk and leans forward, is much more likely to learn, since that "attentive" state allows for better learning. Which state is best for learning? It all depends on *what type* of learning and for how long. In general, you'll want states of:

> *• Curiosity*   *• High challenge*
>
> *• Anticipation*   *• Low-moderate stress*
>
> *• Suspense*   *• Temporary Confusion*
>
> *• Low-moderate anxiety*   *(never high)*

The great teachers consistently engage these states every day in their learners. And, what's more, they are empowering the learners to engage those states on their own to become responsible for their own learning. In these states, you're highly likely to elicit learning. In fact, it's that simple.

The best learning tends to be flowing, self- or outside-orchestrated, from one state to the next. What can put learners into the optimal learning states? Tap into their natural curiosity, sense of surprise or anticipation. Hundreds of stimuli can do it. It depends on what's appropriate for the context you have. Some of the most commonly used strategies to change states are:

1. **Activities:** change from one to another, intensify, stretch, use energizers, go from individual to group work, change locations and do role play.

When a student acts inappropriately, stop all activities and change his or her state

2. **Environment:** change lighting, use aromas, music, ionizers, fresh air, change the temperature of the room, change seating, etc.

3. **Multi-media:** change to video, computers, overheads, music & slides.

4. **People:** the tonality of a voice, the beliefs, change teachers, have a guest speaker, have students teach, switch rooms.

5. **Tone:** change theme, time allowed, goals, resources, rules, opinions.

6. **Focusing:** breathing exercises (inhale & exhale slowly), nostril breathing, use of visualization, mental pictures.

7. **Student input:** learners are motivated to learn when they have control over their learning, creative input, frequency of feedback, positive social bonding, good nutrition, proper learning styles and safety.

The simple fact that our behavior determines our states, leads us to a powerful conclusion. When you are dissatisfied with a behavior, change the state, not the behavior. A student who is resisting any learning does not want a teacher to tell her to "get with the program" or "pay attention." After all, in the state that she is in, she virtually *has to* resist you and stay disinterested. The first thing to do is to change her state. If others in the class are in the same state, change all of their states. If she's the only one, change her state first, the behavior will follow.

Always change the state first before you change the behavior

❖

If learners are in poor learning states, do as much as is appropriate to change their states into more productive ones

Many teachers have already realized this and use this strategy. If one student is in a bad state for learning, you might give the class something to do. Go up to that student and ask her to join you for a brief walk to the drinking fountain, or just to help you do something. Have her do anything physical that changes the body's posture, breathing, eye patterns, all the things that determine state. Once the student is in a different state, it's easy to ask for a behavior change.

Change the state first, then the behavior. Get someone in the mood first, then pop the question. It's so simple, and so obvious. If your spouse comes home from a long day of work and is relaxing, horizontal, on the couch, sofa or easy chair, they are in a "leave me alone" state. That's a bad time to go up to them and say, "Honey, could you do me a favor?" They are in a "No way, Jose" state. Wait until a bit later, when they get up and are walking around the house. Any other posture than the relaxing state. In a different state, you're more likely to get a "yes" response.

Initially, a teacher would want to pay more attention to reading states and eliciting the more productive states. By "managing" states better, the better behaviors of attention, motivation and acquisition will naturally follow. In time, the teacher would want to teach learners how to better manage their own states.

Postures, positions, and states all have their own library of memories

Our Body's Learning Library

Stanford University psychologist Gordon Bower and Howard Erlichman of New York City University confirm that each mental, physical and emotional state "binds up" information within that particular state. In other words, states like anxiety, curiosity, depression, joy and confidence also trigger the particular information learned while in that state. It's almost as if you visit a library and check out a resource while in each state.

Bower says, "It is as though the two states constitute different libraries... a given memory record can be retrieved only by returning to that library, or physiological state, in which the event was first stored." Learners who hear a lecture while a certain baroque music composition is playing will test better if that same music is re-played at exam time.

Maguire confirms this "state-bound knowledge" brain research, as well. How and where we learn is as important to the brain as what we learn. In experiments with color, location and movement, Kallman says the recency effects are enhanced by identifying the stimulus at the time of the state change. In other words, pause and take notice of the circumstances of your learning, and it will trigger itself more easily later on.

The fact that information is "state-bound" also lends credibility to role plays, simulations and acting out learning. This may explain why the physical, concrete learning which occurs when learners act out the learning, better prepares them for the actual event. Pilots use simulators for training, the military creates mock war situations and theater groups do rehearsals. In formalized learning situations, an increase in the amount of role-playing may increase the application of the learning.

Studying and cramming for a final exam presents a problem. If your students study in a stressed-up state, using coffee to keep awake, that's a specific psychological state. The next day, while more relaxed and calm, they may forget much of that same information. It's better to teach students about how their own states can be "matched" for maximum recall, so they can enjoy the benefits.

Or, let's say you're in one room of your house and decide to go get a book in another room. You walk three-quarters of the way there and you forget what you wanted to get. So what do you do? You walk back to the original room and stand in the same place, and let your brain remember what it was you were supposed to get. Then, confidently, you stride back to the other room and retrieve the appropriate book.

> *Practical Application:* Many learners may actually know the material they are being tested on, but may not demonstrate it well during exam time. If they study under low stress, then take an exam under high stress, their brain will not retrieve as much as if they study AND take the exam BOTH under moderate stress. Since it's unlikely that an exam would be a low stress experience; studying that way is less useful. • Role playing is most productive when the same physiological, emotional and mental states are rehearsed that would be needed for the real situation. Fire drills, safety and health emergencies may be best rehearsed under deadlines. Business and social role-plays may be best done with the same intensity as real-life. Learners may want to coordinate their study time, environment and state of mind with the exact time, place and state that may be present at the final exam.

Teach students to manage their states for maximum recall

Specific States For Success

Kenyon, Csikszentmihalyi, Caine and Singer suggest that there are optimal states for much of the learning time. The ideal learning often takes place when the following conditions are met:

➤ **High challenges,** *intrinsically motivated*
(not too easy, not too hard, your own relevant choice)
➤ **Low stress,** *general relaxation*
(not NO stress, just minimal stress)
➤ **Immersed "flow" state:** *attention on learning and doing*
(not self-conscious or evaluative)

51

Very little learning goes on when learners are in poor learning states. In fact, since learning is so "state-dependent," it may be more critical than ever previously suggested to consciously read and elicit the optimal states. When you keep your student in the appropriate states for learning, they will naturally do better. Noted psychologist, Mihaly Csikszentmihalyi says the optimal learning requires a state of consciousness known as "flow." This uninterrupted state, in which one loses oneself in the performance, is well known as a timeless, pleasure-producing absorption in the experience. Children, teenagers and athletes often get into this state more easily than the average adult.

The best learning state is in between boredom and anxiety – a relaxed, challenging, happy concentration... not a forced one

Csikzentmihalyi defines this as "a pattern of activity in which individual or group goals emerge" (as opposed to being mandated) as a result of a pleasurable activity in interaction with the environment. When your skills, attention, environment and will are all matched up with the task, it's "flow." In other words, a situation where learners "go with the flow" while enjoying themselves and increasing their own challenges as they see fit, is optimal. This philosophy allows learners to discover what standards they want to achieve as they incrementally improve (and enjoy). Another benefit of this type of experience is that creativity and learning are maximized.

You rarely can "will" yourself into an optimal learning state. Millions have tried. There are some ways to make it more likely though, such as starting with an easy task and upgrading the challenges until it's just right. Your performance anxiety can be reduced by switching your focus to a particular part of the task.

Let's say you start out learning to play an instrument, speak a new language, ice skate, play golf, jog or use a computer. At first, it seems a bit difficult. You are making an effort. Then, in time, mysteriously, it seems that you are not only getting better, but you are having fun! Time passes without your awareness, skills improve and you seem to learn without struggling. It's the perfect combination of your personal skill level increasing at the same time that the challenge of the task seems to increase. It's the way a child in the snow, at the beach or at the lake, can get engrossed in playing and lose all track of time, learning for hours.

As another example, you get a new computer, open it up and start it. You begin to play around with it, getting used to it. Time passes, you keep learning new things. At a certain point, the phone rings or you realize it's dark outside. You discover you've been at it for almost three hours, but it felt like a half hour! That's being in a state of "flow."

Mandated, step-by-step instruction can work well for the initial stage of learning. It can create focus, belief and motivation. Once beyond that

52

stage, learners can be stifled by it. Assist your learners to get into the "flow" state by setting up favorable conditions for it. Set the challenge high, but keep the stress low. Let the learners set the pace, then provide support to help them to continually improve and re-set goals. This is probably the same way you learned to ride a bike, use a computer, ski, swim, talk, use chopsticks or fix a household item.

Csikszentmihalyi says that we can get into this "magical state" everyday. The formula is simple, he says. "When challenges are greater than your skills, that's anxiety. When your skills exceed the challenges, that's boredom." Match up the challenge and skill levels, and whamo! Jackpot! You get the perfect learning state, or "flow." It is fairly easy to get learners into optimal learning states if you remember what gets you into that state. Have your learners design a complex project that is relevant to them, and then vary the resources to keep the task appropriate to their ability levels. Make it exciting; use teams, simulations, technology, and deadlines, but without too much pressure.

Match challenge to skill level and you'll achieve the learning state called "flow"

Challenge + Intrinsic Goals = Learning In The Flow State

Some say, we lack the luxury of that relaxed play. The critics are more concerned with the accountability of drilling and rote learning. There's a place for some of each, but certainly more of the "flow" states. An example would be when we teach students how to use new software, and audio or video equipment. They tend to get immersed and absorbed in the learning, often losing track of time. This full immersion is critical to include as a whole "package" of learning strategies.

We can encourage productive, purposeful play by understanding how state-dependent learning really is. Then, we can encourage the development of particular states that lead to optimal learning. Naturally, our goal is to empower students to be able to manage their own states. The learning to learn process is partly the ability to decide what is appropriate for the moment and then do it. That means the ability to move from motivation to attention, to acquisition, to meaning states. Learning is more complicated and messy than the list below. But this can be a useful model for the processes, though not necessarily in this order.

Practical Application: Getting and keeping your students in a state of "flow" may be one of the most important roles you have. In that state, learning is enjoyable and learners are highly, internally motivated. Teaching them how to do it is an even better success. At the elementary level, let students make up a "dial" on a piece of paper which lists different states. Ask them to "turn the dial" and change into each of the states listed. At the secondary level, simply let them experience the states through drama and role play. Then help them learn how much control they really have over their own states.

Learning Success Modules

Motivation/Attention: "Why Learn This?"
Managing & eliciting states such as curiosity, anticipation, suspicion, challenge, confusion and interest. Initially, teacher-generated...Over time, students are empowered to manage their own states.

Acquisition: "What to Learn?"
Conscious: can be overt instruction, learner choice, etc. Non-conscious: can be peripherals, peers, non-verbals, voice, by-product learning, stories, etc. When at its best, this is the "flow" state.

Meaning: "What Does This Mean?"
Three Primary Sources: 1) Getting pieces of the bigger puzzle, 2) Engaging emotion 3) Strong personal relevance. This can happen during acquisition or later on.

Self-Convincers: "How I Know That I Know"
Learner-Generated Reinforcement by: Self-Assessment, Discussion, Pair-Share, Presentations, Rituals, Reviews, Teaching, Mapping, Journals, etc.

Long-Term Memory: "Will I Know When I Need It?"
Can be Categorical: improve with links, review, acronyms, pegs, association. Sensory; includes strong emotions, visuals, sounds, smells, taste. Procedural; involves body-learning, acting it out, practice, etc. Contextual; must have a unique location and circumstance.

Eating to Learn

The research on the effects of eating on learning is so conclusive and well-documented, it hardly bears another diatribe. As a reminder, MIT biochemist Dr. Judith Wurtman suggests the follow guidelines:

1. Eat breakfast. The learners who did, made measurable fewer errors, stayed awake in class and had fewer discipline problems. Deficiencies of trace elements like selenium (found in nuts), boron (found in apples) or calcium (common in dairy products) impair learning. Extra B vitamins, wheat germ, lecithin and ginkgo biloba have been known to help thinking, learning and memory.

2. Fats. In one study, those who ate unsaturated fats learned 20% faster.

3. Reduce sugars in the morning. Eat fresh fruits instead. If you're going to eat sugars at breakfast, eat protein with them to reduce the blood sugar swings in the bloodstream.

4. Early Priorities. Schedule fruits and proteins early in day, and carbohydrates later in the day, as an after-school snack or at dinner. Carbohydrates can trigger the release of the neurotransmitter serotonin which can lead to lower metabolic activity (drowsiness).

5. Avoid Dehydration. Drink 8-10 glasses of water daily (allow it in the classroom) and take multi-vitamin and mineral supplements. Water prevents dehydration and keeps alertness stronger.

Nutrition is vital to optimal learning success

Practical Application: There are many ways to influence the eating behaviors of kids. Give parents nutritional guidelines. Talk to them about how to fix better breakfasts and pack smarter lunches. Speak about nutrition at open house. Role model good habits to the kids. Put healthier foods in the school vending machines. Work with the food service staff to prepare more nutritious meals.

Dealing With Difficult Students

Biologically, PET (positron emission tomography) scans often reveal differences between the so-called normal brain and those with more common learning problems like the "hard to reach" or "at risk" learner, dyslexia, ADD/HD and severe discipline problems. There are usually neurotransmitter deficiencies or excesses involved. And a smaller hippocampus (located in the mid-brain area) has been linked to schizophrenia and memory problems. UCLA psychiatrist Adrian Raine says heart rates and sweat rates are slower in juvenile delinquents. They act out just to give their system the "charge" that normal kids get from daily life.

Yet, just because "brains are different," does not mean that's necessarily the problem. Dr. Thomas Armstrong, in *The Myth of the ADD Child,* says that there are dozens of reasons that kids show symptoms of ADD/HD, and they are, in general, misdiagnosed and the whole problem is overblown. Armstrong asserts that the real causes are more likely to be inappropriate nutrition, parenting, lack of clear guidelines or feedback. The labeling of ADD/HD students has become confused by the infusion of funding for "special problem" learners, the inclusion process which is tough for many underskilled teachers to deal with, and a lack of brain-based school environments. This masks the causes, making it very difficult to diagnose.

As an example, a teacher whose dominant teaching style is highly visual may judge student attention and interest in a class based on eye contact and the ability to sit still. Neither of those two behaviors will come from a dominantly auditory or kinesthetic learner. In fact, quite the opposite: you're like to get talkative and mobile learners who can drive certain unaware teachers crazy.

Students who do not give the teacher attention 100% of the time, may not be "attention-deficit," they could have other problems

> ### Difficult Students: their real problems often include:
> - *Undernutrition*
> - *Mismatching of teaching-learning styles*
> - *Over-demand of attentional states*
> - *Labeling by older-style tests*
> - *Bad environment with poor lighting, seating or temperature*
> - *Other masked problems*

As we explored earlier, the whole nature of attention in the classroom is under strong scrutiny. Good teachers have their student's attention for less than 20% of the time. That usually includes attentional states, curiosity, directions, discussion management and a few choice comments. Outside of that, quality teaching is generally going to happen when the learner has choices and can generate their own acquisition at their own pace, with their own tools. So students who do not "give" the teacher attention 100% of the time, may not be "attention-deficit." In fact, they could have other problems.

One of the areas under increasing scrutiny these days is the

EQ (emotional intelligence) of learners. Yale psychologist Peter Salovey proposed this concept in 1990 based on the new brain research. Dr. Daniel Goleman's latest book, *Emotional Intelligence,* explains the fundamental and critical skills:

- *Social skills...handling reactions in others, reading people*
- *Managing your feelings...controlling impulses, appropriate anger*
- *Motivation...the zest, zeal and optimism necessary to vitality*
- *Empathy...the ability to understand and respond to unspoken feelings*
- *Self-awareness...being in touch with your own feelings and knowing when and how to act upon them*

Use brain based learning and you'll be surprised at how many "gifted" learners you really have

 Using a brain-based approach, a majority of students that are labeled as "problem students" would become curious, intrinsically motivated and hungry-to-learn with the approaches in this book. The author of this book has experienced it first hand with thousands of students. The brain is designed to learn and the better the conditions for learning, the greater the likelihood of learning. Implement the ideas and strategies in this book and you'll discover just how many truly astonishing learners you have.

The old approach was to think of the brain as a computer (a poor analogy), and the "problem students" as a discipline problem. But think of the brain as an electrochemical stew (much is more accurate), and your answers are often more sophisticated. One of the more interesting areas of research involves the link between aggressive classroom behavior and the brain's most common neurotransmitter, serotonin.

Dr. Gerald Brown, clinical director at the National Institute on Alcohol and Drug Abuse, has been researching this area for years. He says that studies have repeatedly implicated low levels of serotonin in explosive, destructive and violent behavior. Some studies imply that animals that endure stressful environments produce less serotonin. That suggests it could happen to children raised in violent, threatening homes or neighborhoods. Boys are typically more of a discipline problem but studies show they have a 20-30% lower serotonin level and a 500% higher level of testosterone than girls. Is it any wonder some boys seem like a walking chemical time bomb?

Other areas have been implicated. The wrong levels of dopamine (another common neurotransmitter) have been implicated in depression and attention deficit. Food additives have been implicated by Connors in *Feeding the Brain.* Wurtman, in *Managing Your Mind and Mood Through Food* says poor diet is often suspect. Dr. London implicates excessive fluorescent lighting and lack of natural lighting. Ornstein suggests heavily positive charged rooms can lead to lethargy as well as overheated rooms. The point here is simple: there are many triggers in our environment that impact our body's chemistry. They include lighting, nutrition, seating, temperature and even the electrical charge of the air, that in turn, impairs our learning.

Learning and physical ability have biological cycles of performance

 Practical Application: Make a list of changes you can make. Start with the easiest or the one that will make the biggest impact. Do one change per week or month until you're complete. For more detailed information on discipline from a brain-based approach, see either **SuperTeaching** or **Brain-Based Learning & Teaching** by the author. See appendix for more details.

Body Clocks Run Our Learning

Recent brain research suggests we are far from a "learning machine." Instead, our learning and physical performance are dramatically affected by our biological rhythms. Orlock says that we have temporal cycles that affect us in countless ways, including cell division, pulse rate, strength, blood pressure, mood swings, concentration and learning ability. In addition, these cycles influence memory, accident rates, immunology, physical growth, reaction time and pain tolerance.

Even our breathing has cycles. On the average, we breathe through one nostril for three hours. The tissue then becomes slightly engorged, then we tend to switch to the other side. This has profound influences on the brain of the learner since it affects which hemisphere of the brain we use. Left nostril side, means right brain learning. These cycles are the same, day or night. We are simply more alert during the daytime cycles.

Researcher Englund found these rhythms in his tests that included psychomotor tasks, intellectual tasks, affective states tasks and physiological function tasks. His research tells us that overall intellectual performance (thinking, problem-solving, debating) is greatest in later afternoon and early evening. Although comprehension increases as the day progresses, reading speed decreases.

Scientists have found that our levels of minerals, vitamins, glucose and hormones can vary as much as 500% in a given day. That profoundly affects the brain's efficiency and effectiveness. In general, short-term memory is best in the morning, least effective in the afternoon. Long-term memory is best in the afternoon.

Practical Application: Problems in learning may be a result of lateralization. Learners who are at the peak of the right or left hemisphere dominance may need cross lateral activation to "unstick" them. Dr. Paul and Gail Dennison suggest cross lateral physical activity that moves one side of the body across over to the other side, which can stimulate both sides of the brain and energize thinking. • Options for assessment at varied times could increase learner performance. Vary your presentation hours to suit the ideal timetable for the brain. Provide diversity of activities to suit different learners. Englund even recommends that testing of students be offered at various times of the day to account for these differences. A brain-based school might have assessment on a rotating schedule.

Introduce new concepts to students when they are feeling positive during a high cycle

Ultradian Patterns

Our brains are constantly running on rhythmic learning cycles, says Thayer. The "low to high energy" cycle and "relaxation to tension" cycles are often called ultradian. They are affected by shifts in our breathing and energy levels, and run on 90-110 minute cycles. They dramatically affect our learning and perception of ourselves, he says. But realistically, how would one take advantage of these brain cycles? Thayer claims learners will focus better in the late morning and early evening. Yet they are more pessimistic in middle to late afternoon. Maybe it's better to present new ideas to others when they are more positive. Our thinking can get unrealistically negative at certain low times and quite positive during high cycles. These patterns, or "rhythms of learning," coincide with the ultradian cycles described by other researchers.

Can these ultradian patterns be modified, and are they consistent? Yes, to both. Intense physical activity or emotional engagement will "reset" the brain's normal rhythm pattern. This is critical because the brain is very poor at extended learning. It is better at learning, then a break, then learning, then a break. New neural connections, says Howard, need time to become "fixed" and strengthened without competition from additional novel stimuli. Several strategies can fill that purpose. A short walk, relaxation or even a nap.

Many pre-school classrooms already provide short daily naps. But Rossi and Nimmons report that this idea is perfect for older learners, too. Their research indicates two twenty minute naps per day improve work quality, productivity and alertness. They say studies show that "nappers" out-produce "non-nappers." This research is consistent with the ultradian biorhythms found by Howard. He says that the best time of the day to learn new material is just before going to sleep. Do an introduction to the material, then take a nap, or go to bed. Schools might do well to quit vying for learner's attention six hours a day and begin to appreciate the biology of the learner's brain. And certainly, administrators who judge the quality of learning by how much "attention" the teacher has, would do well to focus on learning, acquisition and meaning instead of the false "holy grail of attention."

Schools might do well to quit vying for learner's attention six hours a day and begin to appreciate the biology of the learner's brain

Practical Application: Teachers and learners may have much more influence over the quality of their learning than previously thought. By understanding patterns and fluctuations, one can learn to take preventive action. Help your learners to become aware of their own best times for learning. Use the influence you have to encourage your learners to manage or stabilize any of their awkward rhythms. They can do that through nutrition, rest and activity. A wise idea might be to offer a time each day for learners to take a short nap and relax. Regardless of the learner's age, they are likely to get value out of it. As a result, concentration may improve and learning may go up.

Greater Use of Natural Memory

How do your students store and recall their learning? Surprisingly, there is no master filing cabinet; your brain does not store "pictures" of people, landscapes, memory libraries, films of scenes in our lives, soundtracks, microfilm or facsimile. Neurosurgeon Dr. Wilder Penfield's famous open brain surgery was done on a patient who recalled incidents when his brain was electrically stimulated. But this only occurs on rare victims with severe epilepsy. Less than 1% of all humans would have reactions like that. Damasio, Rose and Edelman verify that the brain does not "archive" information or memories. So, how do you remember? For long term memories, our brain recreates those images "on the spot." Sights, smells, sounds, tastes and touch are coded, valued and distorted, and stored separately by a poorly under-stood process. When we think we remember, we really only construct enough "fragments" to trigger our thinking.

Once we put information in long term memory, there is no single specific place in the brain where you can access it. When you think of an idea, hear your internal voice, get an image, recall music, see a color in your mind's eye, *you are reconstructing the original.* Your brain composes a memory, pulling pieces from different areas of the brain. As an example, nouns are stored in different places than verbs! As time goes by, our memories fade out if not used or, get more and more "recreat-ed" and less and less true to the event. Your instant recreation of the original takes a split second (usually) and operates a bit like a volunteer fire department: there's no building, office or central system, but when a fire breaks out, the volunteers come from all over, go to one place and, (hopefully), put out the fire.

Taking that analogy a bit further, the more firefighters you have and the more motivated and spirited they are, the better. In the context of memory, the more contextual clues available at the time of the original imprint or event, the more associations available for retrieval. If the firefighters are especially motivated (higher emotional intensity) the better the result. In your brain, emotionally-laden cues create stronger clues for recall because they impact the brain's "memory-fixative" chemicals more than emotion-free clues. On top of that, we remember better that which we understand and relate to well.

Calvin reminds us to *think memory process rather than location* in the brain. Strategies to increase memory might be the use of music, mnemonics, location triggers, intense sensory experiences, theater, motor manipulation or humor. Schacter suggests that *multiple memory*

The mind "composes" memory by pulling from different areas of the brain

locations and systems are responsible for our best learning and recall. His research also shows that different kinds of learning may require different ways to store and recall memories.

Yet, we know that learners tend to remember much more when there is a field trip, a musical, a disaster, a guest speaker or a novel study location. Why? Multiple memory systems are activated. More sites, more associations, more senses, means more likelihood of recall. This has strong implications for learning. One more thing that boosts learning: after any learning, boost your sugar or epinephrine (adrenaline) levels. Studies show that both of them act as a memory fixative (though the later is a healthier choice). You can boost those levels most easily by doing something "mindless" but strongly physical or emotional.

Our short term, working memory, is different. It operates well in the range from 3-15 seconds, almost like RAM memory on a computer, a "buffer" for a printer or the "on-deck" circle in baseball. Most of what our brain "holds" in short-term memory is never transferred to long term memory. Why? The sheer volume of data makes it unnecessary for us to save it. While at times it's frustrating for ourselves or our students to forget so much, it's impractical for most everyday use.

Any system utilizing two or more of the brain's natural memory processes is considered a complex and therefore successful, learning strategy

 Practical Application: Learners may seem to forget a great deal of what is taught, but the problem may be a reliance on a singular memory system. If something is worth learning, it's probably worth remembering. Activate multiple memory systems with a variety of teaching activities, such as reading, listening to a lecture and seeing a video. Then follow-up with projects, role-playing, music, discussion, at-home assignments, field trips, games, simulations or drama. • Some of the best ways to follow up learning include: doing stair climbing, strong humor, dramatic role-play, high-energy games, simon-sez games, dance, running or other body activators.

Your Brain's Three Systems
For Memory & Recall

There are many ways to classify memory (e.g., short-term & long-term, active and passive, surface and repressed, positive and negative, etc.). While there is no single location in the brain marked off for each of these, the brain clearly acts as if we have three systems: 1) semantic memory, 2) body memory; procedural & sensory and 3) contextual memory.

Semantic Memory

Also known as: semantic/taxon/declarative memory/linguistic

Activated by: association, similarities, differences... "this word reminds me of that word"

Time limitation: by time, it can be short-term... it's our "working memory," good for less than 15 seconds unless rehearsed, reviewed or re-learned

Capacity limitation: it is chunk & age related (for a 3 year-old, one chunk; a 5 year-old, two chunks; a 7 year-old, three chunks; increasing to age 15 for seven chunks)

Operating system: in our mind/using words

Motivation: Requires relatively high intrinsic motivation

Examples: rhymes/mnemonics/peg words/similar content

Usage: teacher and student reliance increases by grade level

Brain-compatibility: lowest of the three operating systems... the brain is very poor at recalling books, words, text copy or other forms of "content within content." Have you ever read a page out of a book, then realized you didn't get a single thing out of it? You had to go back and re-read it all!

Semantic memory requires strong motivation and is a very unnatural way to retrieve learning

Semantic memory has never been pinpointed by location other than it is located in the cerebral cortex. The brain is poorly designed for remembering print and text copy. Information embedded in content is usually learned, or attempted to be learned, through rote and by following list-like formats. Semantic is the type of list-oriented, sometimes rote, memory which requires rehearsal, is resistant to change, isolated from context, has strict limits, lacks meaning and is linked to extrinsic motivation. (e.g., she asks, "Remember that article you were reading last night? What was the name of the author?" He replies, "Gee, I don't remember. Why do you want to know?")

This type of memory is unnatural and requires practice and constant rehearsal to keep fresh. That's why most people have the experience of "forgetting" so much trivia. The brain is simply not designed to recall that type of information. Teachers who require a large recall of textbook information are, at best, developing self discipline in the learners. It is certainly not the best way to learn the content. At worst, it creates countless discouraged learners who feel unnecessarily stupid.

Semantic learning has significant limitations in the attention and memory capacity

This type of learning is typified by seated school work and homework. ("Study for Friday's test by reviewing chapter six.") Information learned with the rote, semantic method:

- *is usually out of "real life" context, isolated and meaningless*
- *is harder to update, change and revise*
- *requires extrinsic motivation*

Learning "content embedded within content" (lecture, book, etc.), the brain has significant limitations in the attention and memory capacity. This is also referred to as our semantic memory. Research suggests that the design of the brain is for a limited number of "chunks" of information. It is almost as if we have "slots" for items to be stored. The phrase "Seven plus or minus two" is often quoted as our capacity for storing chunks. That figure is approximate for three reasons:

1. **Variations.** There are wide variations in the human brain. For example, a three-year-old may be able to hold one chunk, a five-year-old may be able to hold two chunks, a twenty-year old seven chunks and an eighty-year-old, five chunks.
2. **Source.** The original research was done on nonsense syllables. It's very unlikely to find someone who has to memorize letter groupings like DGR SDE NVM. Our ability is related strongly to meaning. The more the meaning the greater the capacity. You can memorize larger amounts as long as they have meaning.
3. **Contamination.** There are always multiple factors contributing. For example, the motivation of the learner, the small amount of context clues and a dozen other factors may contaminate the results.

Should we throw out traditional "book learning?" No. Just because the brain is generally very poor at taxon learning, we shouldn't discard the source. Semantic learning does have its place. When you ask for directions, for example, you want the shortest route from A to B. You don't want to drive all over the city to figure it out (although that would create a stronger "contextual map"). On the other hand, if you ask others what, of significance, they have learned in the last year, 90% of what they tell you will probably be contextually embedded information (vs. "rote" or "book learning").

Procedural Memory

Also known as: body-kinesthetic learning/motor memory
Activated by: association with physical movements, places, events, including intense smells, tastes, feelings, pleasure, sights or sounds
Time limitations: relatively few, often lasts for years... even if you haven't ridden a bike for years, you can usually do it without practice
Capacity limitation: appears to have unlimited storage
Operating system: in our body/in physiological states
Motivation: requires minimal intrinsic motivation
Examples: role play, riding a bike, recalling a favorite perfume
Usage: highest in early primary years, decreases annually except in arts or vocational schooling
Brain-compatibility: the brain is excellent at activating this type of memory. It is also accurate in general ways, such as gross motor skills.

Procedural memory is based on physiological states and is very natural for the brain to use

Motor memory, often called "procedural" (e.g. riding a bicycle), musical memory (the melody of a favorite song) and sensory memory (smell of a flower) is strongly brain compatible. The material learned this way is highly likely to be recalled. These are, in fact, the most commonly used methods for early childhood learning. A child's life is full of actions which require him or her to stand, ride, sit, try out, eat, move, play, build or run. The learning is then embedded in the body. And remembered for much longer.

The brain is also very effective in recalling any particularly strong sensory event. A funeral, a birthday, a car wreck, a snake in the face, an unusual sound, a scream, perfume or cologne. In one sense, these are the elements of phobias. These work best when there is the element of uniqueness; that, of course, provides the special distinctive "coding" and "addressing" for the brain so that memory is uncontaminated and easily recalled.

Episodic Memory

Also known as: loci/spatial memory/episodic

Activated by: direct association with events, circumstances or locations

Time limitation: varies (it's intensity dependent)... can last for years with moderate review

Capacity limitation: appears to have unlimited storage

Operating system: space (locations), time & circumstances

Motivation: requires minimal intrinsic motivation

Examples: "Where were you when...?" (Moon landing? earthquake, flood, bombing, assassination, your last anniversary, your first child was born, the Challenger disaster, etc.)

Usage: traditionally highest in early primary years, decreases annually except in arts or vocational schooling

Brain-compatibility: excellent at a general or gross level, poor at details over long term

Our brain sorts and stores information based on whether it is heavily embedded in context or in content

Our episodic or contextual memory can be described as primarily based on location and circumstances (or context). Research discovered that it has unlimited capacity, forms quickly, is easily updated, requires no practice, is effortless and is used naturally by everyone (e.g., "What did you have for dinner last night?"). This natural memory is visually context-dependent. Kosslyn says our brain has parallel visual systems, one for content and one for locations. So all visual information is coded; it's based on your movement, visual relationships and position in space and time. It's impossible NOT to use this contextual memory; it's a "natural memory."

The formation of this natural memory is motivated by curiosity, novelty and expectations. It's enhanced by intensified sensory input (sights, sounds, smells, taste, touch). The information is stored in a visual fabric or "weave of mental space." It's a thematic map of the intellectual landscape, where learning and memory is prompted by changes in the location or circumstances. In a classroom, it's enhanced by the use of seating or position changes, props, music, thematic teaching, storytelling, visualization, metaphors and other variations.

Kesner verified the hippocampus is the primary area associated with our contextual or episodic memory. O'Keefe and Nadel conducted their initial experiments on rats and later extended their findings to humans. They discovered a critical biologically-based difference between the two ways we deal with new information.

The difference between the two can be described quite simply: Information embedded in context (contextual, procedural, sensory memory) means it is stored in relationship with a particular location or circumstance. Information embedded in content (categorical, semantic, rote) is usually found in a book, computer, list or other information storage device.

> ***Practical Application:*** Reduce the amount of times your learners have to learn material by rote or embedded within content. Increase the amount of meaning that you or they attach to the learning. When giving directions and instructions, use small chunks. To a group of five-year-olds, you may want to give them a sequence of only two things. For fifteen-year-olds, this type of memory requires strong motivation and rehearsal, so be sure to limit the amount of dependence you have on it.

In as much as possible, embed the learning experience in thematic context

An overseas trip would provide our brain with heavy "embedding" in context. Millions of information bits, all in context, would be remembered for years. A two-week study session on Russia, using a geography textbook, is content embedded in more content. It all may be forgotten a day after the "big" test. Granted, the textbook is cheaper; but with some imagination, many teachers create much more "context" for the learning. It can be done with dress, language, food, environment and visitors.

For most teachers, planning time is short, so a simple alternative would work. Ask your students to plan a trip to Russia. They might work in diversified groups. They would have to learn something about the geography, money systems, language, passports, weather, foods and customs. They could each present their strategies to the rest of the class. A well-designed unit would remove the reliance on rote memory. It sure beats saying, "read and study chapter five for a test on Friday." Remember, all of the ideas are presented in this book *as an ideal* - you may not be able to implement every single one, especially at once! Do what you can, with the constraints you have.

There are profound consequences of applying this research. We may have been forcing many to learn in a very unnatural way. We have accidentally created generations of "slow" learners who easily forget what was taught. There may be a much better way to reach learners

SEMANTIC

PROCEDURAL

EPISODIC

▶ **HOW DOES IT WORK?**
By use of language, text, words and symbols.

▶ **TRIGGERED BY**
Word association. Repetition, rhymes mnemonics and peg words are also useful.

▶ **MOTIVATION**
Requires the highest intrinsic motivation.

▶ **STORAGE**
Theoretically unlimited, but practically limited by chunk size. Utilizes both short-term and long-term memory.

▶ **HOW DOES IT WORK?**
Learn by doing, hands-on experience. The learning is stored in our body or physiology.

▶ **TRIGGERED BY**
Movement, position, posture, tastes, feelings, states or aromas.

▶ **MOTIVATION**
Requires low to moderate intrinsic motivation.

▶ **STORAGE**
Unlimited storage capacity.

▶ **HOW DOES IT WORK?**
Associating what's going on with where you are.

▶ **TRIGGERED BY**
Revisiting initial learning conditions, locations, time and circumstances.

▶ **MOTIVATION**
Requires minimal intrinsic motivation.

▶ **STORAGE**
Unlimited storage capacity.

through the use of locale memory, thematic mapping and interactive contextual learning.

There are dozens of implications of this research. It explains why we remember certain things and not others. More of these need to be used in teaching, training and learning. Linguistic and book work (lectures, reading, listening) are usually more semantic, although novelty, pattern changes and other variations can increase their impact.

For teachers concerned with discipline, there are significant implications. First, since students remember very well the location and circumstances in which they are disciplined, all forms of "heavy discipline" from the front of the room carry dire consequences. A student will remember how he felt and his brain's contextual memory will link up that feeling with you, the classroom and the school. After only a few of these episodes, the student walks in the door of a classroom and immediately his locale memory tells him, "I feel badly in this room." That can only continue for so long until he starts missing classes. That, in turn, invokes more discipline.

Then, if he is required to stay after school or come to "Saturday School," his brain again links up bad feelings with school. Soon, just being on campus triggers negative feelings. Naturally, he hates how he feels while he's in school and may drop out. An administrator or teacher says, "He just wasn't motivated." You'd know better. He was a victim of a school that failed to understand how the brain really works. Attach embarrassment, revenge, pain and discomfort to being in school and most any student will soon drop out just to avoid the pain.

In addition to trying the suggestions below, make an analysis of your teaching and training to discover how much of what you do is "content embedded" and how much is "context embedded." Your own analysis may shock you. Contextually embedded learning is usually better. Chances are, you'll want to reduce the amount of semantic memory required. Cut seat work by 90%. Give real world problems to solve in context. Give only homework which requires contextual learning, not lists, problems or pages of unrelated facts. The brain is not designed for textbook memory. In fact, the ability to remember and to forget are biologically balanced to prevent psychosis.

Practical Application: Use more outdoor learning. Use alternative locations, other classrooms, the library. Take advantage of the ease and thoroughness of the locale memory system to embed key ideas by using real life learning in real contexts, musicals, plays, role-play, real world excursions, on-the-job training, motor movement and intense sensory input. Use purposeful storytelling, thematic metaphors, directed visualizations and real-world problems. Review discipline policies. Eliminate any system that does behavior "score keeping." Stop actions which evoke the "bad dog!" feeling in students.

More Immediate Learner Feedback

Research by noted brain expert Santiago Ramon y Cajal has emphasized that the brain needs feedback from its own activities for the best learning and growth. Most "great" thinkers of history like Leonardo Da Vinci have kept elaborate journals of their work. That was their self-feedback. As a child, you had plenty of environmental stimulation, but you also got all-important feedback. When you first learned to ride a bike, you experienced immediate and conclusive feedback: either you stayed up or fell down. Imagine trying to learn to ride a bike *without knowing how you're doing until a month later.* You'd go nuts, *and* you'd still be trying to learn how to ride the bike!

We may impede and retard thinking, intelligence and brain growth, and ultimately create "slow learners," by the lack of immediate feedback. Grades are, too little, too late to be considered useful feedback. They are a summary of the feedback over time. By contrast, feedback and reporting do have a very legitimate role. The brain loves feedback because simply, it gives it the information needed to survive. Feedback makes for better brains and learners. The research of Diamond revealed that while enriched environments were better for "growing" better brains, *rats which were given immediate and greater quality feedback "grew" the best brains of all.*

Delayed feedback has to stop. Elementary, secondary and upper level teachers who allow weeks to go by without giving their learners any way to know how they are doing, are creating high stress, poor learners and frustration. Not only is feedback important to the brain, the reporting of the feedback is important to the learner, his or her parents, the school staff and the community. After all, they are the "stakeholders" in the system and they have a legitimate vested interest in knowing the progress of that student. The brain thrives on feedback.

Our brain thrives on feedback for growth in learning, intelligence and survival

❖

The best feedback is immediate, specific and positive, but almost any feedback is better than none at all

Feedback:
The more often, the better • the more immediate, the better • the more specific, the better • the more appropriately dramatic, the better

Feedback can come in many forms. The most time-consuming is when you give feedback to the learners personally. That, in fact, has been the primary "clog" in the system. Teachers have to remove themselves from "the loop" as much as possible. Why? A 30-1 teacher-student ratio puts severe limitations on the amount of time you have, unless you allow students to get feedback elsewhere.

The most efficient (and quite valuable) method is peer feedback or self-feedback. Research by Druckman and Swets suggest that peer feedback is far more influential in generating long-lasting learning than teacher feedback. One of the most powerful business trends now is the use of a strategy called "360 degree feedback." It involves the use of personal multi-rating assessment, coaching sessions, third-party input and software tracking. The results have been dramatic at Coca-Cola, Shell, Merrill-Lynch, IBM and AT&T. Companies are finding out that their employees can become enormously more productive with better quality feedback, more frequent feedback and more variety of feedback. Feedback makes sense for everyone.

Question: What makes kids invest an endless stream of quarters into video games? **Answer:** Because it gives them challenges and feedback that they can get nowhere else in their lives. When given a choice, kids will chose to do something meaningless over something meaningful if they can just get that all-important feedback! To optimize learning, make it a rule that your learners get feedback every 30 minutes or less. Utilize pre-established criteria from which learners can self-assess, use partners and classmates or simply use the whole group to provide feedback. Generate more self-feedback by providing clear criteria for success, time for reflection, journal writing and simple systems for scoring and analysis.

Use all of your options for feedback: you can hold a class discussion where learners get ideas validated or shaped; you can use peer teaching, debates, mind maps with partners, observations, team discussions or a show of hands. Generate more peer feedback through the use of partners, teams, groups, peer teaching, pair-share and larger projects.

Until teachers remove themselves from the feedback loop, learners will never be able to get the quantity and quality of feedback that their brains need to become intrinsically motivated and do better quality work

---

Practical Application–Tips: 1) Students greet students at the door. 2) Have discussion about previous learning. 3) Allow peer teaching daily, or have weekly reviews. 4) Have learners talk themselves through their thinking, out loud. 5) Students keep score charts for their team and post the results. 6) Encourage the use of a journal. 7) Create and take "mock tests." 8) Have them pair up with other learners and prep for a test. 9) Have them correct their own homework, quizzes, tests. 10) Learners present to the group and get oral or written feedback. Feedback comes in many, many forms!

Multi-Modal Strategies

Hart, Herbert, Restak and Edelman say that the brain simultaneously operates on many levels, processing all at once a world of color, movement, emotion, shape, intensity, sound, taste, weight, and more. It assembles patterns, composes meaning and sorts daily life experiences from an extraordinary number of clues. This amazing multi-processor can be starved for input in a typical classroom. The typical response is often frustration or boredom.

Our brain is processing on many paths, modalities, levels of consciousness, and meaning levels. It's designed to process many inputs at once. In fact, it prefers multi-processing so much, that a slower more linear pace actually reduces understanding. In short, many instructors, trainers and teachers actually inhibit learning by the way they teach.

The work of Botella and Eriksen also verifies the parallel processing methods used by the brain in RSVP (rapid, serial, visual presentation) tasks. We all learn in random, personalized, often complex patterns that defy description except in the most reductionist terms. In fact, the brain seems to thrive immensely by pursuing multi-path, multi-modal experiences.

Sylwester says we are multi-processing in a manner much like a jazz quartet. It's a blend of four different instruments, four personalities, with no overt communication, and they still make great music. Anytime a teacher thinks that they can get great learning by teaching consistently to just one "musician" in the quartet, is going to be disappointed. What our brain does, when used best, is make great music metaphorically and literally!

We are quite used to the fact that we do things **one at a time.** We think of a thought, then another thought, then another one. We get up, shower, get dressed and eat, all in apparently a sequence. These illusions are far from the reality of our brain's true operations. Biologically, physically, intellectually and emotionally, we are constantly doing many things at once, says Ornstein. In fact, the brain can't do less than multi-process!

Our brain is constantly registering perceptions (over 36,000 visual ones per hour), monitoring our vital signs (heart, hormone levels, breathing, digesting, etc.), and continually updating our reality (matching new learning with representations from the past). In addition, the brain is attaching emotions to each event and thought, forming patterns of meaning to construct the larger picture and inferring conclusions about the information acquired. The brain is designed for survival by sizing up vast quantities of information. Here's an example of our brain's simultaneous, multi-modal capacity from physicist Herbert:

- *Each eye transmits 100 million bits of information per second along the optic nerve to the mid-brain relay centers into the occipital lobe.*
- *Our skin sends tactile information, as much as 10 million bits per second into the sensory cortex.*
- *From the ears, 30,000 bits per second of auditory information is sent along acoustic nerves to the brain stem.*

The sensory brain has an enormous appetite! That's why it has so much difficulty with traditional instruction. The contexts that students enjoy the most are usually the busiest: arts, sports, drama, field trips, music... all the "real life" activities. With this tremendous capacity, is it any wonder that a typical learner finds himself bored and frustrated by a linear, sequential delivery from a teacher using dominantly either visual or auditory messages? Traditional teaching is usually incompatible with the brain's natural design. We like to learn individually and often with others. However, we each learn so differently that standardized group learning needs to be dramatically minimized. Hart said: "Any group instruction that has been tightly, logically planned will have been wrongly planned for most of the group, and will inevitably inhibit, prevent or distort learning."

Because the learning process is so individual and complex, it's becoming increasingly inappropriate for schools to embrace traditional group instruction. We process so differently and we make meaning in a unique way. Five senses are taken in, and each is individually prioritized for your own brain's needs. The body's hormones are being released on individual timetables, at specified periods for our own biochemical balance. Learning is all multi-processing; the learner is immersed in sensory input, and the brain makes meaning out of it. In short, any lock-step, sequenced teaching ignores the real complexity of the brain.

Any group instruction that has been tightly, logically planned will have been wrongly planned for most of the group, and will inevitably inhibit, prevent or distort learning

 Practical Application: To utilize the brain's voracious appetite for patterns, emotions, sounds, sights, and novelty – use greater variety and choice with your students. • Get learners outside for a session. Teach a class in the media center. Allow students to watch a video (subject-specific) in the corner of the classroom if they'd like. Utilize guest speakers (particularly from your own school) more often. Play music in the background, use it in concert with what you do or have the students utilize it as part of the learning. Fill the room with poster peripherals, tactile manipulative and learning stations. Have a box of props for the students to use. Allow more partner and team grouping. Encourage multi-age grouping. Let students bring in friends, role models and parents to be classroom guest speakers.

Learning Options:
Which Do You Use The Most?

Real Life Experiences

Being there, on-location learning; excursions, a field trip. Engages maximum contextual & procedural memory. Provides the least control for educators. Requires minimal extrinsic motivation. Fewest educational dollars spent.

Immersion

Simulated on-site, a richly constructed environment. Purposeful, multi-sensory, "another world" (Like a flight simulator). Engages excellent contextual & procedural memory (such as a room designed as a foreign country). Minimal extrinsic motivation required.

Interactive Concrete Learning

Off-site; hands-on; using the skills, materials & tools. A dramatic arts class, personal coaching, training. Engages excellent contextual & procedural memory. Ideal when followed by debriefing. Some intrinsic motivation required.

Interactive Abstract Learning

Teaching & learning using representations, not the real thing. Tutoring, distance learning, CD-ROM, INTERNET. Soon, virtual reality will make this "the real thing." Uses categorical (some procedural) memory. Moderate intrinsic motivation required.

Second-Hand

It naturally would occur, learning outside the context. Examples might be videos, books and lectures. Learner must work to make it active with thinking, discussion, mapping, etc. Uses primarily brain-antagonistic categorical memory. Engages minimum contextual & procedural memory. Greatest amount of educational dollars invested here. Requires substantial intrinsic motivation.

The Auditory Brain

At the Center for the Neurobiology of Learning and Memory on the University of California, Irvine campus, Professor Norman Weinberger, has been researching the impact of sound on the brain. He discovered that the brain is already genetically tuned to the available sounds in our world. Each of our brain's auditory cells are designed to respond to a single frequency. His studies suggest that *the brain changes its structure based on the sounds heard*. More of certain types of sounds mean the brain will allocate more cells to be sensitive to those frequencies. In other words, our brain recycles and reallocates neurons based on what's learned and needed for the future. In musicians, the platinum temporal is larger (it's in the left hemisphere, and associated with auditory processing) than it is in non-musicians.

Can listening to music raise intelligence? One study measured the impact of listening to music before taking a standardized test. The students who listened for 10 minutes (Mozart's Sonata for Two Pianos in D Major), raised their test scores in spatial and abstract reasoning. On an intelligence test, the gain was *nine points after just ten minutes!* Although the effect in the brain is only temporary, the results can be duplicated with additional reactivation at any time. Those who listen only to a relaxation tape or had silence either improved only slightly or stayed the same. Researchers agree that more studies are needed to discover the effects of other music, timing and intelligence scores.

A 1987 National Music Educators Conference report says students taking music courses scored 20-40 points higher on standardized college entrance exams. A college entrance examination board study discovered that students who took four or more years of music classes scored higher on both verbal and math tests. Of the countries with the top-rated science and math results, all of them have strong music and art programs.

Other researchers revealed insights about music and its effects on the body. Dr. Houston says music "raises the molecular structure of the body...." The body resonates at a stable molecular wavelength. Music has its own frequencies, which either resonate or conflict with the body's own rhythms. When both are resonating on the same frequencies, you feel powerfully "in synch," you learn better and are more aware and alert.

How does music do this? It activates more than the right brain. It elicits emotional responses, receptive or aggressive states and stimulates the limbic system. The limbic system and sub cortical region are involved in engaging musical and emotional responses. More importantly, research has documented the role of the hippocampus in long-term memory. This

Certain music can boost attention, learning, motivation and memory

means that when information is imbued with music, there's a greater likelihood that the brain will encode it in long-term memory.

Price says that many learners understand and recall better when music is being played. The percentage of learners who fall into this type of category varies dramatically. Among musicians, you would get a different response than from more visual learners. Learner preference for some low-level background music (such as Baroque, in a major key) will run from a low of 20% to a high of 75-80%. Variables include the cultural background of the learner, the learning styles, the circumstances, the way the music is used, the volume, the type of music and carrier of the music. Best results have come from individual experimentation.

In the early educational years, music is common. Children play music, beat drums and sing. By age 20, all mandated forms of music are absent from the educational curriculum. That's unfortunate. Why? Music energizes and revitalizes the brain! Ear doctor and acoustic pioneer Tomatis suggests cells in the cortex of the brain act like small batteries to generate the electricity you see in your EEG printout. Amazingly enough, the brain's own energy storage was not charged by metabolism, they were charged externally, through sound. Tomatis discovered that specific high frequencies sped up the brain's recharging process. This recharge affected posture, energy flow, attitude and muscle tone. The most powerful frequencies for this are in the 8000 Hertz range. Prior research found that low frequency tones discharge mental and physical energy while the correct higher ones power up the brain. Should you use music in the traditional learning context? Absolutely. It can be a powerful addition to the environment.

> *The right sounds produce optimal learning states and energize the body for maximum wellness and optimism*

Practical Application: Provide complex, multi-sensory immersion environments. Reduce or avoid lock-step whole class instruction. Offer options for learning: in one part of the room, a video. In another, a reading area, in another, a discussion group or study session. Make the room rich with colorful posters, pictures, charts, mobiles and mind maps. Use mastery learning centers, group by interest levels or learning centers. There may be some low volume music being played and large projects going on with multi-status, multi-age cooperative groups.

Nonconscious Learning

The pioneering work of Donchin at the University of Illinois suggests that our brain decides to think, talk and act *before we have any conscious knowledge of it*. This simple discovery has helped him to create "leadership profiles" for the military to assess the nature of quick-fire, under pressure, critical thinking and intuition in decision-making. The best leaders, he found, make decisions after they have first experienced their immediate "gut level" response and then re-evaluated the decision in light of their values, circumstances and goals. Non-leaders went with their "gut-level" feelings without reflection.

His studies into the nature of the non-conscious mind revealed that it constitutes *over 99% of our learning*. Perhaps we should pay more attention to it. Sternberg of Bell Laboratories, found that even when we come up with the appropriate answer to a question, the brain continues to process alternative prospects of the question, non-consciously. It literally *practices thinking!* So much of our brain's work is, indeed, outside of our conscious awareness. The explanation for this has to do with how the brain receives incoming data.

The brain's reticular formation, says Herbert, is constantly asking the question, "What do I pay attention to now?" That's an important question, since we are getting literally millions of bits of data at any given time. We are forced, by the nature of our brain's design to make 100,000 decisions a day on what to give our attention to at any given moment. However, the brain allows us to consciously focus on only one type of sensory input at a time, even though we may be receiving many. This means that even though a teacher is talking, the learners may not be listening, consciously; but are definitely affected by it. On parallel tracks, the student may be paying attention at a normal level, consciously watching something, having feelings or sensations about it, and also day-dreaming or listening non-consciously. That's why Meherabian's often-quoted generalization has much truth in it. In general:

Words:	the content and selection	= 7%
Voice:	tonality, volume, tempo	= 38%
Body language:	gestures, position, etc.	= 55%

While the brain is receiving countless content messages, it is also receiving far more auditory and visual information that may either support or contradict the content. How much is deleted or enhanced by the brain at the time of the event varies tremendously. This research suggests we may want to:

1. *Train teachers in the productive use of their nonverbals*
2. *Utilize greater amount of peripherals, posters, visuals*
3. *Improve voice training for inflection, volume, tempo and tonality*
4. *Train teachers in spatial "anchoring" (where you are when you do things)*
5. *Reduce our dependence on having the learner's strict eye contact*

The Biology of Choice

We know that the brain acts differently when choice is offered. *Choice changes the chemistry of the brain,* says Ornstein. How? When learners get to choose a task, the resources, and the parameters for accomplishment, their stress is lower. They feel more positive about the task and look forward to participating and hopefully, succeeding at it. This, in turn, triggers the release of our own "optimal thinking" brain chemicals. These endorphins consist of two chemicals, each a chain of five amino acids. Pert and Restak say the other critical neurotransmitters involved in feeling confident appear to be dopamine and serotonin. As of today, this natural wonder drug has yet to be synthesized in the laboratory (although some say Prozac™ comes close). However, the brain manufactures it at will. The effects are a general feeling of well-being and confidence.

One of the keys to offering choice is that the learners must also recognize it as such... the perception of choice is critical

Teachers often complain of negative attitudes and depression in their students. They may want to read the article, "Learned Helplessness in Children" by Martin Seligman. A lack of choice changes the body's chemistry and that affects the attitude. On the other hand, when we feel hopeless, lacking choices or depressed, the reaction is chemical, too. The brain produces norepinephrine, a neurotransmitter which has a strong inhibitory effect. In this brain state, morale is low, learning efficiency is poor and motivation is weak. Which comes first, the chemical changes or the outward states? It's probably both, depending on the circumstances. Most learners are given little choice in their learning situations, which are organized, routed, facilitated and structured for them by others. This environment is not optimal for learning, according to the research teams of Deci, Vallerand, Pelletier and Ryan.

When students are given control over the content and process of their learning, motivation goes up, say Mager and McCann. The research is strong: when the learner has choice, both rote and complex creative learning can take place. When the learner feels controlled, you'll only get rote learning. To motivate learners, it is important to allow them to make choices about personally relevant aspects of a learning activity.

In other words, your offering of choice is not enough. The learner has to perceive that choice is offered and value it. Choice and flexibility is usually associated with more intrinsically motivated learners. Students enjoy being able to align self-determined goals with instructional goals. Learners who tend to focus more on fun and friendships may be able to be engaged when there are ample opportunities for self-determination and peer interaction, says Wentzel. These provide ways to meet personal goals and, to some, degree, instructional goals. In other words, the more ways the goals can serve the learner's own agendas, the better.

There are ways to tap into learning, excitement and participation levels for many learners who appear to be unmotivated. Help learners become more aware of their own personal, academic, health, social, athletic and career goals. A student is often willing to work on a team project because there's another person on the project that he likes or would like to get to know better.

 Practical Application: Design instructional experiences that allow more ways for learners to meet their own goals. They need ways to show off, meet new people, be an expert in something, grow, get in shape or become well-respected. Implement as many of the optimal motivating conditions as possible, as much of the time as possible.

Consistent choice and variety is a genuine key to motivation and learning

Caine and Caine suggest that excessive control by teachers actually reduces learning. They say that learners "must have choice and variety." It all comes down to this simple concept that Caine explains so well: "If students are to be predominately self-motivated, they must be given the opportunity to focus on *their* areas of interest and to participate in activities *they* find interesting" (author's emphasis).

In brief, unless learners have a real vote in determining the content and method of their learning, the learning becomes forced, rote, mechanical, short-lived and, eventually, distasteful. As Glasser notes in *Control Theory,* the more learners feel controlled, the more resentful they get. The resentment is either expressed or suppressed. It is expressed in the form of frustration, anger, rebellion, or lack of discipline. It is suppressed in the form of detachment, sabotage, apathy and cynicism about learning. Harter suggests that students who lack perceived control on an assigned task will hold back and give less than their best efforts. It makes sense. Unless you feel like you control your destiny, why invest in someone else's destiny? There are seven basic forms that are universally used to alter a learner's behavior. You'll want to use the best ways *without manipulating or controlling them.* Let's explore each of them.

Strategies of Influence:

1. **Hope:** The request is never made, nor is it even "talked around." It is simply assumed that the learner will figure out what you want & comply. The thought is actually outside the awareness of the learners. Since the learner doesn't know about it, there is *no perceived choice* by the learner with this strategy.

2. **Imply:** The literal request is never made, it is "talked around." The intent is that the learner will infer from the implication. Since there is no overt recommendation made, there's *minimal perceived choice* unless the learner successfully makes the proper inference. As an example, "There are some colored pens in the box on the counter."

➤ 3. **Suggest:** The request is made in a way that illuminates preferred options... Here there is *strong perceived choice.* If you like the options you're likely to choose one. "You might like to use a colored pen for taking notes."

➤ 4. **Ask:** Here, the request is made in a polite, way that encourages one to follow... there is *moderate perceived choice* in this method. "Would you please use a colored pen for your notes?"

➤ 5. **Tell:** (Acceptable instructional level.) To simply give them a directed statement in an expectant tone they have *minimal perceived choice,* they are strongly encouraged to do it. "Using a colored pen, write this down please...."

6. **Demand/Threaten:** The second strongest (also a poor choice) is to absolutely order in a way that they have *minimal or no perceived choice.* "Use this pen now, or you're not allowed back in the classroom!" To choose otherwise would be unsafe or wholly inappropriate.

7. **Force:** The strongest way (acceptable only in an emergency) of changing behavior in others is physical authority, physical presence or extreme coercion. Learners have *no perceived choice,* you make no other option available to them. This is unacceptable unless lives or property are at stake.

You've had a manipulative and controlling teacher before. How did it feel? Teachers who enrich environments their way, use music their way, do their kind of stretching, and design learning stations their way, can create a state of resentment and helplessness among their learners. The ideal rapport with your learners is this: sometimes you ask, sometimes you tell and sometimes you suggest. Too much of any can create problems.

It's ironic because the more you "suggest," the more "permission" it gives you to tell. Students don't mind being told what to do now and then, but a consistent diet of it will create resentment and drive motivation out the window. The teachers who have the toughest time with discipline or motivation are usually doing too much telling, demanding and threatening. That creates a bad working relationship and kids will react by trying to "get back"at you. Over use power and others will try to take it back (and at your expense). Choice is brain-based because your brain responds differently to choice than to control. Even the best planned teaching can fail if it's too controlling. In the long run, all controlling teacher strategies will backfire. Learners will give you less than their best effort and learn to dislike the very subject you wanted them to like. It's better to get student input or elicit learner responsibility for creating aspects like the environment, music, goals and activities.

Provide choices in what your students learn and how they learn it

Practical Application: Provide more options for learners, more choices in what they learn and how they learn it. Give students choices about the learning environment, the methods of instruction and types of assessment. Have discussion groups on the best types of student input. Utilize suggestion boxes, teams and expression areas. Students buy into and take pride in doing activities which they have helped to define and over which they have some control.

The Biology of Influence

Suggestion is simply a non-directed influence. It could be a nonverbal, a peripheral, a tonal shift, an off-hand comment, a choice of how something is done, or a thousand other indirect or even covert influences. These are always present because the brain codifies and makes associations with everything, Lozanov says. In other words, *you suggest, even when you think you don't.* Drawing from a large body of research, including the work of Rozanski, Herbert, Bell, Rosenthal, Mills, Meherabian and others, we know that we consistently influence others without making any directed contact. Yet, how does this happen?

Nobel laureate Sir John Eccles asserts the human brain is highly sensitive to the thought of itself and others. In his words, the human mind can and does exert continual "cognitive caresses" on itself. Donchin can measure the thought itself, before it becomes a word or action. We know from experience, attitudes influence the performance of students. But if positive thoughts or affirmations really boost learning, should a teacher give more positive affirmations and reduce or eliminate fault-finding in students? There's no doubt that they should.

John Stuart Bell, an Irish physicist, won the Nobel Prize for what later became known as Bell's Theorem. Bell's discovery was that once any two atoms have interacted, they remain connected in a type of quantum matter that defies distance and barriers. Later experimental verification of the theory was conducted by John Clauser at UC Berkeley and Alain Aspect at the University of Paris. Einstein's Unified Field Theory revealed the quantum inseparability of all matter. In the book, *Quantum Reality,* physicist Herbert says that non-locality (the ability of one entity to affect another, in another location) applies to the mind. All particles that have once interacted, remain, in some sense, connected. Yet, paradoxically, Herbert adds that we may not be able to use this knowledge, we *simply know that these interactions exist* on an atomic level. The affects cannot be predicted, they are non-specific and non-local, yet we know they exist.

This work fits with the work of physicist David Bohm's Nobel Prize winning work on the undivided wholeness of the universe. Everything is, in some way, connected. British scientist Rupert Sheldrake has postulated the existence of "morphogenic fields" of influence. He says that life forms can affect others *across space and time.* He suggests that once relationships are created, they continue some connection, both on a molecular as well as social level. In fact, many teachers insist that once they've had a student in their class, there is a bond that transcends

*Our thoughts are powerful...
Many assert that they work across
the boundaries of space and time*

Research suggests that positive or negative thoughts can heal or even kill

space and time. How potent are these positive or negative thoughts? Research suggests that they can heal or even kill.

For example, living tissue is quite responsive to the mind's will and intention. Rubik's research, described by Dr. Dossey, showed that bacteria isolated in a petri dish *can be killed merely by negative human thought.* Can humans influence others by merely the way they think about them? Yes. Grad's work suggests that certain people can generate "extraordinary negative effects on living entities." Researchers have done studies where intention, merely our thoughts about something have physically altered white blood cell counts. Other studies have suggest influences on healing, attention, enrichment, decay, growth and motion. Braud's study suggests that positive thoughts can function at a distance to affect others. Byrd's randomized, double-blind study with 400 patients discovered that positive thinking through prayer positively impacted the health of heart patients. They required less surgery, fewer drugs and had a faster recovery rate.

Could this apply to the classroom? Countless adults have learning and identity traumas that originated from a primary school event, and were sparked by an unknowing teacher. An article in the New England Journal of Medicine suggests what we say to each other can be of enormous impact. Dr. Rozanski reports that by voicing negative thoughts, our *sarcasm, criticism and put-downs, increase abnormalities in heart rate.* These aberrations were as significant and measurable as those from a heavy workout or pre-attack myocardial chest pains. If this occurs in the medical field, what might the impact be in the classroom?

The author of *Pygmalion in the Classroom,* Robert Rosenthal indicates that the single greatest influence on learners is the expectations (thoughts) in a classroom climate. In a classroom climate typified by positive challenge and joy, the body releases endorphins, the peptide molecules that elevate our feelings and cause us to feel good. Research by Levinthal and Sylwester suggest that this "positive learning climate" promotes faster learning, better problem-solving and higher quality learning. In short, when we feel good, we learn better!

Many factors contribute to a positive climate; our dress, positive comments, enthusiasm and values. As teachers, our beliefs and attitudes are inextricably intertwined with how we teach. The power of suggestion nonconsciously "suggests" that learning is hard or easy, homework is valuable or not, school is important or not. We also suggest to our students that they may find things easy, fun and challenging, or we suggest that things will be hard, boring and frustrating. Your smile, or lack of it communicates to your students. Your conversation,

Negative comments, whether purposeful or accidental, may be far more harmful to students than previously thought

❖

Learners in positive, joyful environments are likely to experience better learning, memory and feelings of self-esteem

your clothes and handouts all add up the impact of the "collective whole."

Examples of suggestion include seemingly innocuous comments like, "Don't forget your homework," or "Don't make so much noise." Both of those suggest the wrong message: to "forget and to make noise," since the brain has to first process the affirmative command before it can translate it into a negative. Also, "You shouldn't find this too hard; others found it wasn't much trouble," give mixed messages. It's much better to suggest, "You might find this easier than expected," or "Others found this subject a lot of fun." Suggestions are found in directions, asides, content, small talk and even humor. The better teachers can be at the use of positive suggestion, the easier their job will be.

Do the positive or negative emotions of the teacher affect the learning of the students? Yes, according to Mills. He says that learners pick up on the particular emotional state of the teacher/trainer/instructor and it impacts their cognition. Teachers who use humor, give warm smiles, have a joyful demeanor and take genuine pleasure in their work will have learners who outperform those who do not. The days you are in a better mood, it seems that your learners mirror it back to you.

Ornstein, the author of *The Amazing Brain* and *The Healing Brain,* says suggestion is so powerful that:

1. *It triggers hormones*
2. *It impairs or boosts our hormone levels*
3. *It can scar or smooth out skin*
4. *It communicates with the body on a cellular level*
5. *It can enlarge or contract our body tissues*

Ornstein's research on the brain has led him to say, *"...the impact of intangibles like words and symbols, when leveraged through a brain whose major form of exchange is such thoughts, can be powerful. Words can be scalpels. They can generate thoughts, feelings and beliefs in our brain which can be communicated to the cells of our body and even the chemicals within cells."*

The evidence from this field is dramatic. What we believe and what we think, can, does and will directly affect us and others. Here are some of the best ways to take advantage of the influences of suggestion:

> *Training in the art of suggestion may be one of the most potent and rewarding staff development investments*

Practical Application: De-stress, listen to music, use humor or positive affirmations. Get into a good learning state to suggest more positively to those around you. Use positive peripherals, colorful posters, inspirational works. Add flowers, music, bright colors and keep it clean. Use seating which encourages open communication (not factory-style rows of desks). The use of polite language: please, thank-you, avoid all name calling, all labels ("lazy, idiot, wise guy, loudmouth, slowpoke, etc."). Your eyes, gestures, facial expressions and posture is either approachable or not. Be excited about learning and exude joy! Your materials either suggest the learning is interesting or boring. The tests suggest learners can succeed or not. Offer variety and choice. That suggests you care about the learners and want them to succeed.

Positive affirmations will strongly influence your students

Reflection and Analysis

❖ In what ways can you translate the key three or four theories and discoveries presented here into practical everyday useful ideas?

❖ What information in this chapter do you already apply?

❖ Did you think of any questions about this material? What were they?

❖ Did you have an emotional reaction to any of this information?

❖ Specify what was different and new to you? What was familiar and what was review?

❖ How did you react intellectually? Do you agree or disagree with any ideas explored in this chapter? Which ones and why?

❖ Let's say these things are, in fact, true about the brain, what should we do differently? What resources of time, people and money could be redirected? In what ways do you suggest we start doing it?

❖ Generate the most interesting or valuable insight(s) you got from this chapter.

❖ Make a plan for your next step, a realistic, practical application of what you've learned, and outline it.

❖ Can you foresee any obstacles you might encounter? How can you realistically deal with them?

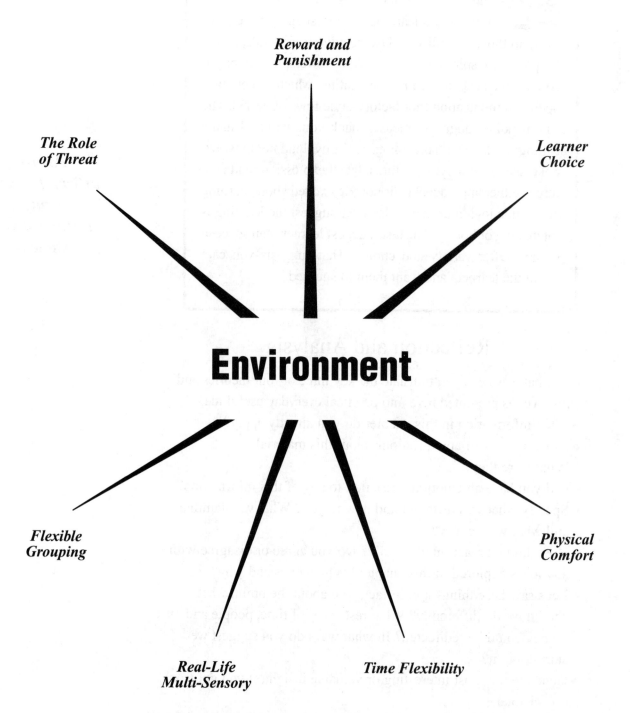

Chapter 3
The Environment

Learning and The Role of Threat

Remember the metaphor of the brain as a jungle? The prevailing "law of the jungle" is survival. The brain is hard-wired to survive and may be run more by natural selection than instruction. As an infant, you learned fastest what you *had* to learn to survive (eating, walking, etc.). As a student, you learned what you *had* to learn to survive academically. A significant part of your brain will insure that you learn, react and adapt primarily for survival. The brain stem area is usually the part of the brain that will direct your behavior under negative stress (excessive cortisol is released into the body) and is most responsive to any threat. The brain wants to make sure that when the negative stress is strong, higher-order thinking skills are set aside in favor of rote, tried-and-true behaviors which may help you survive.

Startling new computer generated images show very clearly that under threats, excess anxiety, moderate negative stress and induced learner helplessness, the brain operates differently. There is increased blood flow and electrical activity in the brain stem and cerebellum area and decreased activity in the mid-brain and neocortex. That means that brain activity has "survivalized." You get more predictable, rote, knee-jerk, reaction behavior when the brain senses any threat that induces helplessness. Survival always overrides pattern-detection and problem-solving. This fact has tremendous implications for learning.

Threat and induced learner helplessness have got to be reduced from the learning environment to achieve maximum potency. Having said that, it's pointless to make learning stress-free. Researchers discovered that learners who were exposed to light to moderate stress and anxiety in their early years became superior learners to those who had no stress at all in their early years. Gazzaniga says it's not stress that's bad, it's *uncontrollable* stress that's bad. Under that type of stress, all areas of the brain are still being used (it's simply a matter of degree), the expression "survivalized" may be much more accurate than "downshifted." It is less capable of planning, pattern-detection, judgment skills, receiving information, creativity, classifying data, problem-solving and other higher-order skills. It's as if your open, receptive arms suddenly close down to new information. The brain is likely to "survivalize" under the following conditions:

- *Potential physical harm from classmates, staff, family, or others.*
- *Intellectual threats (your ideas being attacked, your potential). A test or essay returned with derisive comments. A lack of information to meet the task requirements.*
- *Emotional threats (feelings or self-esteem under criticism). Potentially embarrassing moments. Reward systems that threaten withdrawal if not achieved*
- *Cultural-social threats (disrespect), isolated from peers, working by oneself. Unable to pursue personal values at school. Limited chance to utilize meaningful personal life.*
- *Resource restriction. Constricting time deadlines for performance. Lack of computers, software, knowledge.*

The best learning comes from an emotionally safe non-threatening environment

When your brain perceives "alarm" or "danger," from these types of intense, stressful or threatening situations, the body reacts. Major stress hormones are epinephrine (formerly called adrenaline) and cortisol. When we are exposed to excess stress or threat, the body releases first, epinephrine into the bloodstream, putting it into a state of challenged arousal. That immediately speeds up your heart rate, depresses your immune system, gets your body ready for fight or flight. You know the feeling. When you are threatened, your body feels different. So far, so good. Then after about five minutes, the adrenal glands release cortisol (known as a glucocorticoid), to recreate homeostasis in the system. Over the short run, it's good.

Prolonged exposure to cortisol (one of the body's hormones released under stress), can be devastating. Researchers discovered that when glucocorticoids are secreted, the body is ready to deal with threat and stress on a physical level; muscular activity is enhanced with blood flow and epinephrine. But when you are stressed without the muscular exercise (like in a classroom) those same body systems continue to be stimulated. Studies show that rats (whose brain structure is similar to humans), lose neurons in the all-important hippocampus--an area of the brain critical to learning, memory and emotion--as a result of overexposure to cortisol. Could your students be literally losing their classroom memories over threatening and stress-inducing teachers? The implications of this to our own students, and the levels of stress and threat, are sobering.

The Many Faces of Threat

Teachers who pause and say with a stern voice, directly to the class, "I'll just wait until you're ready to learn" may be doing more harm than good. This threat ("I'll withhold *my* teaching as long as *you* are withholding your good behavior") is a simple example of the continual threats that pervade a typical classroom. Research now tells us that threatening learners may foster more of the same behavior that we are trying to avoid.

A threat is any stimulus that causes the brain to trigger defensiveness or a sense of helplessness in the learner. An example of a subtle threat to the learner is when an assignment or project is given, and the learner lacks the resources to carry it out. That might be not enough time, no pen or pencil or no one with whom to discuss it. The learner reacts and goes into a state of stress. In some cases, the threat may be perceived as indirectly aimed at one's self-esteem, confidence and peer acceptance.

According to Jacques and Leonard, threats adversely affect one's ability to plan for the long-term and to stay engaged at a task for a long period of time. These abilities are critical for learners: some evidence links success with the ability to postpone immediate gratification and go for the long term. This concept is critical to the brain-based approach: Most so-called "at-risk" learners are in a constant state of stress or threat. As a result they constantly make choices that are biologically-driven: work for the short-term, do the tried and true and watch your backside. They are not unmotivated or short-sighted. But the part of the brain that needs to be engaged for long term planning (the parietal and frontal lobes of the cortex) are likely to have less blood flow and be less efficient. Educators that deal with these issues head-on will find more long-term success than those with a knee-jerk reaction that strengthens discipline and demands higher standards.

Perceived threat triggers learner helplessness

Why Rewards Are Brain-Antagonistic

The human brain operates differently under reward systems than when using intrinsic motivation. The anxiety of rewards trigger the release of neurotransmitters which can inhibit creativity, problem-solving and recall. Rewards are manipulative, part of the old school of behaviorism and do more harm than good in the long run. Using the brain-based approaches in this book, motivation will occur naturally and intrinsically. Rewards should be phased out slowly and avoided.

A reward is anything given by an outside agency that has both

1) market value and 2) predictability. A hug, even a predictable one, is not a reward. It cannot be marketed away to another like a cookie, pizza or trophy. A certificate is not a reward unless it is part of a stepladder to rewards. A kind word is not a reward, since it cannot be marketed.

In a reward-based system a learner might be told that if she solves a problem (or has good behavior, perfect attendance, etc.) she will get a sticker, token, food or other reward. With every reward, there is an implied threat of no reward (punishment) for a contra-behavior. Kohn argues that rewards are, at best, short-lasting and at worst, devastating to intrinsic motivation. Spielberger states that learner dependence on "flocking behaviors" (social conformity) and reliance on extrinsic rewards (bribes, stickers, etc.) actually increases with threat. Caine says that threats, even if occurring indirectly through rewards, may hinder our abilities to tolerate ambiguity and to delay gratification, and that it may be "among the most important and devastating of all consequences."

Rewards often impair intrinsic motivation

Another example can be seen with a learner who is constantly disciplined because of his inability to stay engaged in a task or inability to delay gratification. The discipline may actually create a "state of threat" which perpetuates the problem. The so-called "underachiever" who is bribed will learn very quickly how to play the game to get the reward. In "playing the game," *he'll never get a chance to learn what the real rewards are:* learning for the sake of learning and experiencing the absolute joy of discovery. That absence will haunt the learner for the rest of his life, reducing options and shrinking the potential contributions to humanity. Remember, you can only reward for a predicted behavior. And much of the best quality cannot be predicted.

Learners who feel picked on and threatened by adults are least likely to change behavior because the part of their brain that deals with "perceptual mapping" and complex behavior change is unable to be engaged. Both adults and teenagers stay in peer groups for identity and safety. So-called "low achievers" who are constantly threatened, disciplined and bribed with rewards may be unable to work for delayed gratification. Kohn's research demonstrated that even in cases where rewards worked in the short-term for immediate behavior changes, long-term follow-up indicates the *bribed behavior rarely continues.*

The part of their brain they may need to use, the frontal lobes, are less likely to be engaged under a system where others have control, and they feel pressured to perform like a rat in a cage. This may explain many of the common behaviors of gangs, so-called "low-achievers" and the drifting learners who seem unmotivated. The more they are threatened, the more behaviors they'll have which demonstrate a lack of higher-order thinking skills and increased short-term thinking. Any system of learning which uses heavy authority, position, laws, threats, rules, punishments and rewards will, over the long run, perpetuate the very behaviors it is trying to eliminate. The techniques may work initially, but soon the learner behavior will become rote, minimized and stereotyped.

> ***Practical Application:*** Identify inappropriate learner behaviors. Identify areas of threats, both implied and explicit. As much as possible, remove threats from the learning environment and introduce alternative forms of motivation, such as novelty, curiosity, positive social bonding and relevant content. Avoid reliance on extrinsic rewards.

Inter-group competition can exist without reducing motivation

Learner Grouping – Use All Three! Collaborative, Competitive & Individual

The world is highly competitive and it's important to know how to compete. At the same time, the brain learns poorly under excess negative stress caused by anxiety and fear of loss. What's challenging and exciting to one learner may be threatening to another. These fears can happen when the learner is given assignments to complete, without the resources (time, people, information, goals, rules or environment) to do them. Other people can be a valuable resource to help provide encouragement and feedback.

The old model of learning as being 1) an individual only or as 2) a competitor is over. Today's learning takes many shapes; sometimes it's quiet, other times, noisy. Sometimes you'll learn best by yourself, other times with a group. The important thing as a learner is this: if you do want or need the help of others, it should be part of the environment. One ought to be able to get help from others without being ostracized or without a great deal of difficulty.

Allow learners a way to work with others. Collaboration can occur among the learner's peers. Ideally, it is systemic. This is ideal when the teacher, parents, students, administration and community all work together in an atmosphere of trust, mutual respect and cooperation. These are particularly excellent learning conditions because today's problems require creative, innovative thinking. The most creative thinking comes when learners are unthreatened and feel safe with their peers. The brain works most creatively when the stress and threat is low and the challenge and stimulation for novelty is high.

In the last several years, there's been a deluge of research about the advantages and disadvantages of competition in the classroom. Kohn argues strongly in his book, *No Contest: The Case Against Competition,* that competition has vastly undermined educational and business systems. Ames argues that the typical competitive learning environment is strongly detrimental to the learner. Although evidence suggests that some kinds of "win-win" competition (new games, for example) can be positive, he is dead-set against it. He summarizes: *"There is little, if any, viable evidence that a competitive goal structure in the classroom is associated with outcomes that are indicative of positive self-worth, continuing motivation or quality of task engagement"*

Learning challenge and mental stimulation can exist without the risk of win-lose competition

So, does the cooperative learning model fit for everyone? The pioneers of cooperative learning, Slavin and Johnson found that when positive cooperative structures were in place, *some inter-group competition could exist without reducing motivation.* In fact, the more you use cooperative groups and individual learning contexts, the more competition can work. Only in balance can it provide legitimate learning opportunities. Yet so many schools use only the competitive model.

The grading system of a "curve" is a competitive model. The system is a classic case of win-lose. In order for someone to win, another must lose. The model compares one student with another. What in the world does one student's evaluation and assessment have to do with another student's? Either you have a certain level of understanding and mastery in that area or you don't. To prepare our learners for the world of tomorrow, we must role model and teach cooperation, peer support and sharing. This includes re-evaluating "cheating."

Some cheating is counter-productive. It reduces inquiry to "answer-getting." But in contexts of research and exploration, sharing is quite productive. Typically learners experience many barriers which include helplessness or anxiety over content mastery, scarcity of resources, pressure for grades and lack of background knowledge to succeed. While not a panacea, the option to work with others can be more than just motivating; it can be the single greatest boost to confidence and content mastery. Tests can be re-designed in ways that encourage the process of cooperative learning and not the search for the "holy grail" called the right answer.

Practical Application: Teachers can help foster stronger collaboration and trusting relationships with their students in many ways. Some of them include: keeping promises, being fair, being consistent, respecting differences, self-disclosure, being non-judgmental and creating a climate for cooperation instead of competition. It's best to offer choice and variety to boost collaboration. Offer students at least partial choice in who they team up with or work with. Offer time to develop appropriate relationships of trust in the larger groups. Most of all, create cooperative instead of adversarial classroom relationships.

"Invisible discipline"
is a useful strategy
for eliciting
the best classroom
behavior

Brain-Based Discipline

With better classroom relationships, the whole nature of discipline is different. By using a brain-based approach, your discipline problems will drop dramatically. The reason? Students will find the learning to be engaging, real-life, relevant, complex and challenging. They'll have cooperative, "mentor-like" relationships with teachers and cooperative, not competitive relationships with students. They'll feel valued, have input and never feel threatened or coerced. Nevertheless, there will be times you'll have to use discipline strategies. To make it easier, here's a few keys:

Give students appropriate input into the classroom behavior guidelines. Avoid any type of coercive methods, score keeping systems or "Assertive Discipline" strategies. There are two general types of classroom problems: 1) A type you can deal with quickly, easily and often, without anyone else knowing about it. No harm was done and the student is often unaware of their behavior. 2) The second type requires action on your part. It means someone was rude, offensive, group time was wasted or damage was done.

In the first case, your best options are to use "invisible discipline." Only you will know that the strategies you implement and use are also helping students stay on track. Switch teaching activities, change voice tone, change the music, move to a new location, offer some stretching, or deep breaths. Next, discipline the behavior, not the problem. Use a change of ritual, a nod of the head, eye contact, send a student on a errand, regroup into partners – solo or teams, yell at an object, use a gentle touch, drop names, and use a variety of expressions.

In the second case, where someone was rude or damage was done, your response is different. First, never threaten a student with punishments like "If you do this again, you'll stay after school." School is not a prison. If a student is acting out, simply ask him in a straightforward voice, "Tim, can you keep your hands to yourself for the next 10 minutes? Great, thanks..." Or, "Kim, if you can remain quiet for the next 10 minutes, we'll both be happy, is that a deal?" Or, Mark, we've got 20 minutes left. Can you handle yourself? Otherwise, we've got to have a serious talk after class." No threats, no lectures or morality. Just straight talk.

Manage the classroom with meaningful learning instead of control and coercion

When harm has been done to a person or property, feedback is important. The brain learns best with immediate, positive and dramatic feedback. Learners need to know that they were wrong and that they need to deal with the consequences in a positive way. The non-coercive discipline programs that develop a concept of restitution are very brain based. Implement these within an active learning and positive social framework. Unlike the old programs that stigmatize students, these give structure for reparation. It's important for students to learn what damage, if any, they have caused and make up any wrongs. It is based on responsibility, not obedience. Obedience is the old school model of control and coercion. It uses threat and anxiety to manage a class, instead of engaging students in meaningful learning. It's not brain based and should be taken out of the classroom. For more discipline strategies, read **SuperTeaching.**

Physically Comfortable Environments

The physical environment can be either brain-compatible or brain-antagonistic. As an example, how much does seating and posture affect learner success? A great deal, it turns out. Two researchers, Shea and Hodges, did studies to determine the effects of "formal" (hard-backed chairs facing the front of the room) and "informal" (seated on more comfortable chairs, using pillows, occasional floor seating, based on student choice) seating in the classroom. Shea found that students who preferred "informal" seating arrangements performed "significantly" better on comprehension tests. Another group scored much higher in math when they taught and tested in the seating of their choice.

Some researchers (Della, Valle, Hodges, Shea, Kroon) have found that the environment (seating choices, comfort levels, lighting) and learning styles (global, sequential, concrete, abstract, etc.) are a significant factor in determining the success of students. Dunn and Dunn say that at least 20% of learners are significantly affected, positively or negatively, based just on the type of seating options. To be at their best, learners need to have choice. Some students need the floor, a couch or even beanbag furniture to be at their best in learning.

Does location matter? Let's say you go to a workshop and sit on the left hand side of the room. You change the seating at the break and sit on the right hand side. You'll discover that it's almost a different seminar just by switching seats. We may accidentally reduce motivation and learning by keeping learners in a fixed seating pattern. Wlodkowski says that circles, U shapes and V shapes are best. When given a choice, good spellers tend to sit on the right side of the classroom. This may be related to handedness (hemispheric dominance), or left-brain, right field of vision, or the fact that visual creativity is dominant on the upper left side of the eye pattern range.

Mobility, even simply standing up can boost learning. Dr. Max Vercruyssen of the University of Southern California discovered your body's posture affects learning. His research showed that, on the average, standing increased heartbeats by 10 extra times per minute. That sends more blood to the brain, which activates the central nervous system to increase neural firing. Researchers found, that on the average, there's a 5-15% greater flow of blood and oxygen to the brain when standing. Psychologically, he says, standing up also creates more attentional arousal and the brain learns more. While sitting, you are more likely to get bored and lose focus. When standing and listening to another, if it's just for a few moments, your focus is stronger. We may be wasting some learning time by having students sit too much.

A physically comfortable environment can significantly increase student learning

---

Practical Application: When the group energy seems to lag, ask your learners to stand up. Then you can either continue to talk for 1-3 minutes while they stand, or give them a diffusion activity, an energizer, or ask them to start a relevant discussion with a partner. Change seating patterns often. Provide choice and make it easy to change types of seating arrangements.

Dr. London's 1988 experiments caught worldwide attention. London, a Vermont psychiatrist, switched the lighting in three elementary school classrooms halfway through the school year. He was curious about whether the type of lighting mattered to the students. During the December Holiday break, he changed the current fluorescent lighting to Vitalite full spectrum lighting. Although the experiment was not a double blind one, no one expected any particular result.

The results, however, were amazing. London found that the students who were in the classrooms with full-spectrum lighting missed only 65% as many school days as those in the other classrooms. London was not surprised. He said, "Ordinary fluorescent light has been shown to raise the cortisol level in the blood, a change likely to suppress the immune system."

The positive impact of a quality learning environment with strong natural lighting can be powerful and lasting

Dr. Harmon studied 160,000 school-age children to determine which, if any, environmental factors influenced their learning. The results of his research were shocking. By the time they graduated from primary school (age 11-12), over 50% of the student subjects had developed deficiencies related to classroom lighting! To test the hypothesis, changes were made in the students' learning environment, and the same children were studied six months later. The results of the change were equally dramatic: visual problems reduced 65%, fatigue reduced 55%, infections decreased 43%, and posture problems dropped 25%. In addition, those same students showed a dramatic increase in academic achievement.

The experiments have since been repeated with similar results. What about bright versus dim lights? Many students relax, focus and actually perform better in low-light situations, says Krimsky, Dunn and Dunn. Brighter lights, especially fluorescent, seemed to create restless, fidgety learners. Low-level lights seemed to have a calming effect, especially at the younger ages.

In U.S. Defense Department studies, Taylor and Orlansky report that heat stress dramatically lowers scores in both intellectual and physical tasks. In combat tests where special protective clothing was worn, Taylor found that high temperatures were responsible for decreases in performance requiring accuracy, speed, dexterity and physical acuity. While many types of obstacles and barriers are known to reduce or impair learning, heat stress is one of the most preventable.

Choice may be the most important variable in the temperature of the learner's environment. There is a wide variety of perceptions, say Dunn and Dunn, in what constitutes a warm or cool room. The optimal is near 68-72 degrees Fahrenheit for all learners, says Murrain. There are differences among ages, peers, and genders which can change with seasons, moods, and other miscellaneous factors.

In her book, *Smart Moves,* Dr. Hannaford asserts the average learner is often dehydrated. This is caused by the body's necessity to maintain a proper pH balance. Hospitals report that patients improve when encourages to drink up to 20 glasses of water a day. Athletes boost water consumption for peak performance. Theater performers often keep a pitcher of water nearby for the same reason. More and more educators have found that pure water does help learner performance.

Learning specialists recommend from 8-15 glasses per day, depending on your body size, the weather and your activity level. Nutritionists recommend pure water to insure that it is free of contaminants. It's also better to have pure water rather than coffee or tea, which act as diuretics requiring your body to consume even more water to make up the deficit. Teachers have found that in classrooms where students are encouraged to drink water as often as needed, behavior improves, as does performance.

Scientists at the National Aeronautics and Space Administration have discovered that the use of plants creates a better scientific, learning and thinking environment for astronauts. Could their same research apply to learners indoors? Dr. Wolverton, who headed the Environmental Research Laboratory, says that certain plants have improved life for the astronauts and his own personal life at home. He says that they remove pollutants from the air, increase the negative ionization and charge it with oxygen. In fact, according to the Federal Clean Air Council, studies discovered that plants raised the oxygen levels and increased productivity by 10%. The ideal air environment has between 60-80% humidity.

It seems that when it comes to air, the more negatively charged it is, the better. Smoke, dust, smog, pollutants, electrical emissions, heating systems, coolers and traffic are all detrimental culprits. With these, the air becomes more highly electrified (too many positive ions) and humans react. Studies suggest between 57-85% of the population is strongly affected and can gain dramatically from more negative ions.

The impact of negatively charged air on the body is powerful. Originally, it was found to speed recovery in burn or asthma patients. It was later discovered to affect serotonin levels in the bloodstream, to stabilize alpha rhythms and to positively impact our reactions to sensory stimuli. Ornstein reports that rats exposed to negative ionization grew a 9% larger cerebral cortex. The greater levels of alertness can translate to improved learning. Studies by Minkh in Russia, Hansell in the USA, Sulman in Israel, and Hawkins and Barker in England, suggest improved well-being and enhanced human performances on mental tasks.

Everything from plants to air quality affects learning

There are nearly 800 research papers on the effects of negatively ionized air. Dr. Hansell, a researcher at RCA Laboratories, first stumbled on the "ion effect" in 1932. Dr. Kornblueh of the American Institute of Medical Climatology was among the first to demonstrate the dramatic effect that the electrical charge in the air has on our behavior. His work at Pennsylvania Graduate Hospital and Frankford Hospital in Philadelphia led him to make them a permanent part of hospital treatments. Many corporations, including ABC, Westinghouse, General Electric, Carrier, Philco and Emerson now use ion generators in the workplace.

The brain craves enriched, multi-path real-life learning

Practical Application: We may be accidentally distressing our learners by enforcing uniformity in the environment. We may want to have either separate environments or to rotate the type used. Many of our learners are under performing because the environment does not suit their own, best learning style. Add variety to the learning environments you create. Over a span of two weeks, vary lighting, use music, provide silence, provide earplugs and encourage cooperative learning as well as individual learning.

Enrichment: Real-life & Multi-Sensory

In general, the brain craves enriched, real-life learning. Most school children make a distinction between school and the "real world." The real world has an order to the chaos, a rhythm to the cycles and a fullness to the drama. It's three dimensional and full of emotions, challenges, music, smells, voices and things to do. The fact that learners crave the real world experiences can give us some insights into more brain-compatible learning.

Some scientists say that there is very little learning that the brain does best in a school-style, orderly, sequential fashion. In fact, Nobel Prize winning scientist and co-discoverer of DNA's double-helix formation, Francis Crick, says that the functions of the brain "are usually *massively parallel* (my emphasis). For example, about a million axons go from each eye to the brain, all working simultaneously."

We learn about a city best from the full multi-path, sensory experience of it, rather than from sequential information in a book. As a child, we learned our neighborhood from scattered, random input, not from a manual or guidebook. Learning is best when it provides many options and various input. Keep in mind the metaphor of the jungle; the incredible complex capacity of the brain is processing something as simple as crossing a street in five different areas of the brain–visual pattern movement, shape, velocity, sounds and feelings. For a 15-year-old, crossing the street is usually quite mundane. A typical classroom could have double and triple the usual input and you'd still get no complaints from the learners. In fact, your discipline problems would probably cease forever.

All this multi-sensory, multi-modal enrichment feeds a brain often starved for input. But can enriched environments actually build better brains? Yes. In groundbreaking research by UC Berkeley pioneer Dr. Marian Diamond and separately, by University of Illinois researcher William Greenough, an amazing plasticity to the brain was discovered. The brain can literally grow new connections with stimulation, even as you age. The fact that we can "grow" brain, means nearly any learner can increase their intelligence, without limits, using proper enrichment. This discovery was first done on rats, then the findings were extended to human studies. Calvin says cortical area growth does have something to do with "being smart," although the internal efficiency of your "wiring" and connections make a larger difference.

Multi-sensory, enriched environments will build better brains

Many types of rat groups were studied in various conditions. The experiment was divided into three groups: a control group, those in impoverished environments and those in enriched environments. Time and time again, for over 30 years of varied experiments, the rats in enriched environments grew better brains. Brain cells in rats given acrobatic training had greater numbers of synapses per cell than those from rats given only mild physical exercise or none at all. Physical exercise improved neural circulation. Rats in the enriched environments made significantly fewer errors on a maze test and had an increase in brain weight. Greenough found that he could increase the number of connections in animal brains by 25% by exposing them to an enriched environment. Dr. Diamond summarizes the data: *"With increasing amounts of environmental enrichment, we see brains that are larger and heavier, with increased dendritic branching. That means those nerve cells can communicate better with each other. With the enriched environment we also get more support cells because the nerve cells are getting bigger. Not only that, but the junction between the cells – the synapse– also increases its dimensions. These are highly significant effects of differential experience."*

Most importantly, the research of UCLA neuroscientist Bob Jacobs confirms that this research on brain enrichment translates directly to human brains. Jacobs found that in autopsy studies on graduate students, there were up to 40% more connections (dendritic branching) than with high school dropouts. The group of graduate students who were involved in challenging activities (sports, music, drama, clubs, hobbies), showed over 25% more overall "brain growth" than the control group. Yet education alone was not enough. Frequent new learning experiences and challenges were critical to brain growth. The brains of graduate students who were "coasting" through school had fewer connections than those who challenged themselves daily. Small brain slices showed more cellular growth in nearly every case. Jacob's research on cortical dendrite systems in 20 neurologically normal, right-handed humans (half male and half female) evaluated:

For growing a better brain, provide frequent challenges, continual novelty and dramatic feedback which come from enriched, real-life environments

- *total & mean dendritic length*
- *dendritic segment count*
- *proximal vs. ontogenetically, later developing distal branching*

How important is richness, changes and novelty? Dr. Arnold Scheibel, director of the Brain Research Institute at UCLA says, "Unfamiliar activities are the brain's best friend." The fact that the brain is so stimulated by novelty may be a survival response; anything new may be threatening the status quo (potential danger). Once we have grown accustomed to an environment or situation, it then becomes routine. Over time, the reticular formation operates at progressively lower levels and the brain gets less and less stimulation. Do something new, and once again, the reticular formation is alerted. This starts brain growth; more messages are carried by nerve cells and novelty encourages more dendritic branching. That branching triggers new connections, called synapses. It's as if you can almost "grow" your brain at will.

The most astonishing research may have come from Wallace et. al. They discovered that in *just four days, there are significant "structural modifications"* in the dendritic fields of cortical neurons. The measurements were made in the visual cortex and were done on dendritic length and total number of branches. Sirevaag and Greenough found that brain enrichment happens in stages, from surface level to depth growth.

Greater Time Flexibility

One of the complaints at a typical school is the continual sense of "not enough time." The systems of bells, the hurry from class to class and the model of teaching content creates brain-antagonistic conditions. These impair learning because deadlines can encourage stress, create threat, anxiety and induce learner helplessness. What's more, most quality thinking takes time. It takes time to create meaning. It takes time to reflect and time to be thoughtful and responsible. In an environment of "go-go-go," the opportunities for deeper meaning, character development and personal relevance are rare. But there are other considerations.

Two Canadian researchers, Klein and Armitage, discovered that there is an alternating period of dominance and efficiency for each side of the brain. In other words, when spatial dominance is high, verbal is lower. This up-down oscillation runs on 90-100 minute cycles. In other words, learners switch from right brain to left brain dominance throughout the day. The day, for our brain, is defined by 16 cycles lasting 90 minutes each. Every 90-100 minutes, your brain is at the strongest left hemisphere dominance and 90 minutes later, it peaks with right hemisphere dominance. When verbal skills are high, spatial skills are lower.

This discovery fits in well with the earlier discovery that all humans have ultradian rhythms known as the "B-R-A-C" cycle, the "basic rest-activity cycle." These cycles are the alternating periods of REM (rapid-eye-movement) which corresponds with our dream time and our non-REM light rest periods. This nighttime cycle is continued throughout the daytime also.

Orlock says that these 90 minute cycles also coincide with hormone release into the bloodstream, regulating hunger and attention span. She cites experiments in isolation where the subjects consistently "headed for the refrigerator or the coffee pot about every ninety minutes." Sensitivity to pain, appetite and learning varies because the brain is changing continually. She also quotes a study on the hemispheric dominance switches that occurred on learning, thinking, reasoning and spatial skills tests. Once again, the switch-over occurred every 90 minutes.

That's the biological background. So, why is time flexibility an important piece of brain-based learning? Two reasons. First, more time flexibility allows the learner to "even out" the effects of the brain's biocycles. This will affect learners less over a two hour block of time

We may be underestimating the ability of students if we test them at the wrong times of the day

than it would within a shorter 45 minute block of time. Instead of a learner being in the low part of a cycle of brain efficiency every single day, the longer sessions allow them to have both ups and downs in class. It gives time for learners to use more of the multiple intelligences.

Secondly, the brain works best in an environment of choice, low threat and challenge. More time gives the teacher the flexibility to deal with student stress and help the learners feel comfortable and ready to learn. Typically, the brain wants to forge meaning out of the information and to place it in a context. If the learner is given continuous time deadlines, anxiety and the sense of threat goes up. That inhibits learning. If the learner is forced to rush through the material, the focus then becomes "playing the game" or learning for the test. Both of those reduce the depth and quality of learning.

Practical Application: The brain does not learn "on demand" by a school's rigid inflexible schedule. It has its own rhythms. The longer the time block for learning, the more the lows are mediated by the highs. Learners in a full-day schedule at the elementary level will learn more than those in a secondary level lock-step, factory-style, assembly-line format of 45 minutes. Block learning can better take advantage of the brain, while shorter classes are more brain-antagonistic. Secondary schools which make more appropriate use of longer, two-hour blocks will find student learning goes up.

Brain cycles can impact class scheduling

Reflection and Analysis

❖ In what ways can you translate the key three or four theories and discoveries presented here into practical everyday useful ideas?

❖ What information in this chapter do you already apply?

❖ Did you think of any questions about this material? What were they?

❖ Did you have an emotional reaction to any of this information?

❖ Specify what was different and new to you? What was familiar and what was review?

❖ How did you react intellectually? Do you agree or disagree with any ideas explored in this chapter? Which ones and why?

❖ Let's say these things are, in fact, true about the brain, what should we do differently? What resources of time, people and money could be redirected? In what ways do you suggest we start doing it?

❖ Generate the most interesting or valuable insight(s) you got from this chapter.

❖ Make a plan for your next step, a realistic, practical application of what you've learned, and outline it.

❖ Can you foresee any obstacles you might encounter? How can you realistically deal with them?

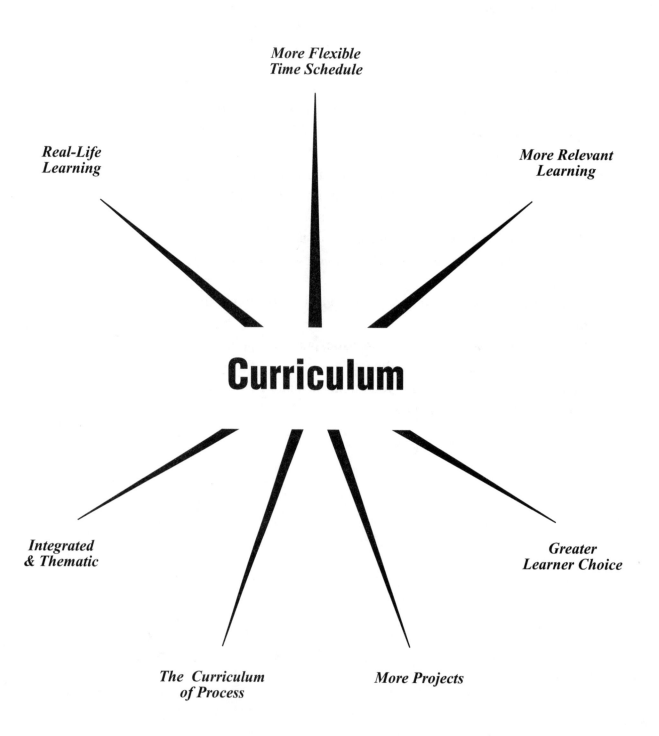

Chapter 4
Curriculum

From Artificial to Real Life Learning

Because the brain is designed to learn for survival, it's very good at learning that which is perceived as useful, practical and real. This type of learning requires the least amount of extrinsic motivation. For example a two-year-old is highly, intrinsically motivated to learn to walk, dress herself, use utensils, eat and learn to talk. These life skills are essential to survival. At a typical technical or vocational school, you'll usually find motivated students who engage themselves in learning every day without rewards, threats or bribes. Those are examples of real world learning.

The best curriculum is real life. It is meaningful, relevant and extends our natural knowledge of the world. In the brain-based approach, the thinking is a reversal of common educational theory. We start with the learner, not the content. The organization of the lesson is based around creating optimal conditions for the best, natural learning. Our understanding of the brain reminds us that the brain rarely learns in a sequence. The common model is ludicrous: "Introduce unit A, learn it, take a test on it. Now go to Unit B..." The brain learns by immersion: jumping into the middle of life-like Unit K, then students introduce real diversions A, D & G. You'll move ahead and backwards, with the next step affecting the previous one, and pushing you in new directions like a Slinky.™ This is the model for how we learn most of what is called "real life."

Closed quarter learning, in classrooms, schools and training, do require some structure. Before the model is introduced, here is a brief contrast between traditional curriculum and lesson planning and the more brain-based thematic interdependent approach. It can provide us with a real awakening.

The Not-So "Good Ole Days"

The old way of teaching was to take a subject like math, science or history and divide it into smaller chunks called units. Then sub-divide the units into daily and weekly lesson plans. Then, each day, present a micro-chunk of the whole. It sounds logical. However, it is not the way our brain is best designed to learn.

Imagine yourself as a five-year-old. You get your first pair of rollerblades (in-line skates) for your birthday. Now you're all excited. You want nothing more than to put them on it and go! Wait... you can't. Your parents have decided that you should learn to rollerblade "the proper way," in the right "order." They will teach you how to use them by instructing you in the following units of content. Would you sit still for this "lesson?"

A. Safety
Personal safety
Use of helmets, pads, gloves
Proper strength
Defensive attitude
Neighborhood safety
Possible hazards
Neighborhood culture
Sidewalk and road safety

B. History of Rollerblades
Laws, customs and social opinion
Original inventors
Purchase price & replacement costs
New vs. used prices for blades
Contingency plan for
mechanical damage
Transportation niche
Advantages and disadvantages
of usage
Comparisons with other modes
Mechanical & product specifications
Materials used

C. The Skills of Rollerblading
The mental approach
The first steps
Proper use of hands
Body positioning
Advanced skills

D. Everyday Use
Storage of skates (locks, garage, etc.)
Permission (when, length of time, etc.)
Extras (special brakes, safety
equipment, etc.)

Naturally, before your parents have finished teaching you unit "A," you have lost interest and gone on to do something else. The brain is far more capable than the list above indicates. Obviously, a more typical child's approach is to get a few bits of important information, pop them on your feet and give it a try.

The brain learns best in real-life, immersion-style multi-path learning...fragmented, piecemeal teaching can kill the joy and love of learning in students. Amazingly enough, most kids learn to rollerblade just fine. If you think about it, that's how you learned some of the most complex things in your life. Your native language, for example. Did you learn rules of grammar first? Did you get classes in it? Did you take tests in it? Of course not! You never were taught formally your native language. You "picked it up."

Relevant, Real-Life Learning
With Choice & Flexibility

Is it possible that our brain can "pick up" other subjects? Is it possible to learn science, history, accounting, geography, math, life skills, literature and the arts by just "picking them up?" Of course it is! That's the way our brain is designed to learn: multi-path, in order or out of order, many levels, many teachers, many contexts and many angles. We learn with themes, favorite subjects, issues, key points, questions, trial and error and application. That is thematic learning.

The underlying principle is that our world is an integrated whole, and that one of the greatest gifts you can offer your students is the connectedness of classroom education to the real world. The thematic curriculum approach urges you to follow threads that weave throughout your student's real world. Instead of a single subject or textbook, use real-life learning. In this fast-moving information age, your preferred sources of information should be a combination of the student's real life experience, magazines, computers, videos, the community, other students and staff, television, the INTERNET, on-line journals and libraries.

Thematic learning is a process closer to the way the human brain is naturally designed to learn best

More Time, More Depth
With Fewer, More Complex Topics

For most learners, school consists of larger complex topics that have been chunked down, dumbed down, watered down and thinned out. It's often boring when a topic or unit is reduced to the lowest common denominator, the smallest information chunk teachable. It's in a chunk, chunk, chunk, chunk, chunk, then end format. The brain learns poorly this way. Typically, secondary academic learning is presented in a linear form. Teach, test, teach, test, teach, test... start new unit, repeat cycle. Yet research shows that we learn best in an immersive environment, with continuous exposure on multiple levels, with increasing challenges and practice. That's why doing projects in multi-age groups, seems to work well.

However, the brain learns more like a spiral: starting out, dropping an item, reviewing it, previewing another, dropping them, reviewing that, starting an item, previewing another. In other words:

• Learning Is Messy! •

You can't take real life and chunk it down into hundreds of little boxes with labels on them and expect the brain to learn it like it does in real life. The more we make school learning like real life, the more the brain, with its rich capabilities, will sort it out.

Diverse, Multiple-Input + Time = Immersion Learning

How does this translate into curriculum? Use fewer topics, spend a longer time on each topic and do a more in-depth study of each. The more rich, the more thematic, the more the sensory input, the more distinctness, the better the memory of the learning. Which would you remember more, a field trip or a page out of a textbook? The longer theme approach, articulated by Kovalik, works best for most subjects. It's explained in detail in her book, *ITI: The Model*. The basic components of it are as follows:

Year-Long Theme: This is a year (or term) long organizational structure consisting of a basic theme (with a learner-grabbing title). If it's unknown by the kids, it's a poor cognitive organizer. Pick a topic that you can work with for a year. The theme should have the following qualities: your excitement, student understanding and excitement, plenty of materials and resources available, application to the student's real world, a clear pattern, a rationale compelling for learners and is worthy of the extensive time invested.

> *Examples might be: The Backyard (grade 1-2). "What Makes it Go?"*
> *(3-5th grade) The Amazon River (4-6th grade) or "Parasites"*
> *(science class, grades 7-8) or Computers (grades 9-12).*

Components: The physical locations and the human issues. Use situations, events, and contributions by students.

> *Examples from the themes above: "The Backyard" (geography*
> *of our own backyard, animals and systems in a backyard, economics*
> *of a backyard, ecology, colors, artwork, foods eaten, the food chain, etc.)*
>
> *"What Makes It Go?" (transportation of the past, the world as a vehicle,*
> *famous cars, unusual boats, rollerblades, making buses, golf carts, bicycles,*
> *the mechanisms, use of computers to build them, etc.)*
>
> *"The Amazon River" (inhabitants, who is affected, geology, unusual*
> *animals, tourist businesses, the folklore, the uses of water, the name itself,*
> *fishing, changes in river paths, flooding, agriculture, weather, maps, rain*
> *forests, etc.)*
>
> *"Parasites" (as meant in nature, the molecular world, society, personal*
> *relationships, economics, medicine, law, history of the word, etc.)*

Make school more like real-life with all the variety of experience, and the brain will sort out the meaning

"Computers" as a semester-long theme can be powerful for many subjects including math, science, history, biology or life sciences.

Topics: A specific aspect of the location or human issues will be studied, about one per week.

Suggestion: Use the newspapers, television, kid's examples and school issues to tie into each of the components.

Key Points: Concepts, skills, knowledge, attitudes, values, models & patterns.

Suggestions: Brainstorm the essential things you'd like students to learn. Ask learners and draw from their own experience. Identify your resources: physical locations, CD-ROM, library, school sites, guest speakers, computers, etc. Your goal is a real hands-on immersion. Study your districts scope and sequence of curriculum mandates. Integrate the child's points of curiosity; what are their "whys" and "wherefores"? You become a learner all over again and will experience the joy of learning.

Inquiries: These are the specific applications of the key points. You may want to use the various levels of Bloom's Taxonomy and integrate the learning into Gardner's Multiple Intelligence.

*Examples: The Backyard (Knowledge: list & describe all the animals in the backyard. **Comprehension:** group them into categories & discuss why and how. **Application:** build a backyard of the future. **Analysis:** write and sing a rap about the daily life of your backyard animals; what is it like from their point of view. **Evaluation:** create a checklist of what is in a typical yard, visit local backyards, and evaluate quality of backyard plant or animal life. **Synthesis:** Use what you've learned from ideal backyard environments, let's pretend visitors from another world came to earth and wanted to make a backyard zoo for humans. What do you think should be in it? Work in groups and draw it out on a huge piece of paper. Discuss and describe to the class).*

> *Create a living, learning, laboratory in your classroom*

To understand it conceptually, picture a spider web. The title is in the center (your year-long theme). If you have nine months, you'd have nine branches coming out from the center of the web, much like spokes of a wheel. Those are the monthly components. On each of the spokes, you'd have weekly topics, four of them. Certainly you can vary it as situations may arise to alter your plans. This thematic style of teaching and learning has been demonstrated far more effective than the traditional unit, chunk, unit, chunk, all unrelated and piecemeal.

The classroom becomes a living, learning laboratory. The learning is connected and the themes are relevant. Think of the classroom possibilities for discussion, projects, plays and writing! Give your students a list of at least ten addresses where students can write for free information including U.S. Government agencies, the Chamber of Commerce and state agencies. Better yet, help them discover for themselves, how to locate addresses, phone numbers and contact persons for each unit. This is a terrific way for them to become a lifelong learner.

Real World Mathematics

For math to be more brain-based, it has to tie into the rich lives of the learners. Math is no strange new language. We live in a mathematical world. Math is all around us. Many geometry teachers introduce triangles, cylinders, cubes or parallel lines as if they were some new concept. How ridiculous! Take your students outside the classroom and stand and look around. There are cubes (buildings, boxes, etc.) everywhere. Take them to the street corner. There are parallel lines everywhere. It's almost that simple. Circles? There are circles throughout the math world. Angles? They are everywhere. The secret is to see that they are all in real life and make the connections. Two math teachers, Geoff Peterson and Rob Meek give us some visual examples of the relationships within the math world. These examples are simple ways that learners can relate better to something that ought to be easy. Math is the most pure, logical and rule-following discipline there is. It could become the favorite subject of countless learners if they were introduced to it in a more relevant way.

The old way was: math is an end unto itself. Learn to do this problem because it's good for you. The new way is different. The learning of math is *a by-product on the way to solving the real problems of everyday life.* The new math projects engage student teams who then need to learn the mathematics in order to solve the problems.

Let's say it's an algebra class. The student problem regards the potential purchase of two plots of land. One is zoned single-family and the other is zoned multi-dwelling. Each costs a different amount, each is on the same size acreage. They have a 30-day purchase option on each of them. Given potential costs, potential revenues, license, taxes, city ordinances, trends in housing, projections of land values, your personal cash flow, your family needs, environmental issues and interest rates, which one makes better financial sense and why? That's a very complex problem that requires the use of formulas, graphs, estimates, interviews and projections. The students may interview real estate agents, bankers, city council persons, consult their teammates, use calculators, go to text books, use computers or ask the teacher for help. Projects like these are engaging and motivating. Most important, they're real life. It's brain-based learning.

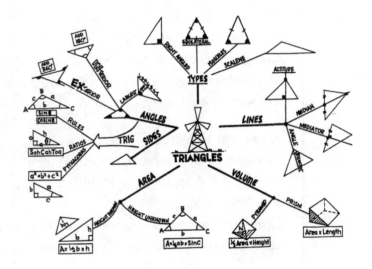

Implementation of this new framework is an on-going process. Initially, will take about two to four years. Some teachers are fearful that their old "stand and deliver" style is being threatened. It is, and it's about time! Textbooks are being abandoned in droves by up-to-date teachers. Suddenly, more teachers are acting like catalysts and learning coaches instead of an all-knowing teacher or professor.

Ultimately mathematics would be integrated across the curriculum. All subjects would be taught by a team of teachers. In one program, 120 high school age students are taught by four teachers who each have their specialties, but all know something about each other's areas. This team of teachers stays with the students the entire time. Sometimes the whole group is collected; two will be team teaching, while the other two handle special needs. Other times, they'll be in four rooms, with four teachers. There's no better way for learning and teaching, than for teachers to have the support of knowledgeable colleagues. That's the brain-based way.

Math Strategies

Approach: Extending natural knowledge
Concept: "Known to the unknown"
Example: in geometry, make lists of shapes from real-life like parallel lines, circles, and triangles. Students generate qualities and rules of items. They organize that information and make observations about those items. Mind map it.

Approach: Real life problem-solving & realizing dreams
Concept: How to create a lifetime real estate cash flow
Example: Mock purchase, renovation & ownership of rental units. Sort, find, select potential rental property. Apply for loans, doing financial projections. Do mock remodel on a property, rent out & do profit analysis.

Approach: Community problems
Concept: How to solve the touchy dilemma of whether to develop land or turn it into more shopping. The IMP (Interactive Math Program) uses problems like Meadows or Malls.
Example: Students do extensive analysis including the use of matrices, graphing, statistics, posing problems, asking for outside help to help make decisions on land use.

Approach: Small business success
Concept: How to maximize the profits in an ever-changing small business which produces "Widgets" or a fast food outlet.
Example: Students ask questions, formulate hypotheses, test them out, use equations, cash flow analysis, and outside help to help make decisions on how to run the business.

Approach: Using mass media to teach
Concepts: Produce a weekly cable TV show on that chapter .
Examples: Class is run like the FYI TV show on "Murphy Brown." Week after week, ideas are learned on Monday & Tuesday, group discussions held Wednesday, script created with graphics on Thursday, and Friday is taping day.

Language and the Brain

The biology of the brain tells us that children are born with a pre-wired understanding of how language works. An infant may not know what the word for table is but he or she knows that it is a thing, an object. In fact, research has demonstrated that when a parent or teacher says "This is a table," children understand that the teacher is referring to the larger object, not the *color* of the object, or the *material* it is made out of and certainly not the *act* of pointing out a table. The child seems to intuitively know the general and specific details of what the teacher means. Now, this may not seem very important or relevant, but it is.

Human beings have the genetic storage of the systems of language. We don't know all the vocabulary words but we do, genetically, understand syntax. Point to a cat drinking milk, and say "cat." The child knows you are referring to the cat, not the act of a four-legged furry mammal drinking milk. In fact, even the best scientists have failed to build a language-learning robot that can understand all the "rules" that a 3 year-old knows. The point is, we don't need to teach language structure when we teach our native languages. So why do we do it in a foreign language class, when in many cases, it's the same as our own language? It's time to take into consideration how the brain learns languages best. Languages are learned through acquisition, not formal instruction. Steven Pinker, linguist and researcher, says, *"It is in the detailed analysis of grammar that evidence is provided for the deep biological nature of language...Nowhere does the old idea of tabula rasa fall on its face with such force. Children reveal to us that huge aspects of the mind are built-in."*

As an example, language learning is best done during the time that the brain perceives the need to learn it to survive. Meaning from ages two to ten, we have our greatest growth in vocabulary and syntax. William Calvin and George Ojemann, authors of *Conversations with Neil's Brain,* say that our native language is learned far more efficiently and takes up less space in the brain than our second and third languages. The brain is organized to learn languages early in life much better than it is after age ten. Yet in schools around America, second languages are often introduced in middle school and high school. From the brain's point of view, it's ridiculous. The brain begins the "neural pruning" process early and what isn't taught at the best biological time becomes harder and harder as we age.

Because Henry Kissinger's younger brother learned English when he was in elementary school, he has no discernible German accent.

Language is best learned during the time the brain perceives the need to learn it to survive

Certainly adults can learn foreign languages, but there is a price in efficiency and result. Keep a mental note of the Edelman paradigm: "The brain is designed for selection survival, not instruction." If language is perceived as necessary, early in life, it will be learned.

Language learning is universal, from native to "foreign" languages. Using the right brain-based principles, every one of us can learn virtually every language on earth. How? We are wired to genetically understand them. All we need is the NEED to learn it. There are, of course, better times to learn it than others. As we mentioned earlier, foreign languages are learned best from ages 3-10. Waiting until middle school or high school is NOT brain-based and is an enormous waste of learner potential. Using the brain-based approach, teachers are most likely to do the following:

Foreign languages are best learned from ages 3-10

- *A complete immersion environment simulating a foreign country complete with music, posters & dress*
- *All mistakes pointed out indirectly, emphasis on using the skills, save the grammar for later (learn it the way we all learned our native language)*
- *Absolute minimum of grammar, syntax and rules*
- *Use of music, role-play and celebrations*
- *Real-life situations, no textbook learning; learning is thematic everywhere*
- *Use of alternative characters: puppets, assumed identities— students take on full characters and roles*
- *Multiple contexts for memory embedding: inside and outside the classroom, a restaurant, a civic event, a festival*

The immersion approach is alive at the University of Massachusetts, where Dr. Lynn Dhority has been using this philosophy and these strategies to teach German. Instead of the old way of language, starting with sentences and vocabulary, using singular, lock-step, sequential, one-bite-at-a-time lesson planning, initially Dhority uses a virtual overload of stories, conversations and re-enactments. This explosion of ideas elicits curiosity, intrigue and prompts the learner to discover meaning for him or herself. Dhority consistently floods his students with more German than they can possibly grasp. Over time, it all gets sorted out by the learner, brilliantly. If that sounds like the real world of learning one's own native language, you're right. Dhority has been consistently one of the most effective language instructors and is one of many teachers who embodies a successful brain-based approach.

In learning a native language, students can learn everything from origins of grammar, to writing skills and literature in a more brain-based way. Here's an optimal place for thematic, patterned learning. The secret is to keep the threat low, expression high and the use of peers strong. Use theater works for learning about literature. Use teams to learn the rare, small amounts of more rote, repetitive information. Avoid all rewards in the expression of creativity and writing skills. Employ greater use of videos, guest speakers and outreach projects. Immerse the language learning in the culture of that language. Have students pick more than names in that language, have them choose a whole new identity; a job, friends and family. The more the contextually-embedded cues, the quicker the learning.

Real World Biology

Give the students an opportunity to learn how the sciences affect their own lives. The study of biology can be as boring or as engaging as a teacher makes it. Students can learn about biology through assisting with community outreach programs or starting public discussions on alcohol, drugs, pregnancy, AIDS or other STD's. Or, they can decide how to build a human helper-robot, a "droid." This means they would need all the knowledge of biology (and more!). They could understand how others around them develop Parkinson's or Alzheimer's Disease. A real-life project might be the following: you discover your mother or father is getting Parkinson's Disease. Find out what causes it and how it will affect your parent. What are the traditional treatments and what alternatives can you locate? When offered as an opportunity to fill needs (like love, health, thinking, parent bonding or sex) this course becomes a high interest priority to the learner's brain.

Get your students involved in "real-life" biology, and it becomes more personal, therefore, more relevant

Geography/Global Studies

Some of the possibilities that you may be interested in using, include:

- *Students have some choice in how they learn: computers, videos, phones, teams, partners or by themselves*
- *Learning is thematic: tied together with larger meaning patterns*
- *Large, consuming projects are developed:*
- *learners develop mock economic/social aid packages*
- *students develop mock communication/satellite companies (Motorola has done this)*
- *Travel plans are developed in detail for round-the-world trips including visas, passports, tickets and packing lists*

115

For a geography project, learn the United States as a unique month-long or even year-long project and challenge. Class teams pretend they have just immigrated to America (or any other country) in the year 1850. They arrived from Europe, are in Virginia and now want to go to California. There are two families. What season of the year might they travel? Consider the following: weather, Indians, bandits, transportation modes, food supplies, money available, skills, geography, health, etc. What path would they take? What obstacles are realistic? What cities would not even be started in 1840? What documentation is there available? What would the trip be like? Plan it out in complete detail. What would the equivalent trip be like today? For six graders, this might be a 10-week project. In a science class, your class could plan a trip to Mars. Think of the math, astronomy, biology, global studies, language, and science required to make THAT happen! These ideas are not necessarily new, but they work. The philosophy of brain-based learning is being carried out in this subject by teachers worldwide. The structure varies dramatically from classroom to classroom, but the results are always the same: motivated learners who gain an authentic, in-depth understanding of the material.

Allow learners to gain an authentic in-depth understanding of the material through experiential exploration

The Curriculum of the Process

Part of brain-compatible learning is the long-term *content* planning (thematic curriculum). Another key part is the long term *process* of learning. There are four stages for a learner to develop understanding and meaning. In general, they tend to happen in order, as the brain develops greater neural mapping in the subject area. They can also happen out of order, since the brain works randomly, processing multi-path and in parallel sequences. Every learner will have their own path, and their individuality ought to be respected. It's important to not only give learners choice about their learning, but also provide a blueprint. Talk to them about what it's like to be a "expert learner." Get them excited about these four levels so that they want to progress further.

Levels of Understanding

Level #1: Starter Knowledge

Content: information or acquisition • This level is the acquisition of specific data. • It is usually the memorization of key facts. • *Process:* the learner has no awareness of how they are learning • It is a case of non-conscious competency • An example, in history, we are often taught the principle reasons for the Vietnam War, the Cold War, the Gulf War or World War II.

Level #2: Relational Knowledge

Content: thematic mapping, greater content associations • At this stage, the content is making more sense • It's not just dates in history, it's the rise and fall of political systems • It is cycles of corruption of power (as an example) • *Process:* Learning how to learn: reading, finding, integrating, mapping, etc., • An example is learning to see related non-political, economic and financial reasons for the Gulf War. Now, we understand how the World Bank, NATO and upcoming elections can influence military policy.

Level #3: Globalize Knowledge

Content: Able to relate it to self, community, planet • The learning has strong personal meaning • The learner is likely to make it a lasting part of their life • The learning is contextualized into the local impact, national impact and global impact as well as your own personal feelings • *Process:* Processing the process; metacognition. This is the ability to think about, how you were thinking about things • As an example, you now ask yourself, "How do I feel about this issue?" In another sense, what do I do, in some little way, on an everyday basis, that either contributes toward or impairs world peace?

Level #4: "Expert Knowledge"

Content: Here is genuine mastery, deep meaning, expert learning, new insights & even the ability to think "outside the box," a paradigm-creating pioneer • *Process:* Re-contextualizing it • The generalization systems mastery, skills to empower local and global learning organizations • As an example, you locate community resources and gather information. • You learn about Gulf War diseases and form a local support network for Veterans with war-related health problems.

Keep mental notes of your learner's progress. Your goal may be to inspire them from the introductory level to the next one, or as far as possible. In some cases, getting to level two or three will be a major victory. In other cases, your goal and the learner's goal might be to get to level four. It depends on their age and motivation.

Transforming Curriculum
Paths of Progress

	Elementary	**Secondary**	**Upper Level**
Initially	more relevant units that children relate to	more project-based complex learning	hands-on and practical
Long-Term	year-long themes multi-disciplinary	multi-subject team-teaching	apprenticeships in community

School districts around the world are adopting interdisciplinary, integrated curriculums. For example, the Canadian province of Ontario has begun the change process. They've tackled three major assumptions from the old paradigm in education by making these changes:

1. *Creating top quality learning in every student*
2. *Making life skills as important as content knowledge*
3. *Using less teaching and more constructing of knowledge*

While the terms are hardly new, there's a difference between thinking something is a good idea and making it policy. The schools around the world that are succeeding are:

1. *Identifying what they want and the direction they want to go*
2. *Making it policy*

They give the staff time, support and resources to make changes. They educate the parents and the community so that they gather support, not alienate.

Practical Application: Examples include: Publications: research & create newsletters or cookbooks • Use one book, a play or poem with its current applications • Do major, long term, travel planning • Write and publish poetry or journals–theirs or others • Make local movie & restaurant guides with ratings • Historical re-enactments; create a mini-Hollywood • Create & publish comic books in other languages • Do the whole process of applying for grants, etc. • Write, choreograph and sing music on relevant topics • Create wall-sized timelines, murals, graphics for the public • Create a photo yearbook for sale in the community • Visitation to other cultures, other parts of the city & country • Community service to learn languages, provide services • Theater groups–Put on plays, visit plays in town • Run an on-campus student store, do the finances • Artificially buy and renovate real income property • Investigate buying a business franchise; assess the finances • Students involved in ordering school supplies • Mock home purchases; designing or remodeling a house • Inventions - significant projects that solve student problems • Community projects that address real needs • Projects on the INTERNET • Team student-teaching of key areas of the course • Travel within school, the community or outside • School clean-up; campus beautification • Outline and implement a school recycling program • Interview others for a book, newsletter, etc. • Whole class makes a video guide for local tourists • Switch families for a week/month • Job shadowing; become an apprentice for a month • Volunteer work to learn other cultures • Plan a detailed, round the world trip • Produce a community event; a fair, health or sporting event • Publish community alert bulletins • Archaeological digs in your own community.

Reflection and Analysis

❖ In what ways can you translate the key three or four theories and discoveries presented here into practical everyday useful ideas?

❖ What information in this chapter do you already apply?

❖ Did you think of any questions about this material? What were they?

❖ Did you have an emotional reaction to any of this information?

❖ Specify what was different and new to you? What was familiar and what was review?

❖ How did you react intellectually? Do you agree or disagree with any ideas explored in this chapter? Which ones and why?

❖ Let's say these things are, in fact, true about the brain, what should we do differently? What resources of time, people and money could be redirected? In what ways do you suggest we start doing it?

❖ Generate the most interesting or valuable insight(s) you got from this chapter.

❖ Make a plan for your next step, a realistic, practical application of what you've learned, and outline it.

❖ Can you foresee any obstacles you might encounter? How can you realistically deal with them?

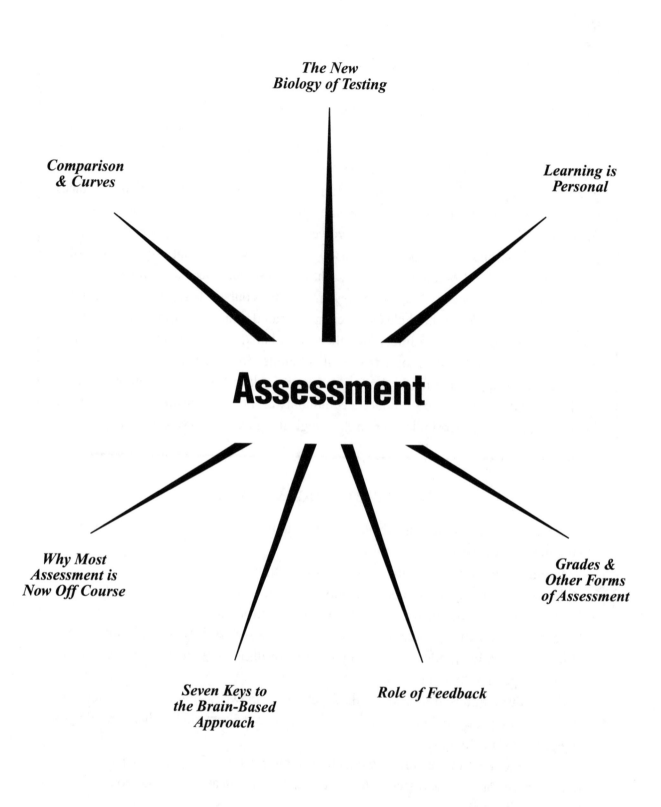

The New
Biology of Testing

Comparison
& Curves

Learning is
Personal

Assessment

Why Most
Assessment is
Now Off Course

Grades &
Other Forms
of Assessment

Seven Keys to
the Brain-Based
Approach

Role of Feedback

Chapter 5
Assessment

The New Biology of Testing

Can we make links between current neuroscience and our assessment dilemma? There are connections to be made, and, they have to be made. The current forms of testing are often poor indicators of true learner knowledge. Learners commonly dislike testing because it can make, on any given day, even the best prepared learners, feel stupid. It's stressful and often irrelevant. It rarely lets us "shine" as learners. There has been a great deal of insights and discoveries about the brain in terms of learning and memory, but crucial questions remain unanswered.

These are old questions, but they remain important. How does the brain best learn and recall? What is learning? Can it even be measured? How do we really know what we know? What causes us to want to learn more long term? Are some types of learning not measurable? What about memory reliability? These questions get us away from the old model of testing which asks only the questions, "What do we teach and did they learn it?" Formal and informal testing have been around for a long time. Basically the old model of academic testing is quite simple. It goes something like this:

The teacher, committee or bureaucracy decides what is to be learned
followed by
The teacher teaches and makes up the test
followed by
The students study what they think will be on the test
followed by
The students take the test
followed by
The teacher grades the test, based on what he or she decided was important
followed by
The students forget what they studied a few hours or days after the test
followed by
The cycle repeating itself

Typically, assessment can cause narrowed learning simply to "make the grade." Particularly stressful is any grading system which has enormous delays and high stakes. You don't need to be a rocket scientist to realize the stress and lunacy of the system above. The teacher makes most of the choices, and the student narrows the learning to exactly what's predicted to be on the test. Then, of course, to get school achievement scores higher, many teachers are encouraged to teach directly to the test. Not good. It's a manipulated system of control with fixed outcomes and it encourages cheating. It is certainly a poor assessment model for preparing our citizens for the next century.

In education, we rarely test for real learning... We test to determine how well the learner is playing "the testing game"

Many educators think they measure learning everyday. They don't. Neuroscientist Gary Lynch of The University of California at Irvine says learning is defined by synaptic growth, connections among dendrites and changes in the density of neural networks. Do you have a test that measures that? Biologist Ira Black, in his book *Information in the Brain: A Molecular Perspective,* says that learning is defined by "modifications to the neuronal pattern of connectivity." Do you have a test that measures that? It's time to say, "The emperor has no clothes!"

The standard dictionary definition of learning is simple: it's related to knowledge and understanding. Yet, many of the world's top neuroscientists would have a tough time defining learning. Why? *Much of what is important in learning cannot be measured at this time.* Examples of the "hard-to-measure" include our so-called "mental models" of how things work, critical neuronal connections, our values, our capability beliefs, the degree of personal transference and level of depth of meaning.

Outcome-based education where there are specific, defined, measurable outcomes would be brain-antagonistic unless the learners have a say in them. It still operates out of the "demand model" of learning. The notion of some bureaucrat in Washington who knows nothing about the brain, making national goals for learning is ludicrous. You simply cannot measure, with current technology, at this time in our neurobiological history, most of the truly important learning the brain does.

In other words, most assessment is off course. Certainly you can measure if a learner can create and manipulate prose arguments or summarize what the teacher has said, *but is that the only thing we want?* What will serve the learner in a competitive global society where the greatest advantage may be in learn-to-learn skills, teamwork, model-building, problem-solving, systems thinking and communication skills? The vast content knowledge base will be accessible to anyone who has a computer, television, phone or fax. With this in mind, should we ask that an increasingly larger body of knowledge be memorized and replayed at test time?

Ultimately, learning is judged by someone who expects immediate, tangible, measurable results. The problem is that *the best learning takes time.* Over and over again we have all witnessed students who seemed to vehemently resist learning ideas, programs and disciplines only to emerge years later as far wiser and better rounded than the learners who got the highest marks on the spot.

We all know the opposite: a learner who does what's expected, fills in all the boxes perfectly and graduates with little skills for living in the real world. That's also why "pop quizzes" should be banned. They create stressful, adversarial ("teacher vs. student") relationships and provide little useful information. In fact, they are often used to give students a "wake-up call" by showing them how little they know. Unfortunately, they are usually surface level. And, brain-based learning environments should provide such a rich flow of feedback that most interim testing is redundant.

Biologically, the best, most valuable and deepest learning does not produce any tangible results for a considerable time

The Right-Answer Fallacy

The other fallacy of typical grading is the obsession with success and "getting it right." The more we emphasize the right answer and the correct reasoning, the more we box in our learning. In *Society of Mind,* Minsky says, "...confining ourselves to 'positive' learning experiences alone leads to relatively small improvements in what we can already do." We had to already have some concept of how to figure out the problem and how to succeed before we even started. So, where's the learning if it's all success-directed? A Canadian researcher, Powell discovered that wrong answers provide far more clues to learning than the right answers. Whereas the right answers simply say you knew it, or guessed it right, the wrong answers illuminate models of thinking.

In the end we must learn to teach the value of thinking about our thinking and then value it. If we continually mark down students for getting the wrong answer, the message is, "Learn to get right answers and play the game." There has to be room to fail in positive ways. Our culture must learn to value the failures and the opportunities they present or students will continue to "play the game" and walk away with shallow learning and a worthless diploma. Educator fears that this style of learning will degenerate into a "intellectual free-for-all" are groundless. As you'll soon see, there are many appropriate new ways to assess learning better.

Comparisons and Curves

Developmentally, the brains of normal learners can have as much as a three year difference. It's unrealistic to hold each learner to a specific standard or group norm. That ignores what we now know from research in neuroscience.

What one student is doing academically is totally separate and unrelated to another student. Their brains can be quite different. Their backgrounds can be a world apart. A curve or any comparative rating system is unfair and irrelevant to real learning (that includes the famous "bell-curve"). The only thing that really matters is, "How is that student doing compared to that same student a week, a month or three months earlier?" Each learner should not be competing against other learners, but rather against him or herself.

Grading on a curve creates an unnecessary stress for learning. It gives the wrong message to our students who need to cooperate for success in life, not lose if another wins. Curves are a zero-sum game where some are doomed to lower scores. They destroy collaboration and community. They create a false sense of quality ("I'm good because I'm better than someone else."). Real quality is not based on "better than." It's based on exceeding a set of agreed-upon standards of measurement.

Learning is Personal

If we make a distinction between knowledge (usually surface knowledge) and meaning (something of value or something that helps our own world make sense, or that extends our existing natural knowledge) then it is clear that *we are after meaning* in our students, *not just knowledge*. The surface knowledge will be forgotten shortly after any test given and what's lasting is the meaning. Teachers, schools and districts who compare students against one another are doing a disservice. Also, if in fact, all learning is personal, how could you compare two students? You can't.

Here's the crux of brain-based assessment: Most of time when we think we are assessing learning, we are merely *getting feedback on the student's ability to play the "testing game."* Most of what is *easily assessed is biologically and personally irrelevant to the brain.* That's why grading for effort is crazy. Students who learn very little but work hard at it are rewarded for **not** learning from their mistakes. Their conclusion may be that they are deficient. Those who learn a great deal with little effort are punished, in a sense, for **not** struggling.

Comparing one student to another is one of the most irrelevant and damaging assessment strategies ever devised

One of the greatest sources of low self-esteem in students is comparisons

"Authentic assessment" is an incremental improvement over traditional, formalized testing. Broad-based assessment using the multiple intelligences is much better than a strict pencil and paper test. However, let's not kid ourselves. Most of what is important to the brain, that which truly shapes our understanding, our thinking, our meaning and our character is *relatively difficult to assess*. In order to decide if your assessment is on the mark or if it misses the real learning, use these seven brain-based guideline categories. The seven approaches listed below can become the basis for a more accurate way to assess. Is there any proof that these are better than what we have? Just as with other forms of assessment, it will take time to validate these more biological approaches. We are on the threshold of a revolution in learning and those who are leading the paradigm shift are often "naked" without the usual evidence that comes with time.

Seven Approaches to Brain-Based Assessment

Traditional method of content mastery ought to be just one of the ways we assess. The push for "authentic assessment" and "multiple assessments" for multiple intelligences are useful only in part. Much of it is still "playing the testing game." Granted, it takes more thought and more time to measure other ways to learn. But in the long run, it will be a much greater service for you and the learner. Einstein once said, "Everything that can be counted isn't worth counting, and everything that is worth counting isn't always countable." Taking some literary liberties with that, we get: Let's make what's important more measurable, instead of making what's measurable, more important.

Having said that, are there better ways to assess? Certainly. In the next few years, more and more of us will be finding out ways to measure the more important things in learning. We'll move away from the "bean-counting, box-checking, please the teacher" testing and move more into the neurobiological arena of genuine learning and assessment. This is no trendy fad. This is the wave of the future. These are the most accurate ways in which the human brain can "evidence" learning:

True learning is tough to assess. Comparisons are irrelevant. Tests are usually too little, too late, for feedback

> ### Assessment Keys:
>
> ✔ Observable Behavior Changes
> ✔ Learner's Acquired Subject Bias
> ✔ Relational Thinking: Interdisciplinary
>   Application & Generalization
> ✔ Quality of Mental Models
> ✔ Personal Relevance & Integration
> ✔ Strategies & Skills
> ✔ Content Mastery

Make what's important more measurable, instead of making what's measurable, more important

1. Observable behavior changes... Many neuroscientists would say that unless there is a corresponding change in physical behavior, we cannot say that biologically, something has been learned. In other words, cognition or auditory descriptions of content understanding is not integrated until the whole body is involved in learning.

The best way to do this is to give students projects to work on. Give them the choice of working by themselves or with others. During this time, make observations and listen. Give students a problem to solve which can be solved many different ways. Just for fun, let's use the example of a man and a woman out walking, starting from the same place. The man takes two steps for every three the woman takes. They start out together, and immediately lose synchronization. After how many steps will they be back in "synch" again? That problem can be solved using just about every one of the seven intelligences. Which one is chosen by the students?

Give students a choice in activities and games to play and watch. Discover which ones they pick: Pictionary™, Monopoly™, crossword puzzles, manipulative puzzles, charades, music recognition, etc. Then observe what they do during the game. Use discussion, and reflection after a play, movie or musical. After students watch one of these, ask which parts struck them most and were really memorable – was it the music, the action or the relationships? How often are behaviors chosen?

0 << Never–Rarely   4   Often–Usually   7   Most of the Time >>10

Watch for the type of learning and intelligence that is most used. Students tend to do what they like or are most successful at doing. Find out who are the questioners, the noise and music-makers, the artists,

126

doodlers, the active learners, the talkers, the loners, etc.

Your observation can be in inventions and model-building. Give students a chance to design, build and use some kind of a physical representation of the topic learned. Observe what parts of the task they like and excel in most easily. You'll learn a great deal about how each student learns.

2. Learner's Acquired Subject Biases. Assess a love of learning? Absolutely! You may have experienced a "learning block" in some subject before. What's the point in doing well on a test if you'll hate the subject for a lifetime? That's why it's an important question to ask, "What are your attitudes, perceptual biases or opinions about this topic?" How you feel about a topic or subject *does* matter a great deal. Do you feel positive about the topic, like it or want to learn more? If a learner can pass a written test but has learned to hate the subject, what has been gained?

We know this to be intuitively true, but what's the evidence on this? New research suggests that the synaptic connections may be less important than the broader chemical balance in the brain. Neurologically, this is critical because the neurons have "synaptic gates" which either open (excitatory) or close (inhibitory) *based on the neurotransmitters present at the time.* Peptide messengers in the brain exert influences far from where the neurons have matching receptors. This means these neuromodulators, which play widespread and critical roles in our moods (like joy, sadness, helplessness and dislike) do influence our future likelihood of wanting to learn a topic. Restak says the emotions present can trigger the chemicals to open gates easily to allow for future learning, or close them to create a blockage.

That's why our feelings about a particular subject are important. The peptides and other brain messenger chemicals in the brain *have been discovered to be present in the adrenal glands, spinal cord, sexual organs and the stomach.* These chemicals can influence mental processes, whether they are located in the brain or not. In fact, the mind, body and feelings are inexorably linked by a common chemical transmitter. The new models of brain research indicate the mind is modulated by hormones, and they are not just in the brain. They are located throughout the body. This fact may help us understand why we have the expression, "I have a gut feeling about this." In short, there is a biological basis in brain chemistry to subject matter bias. The best way to evidence this is through interviews, theater, essays, art, drama, journal writing, discussion or speeches.

Our mood influences our future likelihood of wanting to learn a topic

127

Some educators have done things as simple as pre and post surveys. These are not what some educators like to call "objective" but that's the whole point. We are emotional beings and until we begin to integrate feelings into our instruction, curriculum and assessment, we are still ignoring the entire focus of learning, the brain. Surveys can be an initial stage for determining the students attitudes. A simple survey might look like this:

Subject Survey:
Please answer the questions honestly, the best you can. Thanks.

1. When you first thought of taking this subject, your first feelings about it were:

   _____

2. What are the chances you'd pick up a book or watch a movie on this topic?
   Please circle the number below that best fits, with "0" being "least chance" and a "10" is "greatest."

   0   1   2   3   4   5   6   7   8   9   10

3. What is the likelihood that you would take up this subject/topic as a profession?
   Please circle the number below that best fits, with "0" being "least chance" and a "10" is "greatest."

   0   1   2   3   4   5   6   7   8   9   10

4. Overall, on a scale of 0-10, where would you rate **your** interest in this subject?
   "0" means "extreme dislike" and a "10" is "you really like it"

   0   1   2   3   4   5   6   7   8   9   10

---

3. Relational Thinking. This includes the concept of relating the learning to other disciplines, other formats of thinking. Certainly the whole issue of contextualization and generalization comes into play. Now that you have learned ABC, how can you apply it to DEF or HIJK? This process takes the learning from one domain and asks the student to map it onto another domain. It's the perfect example of complex neural mapping and is how our brain develops "expert intelligence." Much of the brain models today deal with the interplay between the mental maps, models or neural mapping – that's *real* relational thinking. These systems connect and glue together widely distributed pieces of information.

In the example of the Oklahoma City bombing, it's one thing to know the simple facts. We can learn how many were killed, where, who and when. Relational thinking asks us to put this in relationship with other knowledge. Is there a link with the increasing number of militia groups? What about the link with politics, the tax structure, Waco, Texas, the school system, FBI security effectiveness, dysfunctional families, state laws on accessibility to explosive-building materials, the criminal justice system or radio talk shows? The ability to make these relationships is one of the critical pieces of the learning puzzle.

Sternberg and Wagner say that intelligence is related to the ability to generalize learning to perform in novel contexts. To do that, they say, requires, "...the use of widely applicable performance components" – planning, metacognition, and both inductive and deductive reasoning. While teaching students about thinking and learning, we are also providing them with the framework to succeed on their own in the productive work world.

4. Quality of Mental Models. A mental model is a way of thinking about something. Mental models are also a set of organizing principles which describe how something works ("a democracy is run by special interest groups" or "democracy works best when we all participate..."). It includes, but is not limited to, your beliefs about it, your biases, your understanding of the content, the systems and, most importantly, how something functions. Our mental models provide an operating framework for how we'll deal with that area for the rest of our lives. They also, Minsky says, give real insights into the brain's neural patterns.

Ask a five-year-old to build a house with blocks (The "How" question would be, "Can you show me how to build a house out of blocks?"). The way they demonstrate it may have some similarities to asking the same question of a general contractor. "Explain simply, how do you build a house?" This tells you their understanding of many things from science to finances, physics, and values.

Harvard psychologist Howard Gardner points out in *Unschooled Mind* that most mental models are formed before adolescence. As a result of early formation, we are rarely conscious that we even hold a model. For most math students their mental model of solving math problems is either success or failure. But a math teacher has a successful mental model of how to do mathematics in his or her mind. If only they could provide that model to their students, the majority of them would enjoy significant success in that subject. Maybe their model

Provide good mental-models for your students to insure significant success in a particular subject

looks like what you see on the next full page. In school, the best way to elicit this type of understanding is through drawings, interviews, graphic organizers, projects, demonstrations, speeches and role plays.

5. Personal Relevance & Integration. The learners ought to be able to talk about how the learning has become personally meaningful and what are the specific links to their own life. This is the learning that is going to last. It is the learning that makes school and education rewarding, rich and timeless. It's also the kind of learning that spurs the intrinsic motivation to learn.

The subject should be personally meaningful in order to increase intrinsic motivation

If I have studied ecology as part of a year-long theme, and I can pass a test on it, is that enough? Or have I just learned to "play the game"? What's really needed is for the learner to start asking questions about a better process to get rid of garbage in their own home. How important is personal relevance? This is the difference between: 1) one student who went from 0% home recycling to 75% of all home waste products being recycled in a one month period, or 2) another student who passed a written test on the facts of recycling. Which type of learning did you want to occur? The best way to determine this type of learning is through interviews, journals, discussion groups and demonstration.

6. Strategies and Skills... These are usually embedded as procedural memories and are often called "body learning." Examples would be: playing an instrument, building a model, hitting a baseball, working a microscope, etc. The easiest way to assess this is with demonstrations using clearly defined criteria. Is the learner demonstrating behavior that shows the learning is embedded? Here are some examples:

- *Shows the behavior of courtesy, cooperation and respect*
- *Demonstrates the ability to use equipment, tools and machinery*
- *Completes a hands-on task or accomplishes a large-scale project*
- *Creates an artifact; wood, metal, paper, plastic, etc.*
- *Uses performance (dance, art, sculpture, music, drama)*
- *Athletic skills*
- *Locates and uses appropriate resources for learning*

7. Content Mastery. Content mastery is still important. What do you know and how do you know it? This is the most traditional area of assessing for associations, themes and relationships. It includes all the traditional "bits of knowledge" and facts. It also includes them in context only. This means no more rote trivia, no more math facts. Instead, it is also the big picture. For example, in mathematics, can your

Sample Mental Model
For Mathematics

Start With
Success Mind Set

Determine
Problem

Set
Goals

Establish Rules
& Procedures

Begin
Problem Solving

Success   *Setback*

Recheck Figures
Re-define Problem
Reread Problem

Success   *Get Help:*
                       Buddy-Partner
                       Books-Computer
                       Teacher-Aide

Success
or
Regroup

students take a concept like lines and demonstrate where and how they are expressed mathematically? Help your learners to see how lines are prevalent in every aspect of their lives.

Find the connected information and weave it together to form meaning. This information can be gathered many ways. The learner can present this using mind maps, creating a video, writing essays, an open discussion or more traditional tests. Allow for the use of music and sounds. Students can create jingles or songs about a unit. They can create a song and perform it. They can re-do the lyrics to a song using new key words. You may find a "process-folio" is the best vehicle for the overall assessment process. Suggestions and strategies have already been given for the other important ways to assess (items 1-6 above). Use any of the choices below to understand what's being learned and the quality of the learning in the content area. Here are some examples of how to assess content.

Typical classroom assessment is a poor indicator of real learning

- Give students a choice on the type of assessment

- Use a journal or diary with reflections and personal growth

- Get credit for community or business work

- Produce a videotape (or audio tape)

- Peer assessment (with your established criteria)

- Student interviews with you

- Take a written test (students help create the questions)

- Make a chart of progress in the course

- Write a story or article

- Make graphic organizers, mind maps or diagrams

- Make an advertising flyer for the course/subject

- Produce a large mind map

- Self-assessment using personal or course goals

Balancing Assessment & Feedback

As we indicated earlier, genuine assessment of learning can be quite challenging, but feedback is not. Typical classroom assessment is a poor indicator of real learning and should be substituted for dramatically increased feedback. Learners are over-tested and get far too little feedback. As teachers and administrators, our newer approach would be, "Down with old-style testing and up with feedback!" Learners crave feedback, the brain thrives on feedback, *yet most learners are starved for it.* While a five-year-old student may get some kind of feedback many times a day, a typical high school student may go all day without getting any feedback. The alternatives that students usually take, in their quest for feedback, are the following:

1. **Athletics & Clubs.** At least a coach will give them frequent feedback, good or bad. Drama, music or academic clubs often provide a rich source of feedback.

2. **Peer groups.** Many will join cliques, gangs and clubs to get the interaction they crave so much.

3. **Inappropriate behavior.** Many, particularly boys, will become a discipline problem. Here, some feedback, even negative, is better than none at all.

4. **Detachment.** Failing in their quest for feedback, they decide that if they can't win at the game, they won't play the game. The student becomes bored, listless and apathetic.

There are hundreds of ways that teachers can generate more feedback for their students. A primary problem has been the student-teacher ratio. That relationship has meant that the teacher only has a certain amount of time per student, per day. In many cases, the ratio is one teacher for 30 students. But the model is all wrong. Feedback can be generated from all sources, not just from the teacher. As soon as the teacher can get out of the feedback loop, the amount of feedback learners can get can go up dramatically. It simply has to become much more learner-generated. When teachers reduce the feedback they give, they can increase the amount the students receive.

Students, to be able to learn best, have to have constant feedback, whether they generate it on their own or get it from peers. How long do you think a kid would play a video game if it never kept score? The

Teachers are the primary source of feedback for their students, and do often unintentionally starve them of it

research shows kids won't play! True quality assessments take time. Ban all unannounced pop quizzes, all announced teacher-generated quizzes and all testing that occurs over a period of less than one month's time. Why? Learning takes time. Replace the void with a massive increase in daily feedback that every learner gets. The feedback will make the single biggest impact on the learner in building intrinsic motivation. With other brain-based approaches in effect as well, you'll never again hear that dreadful question from a student: *"Will this be on the test?"*

We may have 7 types of intelligence not just one or two

 Practical Application: Do testing less often. Feedback can come from peer assessment, smiles, team evaluations, peer teaching, hugs, post-it notes, letters home, talks after class, mentioning something they did, greeting at the door, collaborative projects, community work, public acknowledgment, etc. Many of the best forms of feedback are not from the teacher. They are from peers, learning logs, journals, goal listings, parents, other teachers and the community.

Multiple Assessments For Multiple Intelligences?

Harvard graduate professor Dr. Howard Gardner suggested we may have seven intelligences, not just one or two. Instead of just mathematical-logical and verbal-linguistic, Gardner says we also have interpersonal, spatial, intrapersonal, musical-rhythmic and bodily-kinesthetic intelligences. A whole new movement has grown (some would call it an industry) that promotes not only the teaching of the intelligences (a good idea) but also assessing in those intelligences (not always a good idea). Why would this be true? There are two important reasons.

First, just because it is a good idea to ask infants and young children to do cross crawls to develop their brains properly, doesn't mean we should test them in crawling. Because relaxation, humor and play have important functions for the brain, doesn't mean that we should test for them. And just as importantly, just because we think there are seven intelligences to develop, doesn't mean that we should assess in all seven intelligences. Everything that should be taught should not be assessed. But everything that is assessed, should be taught.

Second, if we offer the option to be assessed to a student in a method of assessment other than that which is most appropriate, we demean that learner. For example, avoid asking an adolescent to sing or do role-play instead of using his mathematical-logical intelligence in problem-solving. Every learner can learn to solve math problems, at all pre-college levels. Learners are not inherently stupid or incapable of using a pencil to work out math problems. By avoiding the reality of having to do real-life math, with a calculator, pencil and paper, we are underestimating their true capability and destroying their possibilities for a lifetime. Teach in all the intelligences, but assess in the brain-compatible ones.

The Bottom Line: Grades

Do learners have to get grades? Certainly not in the traditional format. What does make more brain-based sense is a simple rubric based on the seven brain-compatible keys listed above. Nearly any student, in nearly any class or course, could use a grid like this. Teachers should tell students about the grid from the start. Students may want to have (and should have, when appropriate) input on the criteria used for each of these. There are seven categories listed below. Either a student is EA (early so far; not much evidence yet), EM (emerging in competence) or EX (extending well or beyond course goals). An EA could be worth one, and an EM, two points and EX three points. With seven categories, that's a possible of 21 points. Here's a sample of a student's "grade grid":

Assessment Possibility:			
	EA	EM	EX
For: (student name)			
Class/Grade:_____			
Observable Behavior Changes		X	
Learner's Acquired Subject Biases	X		
Relational Application & Generalization		X	
Quality of Mental Models		X	
Personal Relevance & Integration			X
Strategies & Skills			X
Content Mastery		X	

The student above has 2 ones, 3 twos and 2 threes. That gives her a 14 out a possible 21 points. Is that a passing grade? Students and teachers could decide well in advance what is an A, B, C, D or F. Maybe a 14 is a C. You might say, "Well, here we are, back to a grading system. What's changed?" The answer is, everything. This format has the following key qualities: 1) it's based on how the brain really learns 2) it involves choice from the learner 3) there's no surprise about it. This way, when a learner gets an A, it means something more than the learner just learned "how to play the game."

Teacher Assessment

Assessment must begin with ourselves

If we, as educators, think it's so important to evaluate our learners so that we can help them improve, the theory must hold true for us, too. More and more, teachers are realizing that they need their own reminders of sound brain-based educational practices. While everything, the whole "teacher package" is important, I have been asked many times for some guidelines. They are printed on a list in the last chapter. *These are for teachers to use for themselves,* not for someone else to use on a clipboard to evaluate a teacher. Once a teacher has exposure to the brain-based approach, discussion, support and gentle reminders like these will keep the process in motion.

Reflection and Analysis

❖ In what ways can you translate the key three or four theories and discoveries presented here into practical everyday useful ideas?

❖ What information in this chapter do you already apply?

❖ Did you think of any questions about this material? What were they?

❖ Did you have an emotional reaction to any of this information?

❖ Specify what was different and new to you? What was familiar and what was review?

❖ How did you react intellectually? Do you agree or disagree with any ideas explored in this chapter? Which ones and why?

❖ Let's say these things are, in fact, true about the brain, what should we do differently? What resources of time, people and money could be redirected? In what ways do you suggest we start doing it?

❖ Generate the most interesting or valuable insight(s) you got from this chapter.

❖ Make a plan for your next step, a realistic, practical application of what you've learned, and outline it.

❖ Can you foresee any obstacles you might encounter? How can you realistically deal with them?

Chapter 6
Organizational Approaches

Change and the Brain

There are some powerful change theories from widely divergent fields of science that we can integrate into our educational systems. Wheatley has written much on the subject of how we can integrate areas like physics or quantum mechanics in our organizational systems. But in the context of this book, a more relevant question is, "What do we know about brain research that tells us about how to organize and structure our schools?" It's a very delicate issue because *the researchers who know the brain best are often the least likely to talk about the practical implications of the research.* Here are some of the discoveries that may have some connections to changes in organizational structure:

The Brain's Response to Threat. Research suggests that when the brain senses threat, we tend to become more territorial, defensive, closed to options and resistant to change. The brain's fear response is predictable; more protection of territory, less willingness to try new things. Administrators who are considering rapid or dramatic changes are forewarned: if you don't deal with the staff's concerns and fears first, the project will be sabotaged. Take the time to discover the fears of your staff. Ask them for their concerns and their own solutions.

The Role of Staff as Influencers. The strong amount of sensory input that the brain "sponges up" means more attention to nonverbals. *How* you say something is as important as *what* you say to your staff. When you convey excitement, the staff will see it, hear it and feel it. When you give mixed messages, it can undermine your efforts to communicate the enthusiasm of the project. In another sense, we can only ask of others what we role model ourselves. All of us in the change process must be concerned with our whole presentation and model the very qualities that we are preaching.

Paradigm Shift Problems. Be careful of large, imposed change. *The brain is poorly designed to take on whole new paradigms at once.* It is better designed to "nibble away," building a model over time. Remember, while trends are last to be detected, any "will" emergency garners all of our immediate attention and resources. This means that changes are best done slowly, as the new models are built or emerge. The secret is to start with what a staff already does well. Allow them to see, hear and feel what is working. Add a new strategy. Let it get settled in. Add another new one. Step by step, it will work. Naturally, if you have a new staff or new school, you can implement change much faster than you can with a school of 100 staff members that are all 30 year-veterans.

Cut the Red Tape. Most of today's top neuroscientists, including Nobel laureate Edelman, say that our brain has no central command post. Restak says it's modular in function and very good at communicating with itself. That means resources do not need to be duplicated, lag time is short and decisions are usually quick. If the brain works well without a bureaucracy, why not reduce the bureaucracy in schools? It helps adaptability and chances for survival. Increase the feedback for everyone; cut the red tape. This sensible, light evolving system will be able to make changes quicker.

Choice and Empowerment. Research on the value of choice is solid. Our brain generates different chemicals when we feel optimistic and in control. These endorphins insure pleasure, the "flow state" and intrinsic motivation. Make sure that everyone has some role in the change process. When anyone feels forced, manipulated or threatened, you'll get resistance. Allow everyone to contribute, to provide feedback and to take the credit.

Larger Systems Thinking. Researchers Pribram, Alkon, Restak and Gazzaniga tell us that the brain works as a single system. An impact on any part of the body affects the brain and vice versa. In other words, to affect one part of the system is to affect another. We cannot demand students perform unless we, as educators, demand accountability among ourselves. This is not a top-down or a bottom-up theory of management. It is participatory at all levels. It is the understanding and reaction of everything at the larger system-wide context that enables us to make true changes.

Progress in one area may be sabotaged or undermined by progress in another. Your brain operates as a single system, your body operates as a single system. So does a family, a car, a home, a business, a government and a rain forest. Everything, in some way, affects something else. If the community or school holds high standards of excellence for their students, those standards will fail every time. Unless the high standards also apply to the staff, the system won't work.

Recognize that piecemeal solutions are short-term and short-sighted. Every issue: motivation, curriculum, school or district policies, staff development, budgeting and nearly everything else is part of a larger system. In fact, to remain intact, change will have to be developed at the following five levels:

Individual Change

Unless each member of an organization is practicing what is being preached, it creates an uncomfortable dissonance. This often means staff members will have to face up to their fears, guilt, stress, uncertainties and weaknesses. It means being willing to admit mistakes. It's important to support each member to create a personal vision, guiding life principles and both long and short-term personal goals. Staff must locate, look at and discuss their own "sacred cows." The things that we ignore or refuse to acknowledge may be part of the problem. As long as we think the problem is "out there" we will never solve it.

Structural Change

Understand the fundamental systems that are causing our problems and challenges. From a larger, broader perspective, we can create better solutions. For example, student dropouts and graffiti are not a discipline problem. Create more security and heavier punishment and you miss the real problem. The learners need more choice, control, responsibility and connectedness, not threats and punishment. Examples of structural change include changing the lines of accountability and responsibility, creating work-time flexibility with teacher's unions and freeing up time during the teacher's day for quality planning time with grade or subject level peers. Start thinking of our roles as interactive catalysts (not teachers), our institutions as flexing systems, not factories where we can add one new piece of machinery to change or upgrade.

Symbolic Change

This form of change is important because it is the type most often communicated. It means dozens of surface level changes that may simply

Change will need to occur on five levels

represent the larger, more meaningful changes. Examples include a new mascot, press releases, a kick-off assembly, special T-shirts, a sweeping new vision statement posted up or a change of name.

Cultural Change

The culture of a school is very powerful. What's the conversation in the lunch room? What's the reaction to new ideas? What's the dress standard? What about calling in sick when not sick? How are kids spoken of behind their backs, when they are doing poorly? All of these are examples of the prevailing school culture. How do staff members speak about the end of the day, end of the school year or retirement? At some schools the teachers horde their ideas. Every single problem has already been solved by someone, somewhere else. No need to reinvent the wheel! With modification, other solutions may work for your staff. Does every teacher at your school know the best 25 ideas of every other teacher? They should! These realities are all part of the prevailing and accepted school culture.

Political Change

Certainly local politics play a part in the change process. Get every other player or stake-holder involved in brainstorming, solution finding and implementing. This requires partnerships, teamwork and fair play. The parents, school board and community will need to buy into your ideas. This means a real concerted effort to communicate what you want to do, to answer concerns and include them in the process.

That's the theory, here's a true example: A high school with poor attendance decided that they would solve the problem by giving students certificates ("caught you being good") and rewards for perfect monthly attendance. At first, the system worked. Then, it fell apart. Why? The real reasons kids stayed away from school were not addressed (poor communication, irrelevant curriculum, stress, threat, embarrassment and failure). It was a system's failure. Nearly everyone at the school contributed to the problem, from rude P.E. coaches and burned-out teachers, to unfriendly cafeteria staff and an out-of-touch principal.

Implications For Year-Round Schools

Since more and more schools are moving to a year-round schedule, the question often asked is, "Are there implications for learning from recent brain research?" Yes, there are; and many more may be discovered.

Everyone contributes in some way, to a school's failure or success

1. Memory and retention. The typical three month summer break is deadly for many types of recall. The most useful recent studies quoted in Learning and Memory (Wittman and Healy; King; Sinclair, Healy and Bourne; Crutcher) separate the various types of memory tasks tested. Typically, these are procedural (task-oriented, motor memory), categorical (content) and contextual (spatial or temporal–involving location and time cues). Review or warm-up periods enhanced recall in all cases. Healy and Bourne report excellent retention across a one month interval, but weakening retention afterwards. The overall results suggest that even a break of one week impairs memory, but six weeks is quite harmful. It is naturally, not nearly as bad as three months or one year.

There are two questions that arise out of this. One, did it matter which type of memory was being used? The answer is yes. The procedural (body learning) and contextual (temporal and spatial) *lasted much longer,* as suggested they would in an earlier chapter on instructional strategies. The recall was quicker and stronger. These, of course, are much more brain-based than the traditional categorical or rote type of memory used for most content.

The second question has to do with appropriateness of memory. Is it even appropriate that we emphasize a reliance on a library of facts? Yes, to a degree, although not to the degree it is utilized now. Today's learner must be able to make critical decisions, form cooperative groups, locate resources and apply the knowledge. The days of memorize and memorize, are long outdated.

2. The Effects of Natural Lighting. Year-round schools means a longer time in the classroom during the summer months. Those months have 20-30% more hours of daylight. Can that affect learners? Yes, says the research of London, Harmon and Orlock. Learners in natural or non florescent lighting had fewer visual problems, less fatigue, fewer posture problems and increased academic achievement.

The pineal gland, located within the brain's blood-barrier is most affected by outdoor or indoor lighting. Interestingly, it has the largest concentration of serotonin in the body. This neurotransmitter is known to affect our waking and sleep cycles, depression, relaxation and alertness. Research suggests that during the shorter daylight months it may be responsible for Seasonal Affective Syndrome (SAD). The symptoms are depression, listlessness and carbohydrate cravings. While longer daylight can mean a more positive outlook and a better attention span, shorter days can mean depressed learners. Over ten million Americans have a strong reaction to shorter hours of sunlight, and 25 million are

The days of memorize and memorize are long out-dated

143

affected by it. The dietary implications are strong, but the direct influences on the brain are worthy of note, as well.

3. Dietary changes. Increased carbohydrates may help us boost depressing moods during the darker winter months, but the affect on learning can be powerful. The increased levels of carbohydrate intake can have a negative impact on concentration, too. Alone or with sugar, they create a troubling combination for the brain's attention and memory levels. Research by Wurtman suggests that these brain-poor diets can impair alertness, thinking and memory. The typical diet changes during the summer and some of it is good for learning. Many learners eat more fresh fruit and vegetables, which have critical trace elements for learning such as vitamin C, boron, niacin, folic acid and selenium. The diet is often leaner on fats. Studies by Professor Greenwood at the University of Toronto found that rats on a diet of polyunsaturated fats learned 20% faster than those eating saturated fats.

Future applications of recent brain research will become more and more evident over time

4. Stress levels. A year-round school schedule can positively effect both the teacher and student stress levels. For one, there's less build-up of stress, since there are more frequent breaks. Second, during the summer months, more students are physically active. Research by Ned Herrmann (edited by Michaud) suggests exercise lowers stress and boosts learning. Learners with lower stress will be more attentive and recall more, says a study by Kushner at Scripps College in Claremont, California.

5. Relationships and Family. Time away from school can mean more time for family and friends. This can be a stress inducer or inhibitor, depending on the particular situation of the learner. More studies will have to be done in this area to determine the overall effect.

As time goes on, applications of recent brain research for year-round schooling will become more evident. For now, the evidence suggests it's a fair bet that year-round schooling is better for attention, learning and memory.

Defining A Brain-Based School

Can one define a brain-based school? It's an organization which operates based on the best knowledge about the brain and how it learns. An automotive engine can have many things wrong and still work. It can have many things right about it and still not work. Brain-based schools are not perfect. They have not solved all problems. How they

144

are different is simple: it's like the manager-executive difference. The manager does things right, the executive does the right things. The brain-based school *does most of the right things and usually does them the right way.*

There are several ways you can tell immediately. As you walk around your campus, what do you see? Do you see students who are enjoying being at school? Do they work together in groups outside of class? Do they do extra work on their own? Do they bring things to school from their personal life, without being asked? Do they make it to class on time? Is attendance high? Are teachers highly regarded and spoken of well, in private? Brain-based schools have a different "feel." There are hundreds of schools who have begun to embody the principles of this book. What else makes the difference?

In brain-based education, teachers think of themselves as "learning catalysts" instead of teachers. After all, teachers teach. The old definition is basically more of the same, top-down, "I'm in power, you, the student, are not." Instead, a learning catalyst *changes the role to promoting learning in whatever form is appropriate.* They are fully skilled in the use of multiple intelligences and learning styles. They are skilled at reading student states and managing them appropriately. They utilize and integrate technology, mind mapping, accelerated learning, peripherals, music and art across the curriculum. They give learners choice and variety, with plenty of feedback. More importantly, they think of themselves as learning catalysts, not a "stand and deliver" teacher. They use these methods more consistently and with confidence. They enjoy learning and trying new things; they "walk the talk."

If you don't "live it," you don't believe it. A perfect example of this is a staff development day. To make it brain compatible, it makes sense to use the following brain-based strategies:

1. Offer choice to the staff in the content & process
2. Make it safe and threat-free to ask questions & challenge
3. Insure it's multi-sensory, hands-on, with handouts
4. Enrich by using thematic content, not unrelated piecemeal topics
5. Use contextual memory, mind-body state management
6. Offer & receive plenty of feedback

The previous chapters provide the initial framework for a more brain-based school. The next page gives you some *(reproducible)* additional specific distinctions and examples.

If you don't "live it," you don't believe it

Summary of Brain-Based Learning Strategies

Not Brain-Compatible	YES: Brain-Based
Low emotional impact	Appropriately high emotional arousal
Fragmented, sequential only	Global, unified, holistic, thematic
Concern with being "on task"	Alternating focus-diffusion learning
Standard boring illustrations	Colorful abundant memory maps
Suppressing learner energy	Utilizing & expressing energy
Lecture, more didactic	Multiple intelligences served
Emphasis on content	Emphasis on context, meaning & value
Resigned to the learner's state	Positively conditions the learner & states
Mistakes recognized directly	Mistakes noted indirectly or re-framed
Learner association with failure	Use of alter-ego, other fun characters
Emphasis on quiet learning	Often rich with talking, music, activity
Assessment by standardized tests	Feedback quality & quantity is increased
Belief that learning is difficult	Attitude is: it's easy, fun & creative
Create tension & stress to learn	Keeps stress low and enjoyment high
Learning as only mental/cognitive	Learning also emotive, action, movement
Central focused stimuli	Use of significant peripheral stimuli
Extended presenter lecture time	Alternate focus & diffusion activities
Assumes authority from role	Creates constant respect & credibility
Finish when time's up	Finish with celebration
Subtle or obvious threats, helplessness	Remove threats; focus on support
Focus on learning in classrooms	Real world, simulations, trips
Institutional boring rituals	Positive, purposeful rituals
Infer, threaten, demand	Suggest, ask & tell, suggest, ask & tell
Watered down micro-chunk curriculum	Year-long real life thematic curriculum
Insistent focus on conscious learning	Use of strong non-conscious learning
Minimal open & closing time	Longer open & close, shorter middle
Delayed, indefinite vague feedback	Immediate, positive & dramatic feedback
Teach for the test, with stress	Learn for the joy of learning & real life
Sit at desks & limit interactions	Mobility, face each other, partners, groups
Abrupt exposure to content	Purposeful & consistent pre-exposure
Introduce topic, forget it	Multiple exposure & activation at 1-3 days
Outcome-based learning	Learning is often a by-product of play
Constant use of negatives; "don'ts"	Use of totally positive language
Artificial, contrived textbook learning	Using real life problems in the real world
Use of bribes, rewards, gimmicks	Intrinsic motivation elicited
Starve the brain for stimulation	Enriched: music, sights, aromas, movement
Disciplined, ordered, quiet, repressive	Expressive, changing, noisy, music
Single topic only by teacher choice	Learner input on topics, directions & depth
Standardized "objective" assessment	Multiple brain-based assessment strategies

Where Is All The Research?

You may ask, "If this brain-based approach is so great, where are all the studies that back it up? Show me a school or better yet, a district that used it where their standardized achievement scores actually went up. Prove it to me!" I'm trusting that by now, you've come to some important conclusions:

1. Only the tried and true, that which is **not new** has all the supporting data. By the time it gets the data to back it up, there may be something better.

2. There already are quality schools around the world that do use these general strategies and enjoy terrific success. They may not call themselves a "brain-based school." What you call yourself is less important than what you do.

3. Many things that are absolutely essential for students and great for the brain *will never, ever show up on the state or national achievement tests.* As pointed out in Chapter 4 on assessment, the whole paradigm of what and how we test is now being called into question. Trying to make brain-based achievement fit on traditional question-answer boxes is like "street testing" the space shuttle on how well it stops at red lights and parks. The shuttle was never designed for city traffic and it's an irrelevant form of assessment. *Until assessment changes, brain-based learning will never fit the statistical mold–it's not designed to!* The author maintains a newsletter and e-mail for listings of current schools using these methods. Feel free to contact them. This path is a long-term process, not a quick-fix. But it's well worthwhile!

Reflection and Analysis

❖ In what ways can you translate the key three or four theories and discoveries presented here into practical everyday useful ideas?

❖ What information in this chapter do you already apply?

❖ Did you think of any questions about this material? What were they?

❖ Did you have an emotional reaction to any of this information?

❖ Specify what was different and new to you? What was familiar and what was review?

❖ How did you react intellectually? Do you agree or disagree with any ideas explored in this chapter? Which ones and why?

❖ Let's say these things are, in fact, true about the brain, what should we do differently? What resources of time, people and money could be redirected? In what ways do you suggest we start doing it?

❖ Generate the most interesting or valuable insight(s) you got from this chapter.

❖ Make a plan for your next step, a realistic, practical application of what you've learned, and outline it.

❖ Can you foresee any obstacles you might encounter? How can you realistically deal with them?

Who is Part
of the Entire
Change Process

Parental
Involvement

Before You
Make Any
Changes

The Next Step

Teacher's
Guidelines

Suggested
Time Line

Reminders for
Success in the
Change Process

Year-Round
Schools

Chapter 7
The Next Step

Before Implementing Any Type of Change

We know that not all change is good. Some types of change just create more problems. Before your school begins any changes, regardless of whether they are brain-based or not, stop and take notice. Research by school reform experts Ryan, et. al., Paris, Ryan and Stiller, and Covington all suggest that ***educational leaders may want to consider (and avoid) these fatal paths:***

- forcing change on a staff without their input (or too fast, too rigid, etc.)
- non-thematic curriculum mandates (removes student choice & buy-in)
- high stakes testing (creates teaching to the test and causes students' brains to "minimize"). Instead, create more frequent assessment
- short-term assessment (much short-term learning is useless – instead provide a rich and constant source of learner feedback)
- outcome-based learning that focuses only on assessment of immediate results or on measurable results (much of the brain's best learning cannot be measured) instead of learning *how* to learn with joy & passion.
- outcome-based learning which excludes learner input (the "demand model")
- annual testing standards based on the "average" or what's "normal" (better to have wider standards; brains may be from 1-3 years apart & still be normal)
- rigid performance evaluations of teachers (causes teachers to perform according to assessments; discourages creativity)
- strongly controlling classrooms (creates resentment, apathy)
- "stand & deliver" teachers who lecture, lecture and lecture
- special programs for so-called gifted, talented learners or "at-risk" (all students need the same enrichment as "the gifted" are offered)
- controlling, bribery, punitive systems and similar tactics

If you want learning to increase and your students to change, influence the factors you have the most control over. When students get a more responsive environment, their behaviors change, say social researchers Edmonds and Kagan.

Regardless of other educational restructuring and reform, there is one single change that would do more to motivate learners than any other: Make school more real and less artificial; That means more cooperative, rich with choice and complexity dealing with real situations, problems and solutions

Schools and businesses can "change" all they want, but until they make true distinctions between what motivates learners in "real life" and what is going on in their own environments, it will get the same result: good, curious, motivated people who become unmotivated, then branded as lazy.

Make school more real and less artificial; That means more cooperative, rich with choice and complexity dealing with real situations, problems and solutions

Everybody Participates in the Reform

Research shows that the following approaches can work, when done at the appropriate age and grade levels for those involved:

1. Reorganize tasks and activities so that all of the routines involve some kind of team and partner work.
2. Elicit genuine, short-term academic goals from students and align school goals with students' lives, and social and personal goals. Provide students with consistent choice in the reform process.
3. Provide an environment which is responsive to student goals.
4. Infuse student learning with emotion, energy and enthusiasm.
5. Utilize student values such as autonomy, peer approval and responsibility, to provide maintenance structures for school systems.
6. Create a new model of teacher-teacher support so that every teacher knows every other teacher's best ideas.
7. Establish a "bottom-up" administrative approach wherein students experience their beliefs, goals, and values consistently integrated in the school design.

Schools who use the brain-based learning methods outlined in this book are consistently more successful than those who don't. What is meant by successful? There are fewer dropouts, the children enjoy school more, they are willing to take risks, think for themselves, and be creative. They understand how they learn and love to do it. It's more than just applying a few techniques. A school must become a learning organization. You may want to use the following sequence of steps for transforming a school into a learning organization:

1. Assess the Existing Culture
Do this both formally and informally, both individually and organizationally. Be sure to make it safe for others to tell the truth about their organization. Through discussion and genuine dialogue, understand the mental models of each employee. These are the paradigms that shape their decision-making on a daily basis. Find out how they think the system works, and how teaching or learning works. Sometimes this step can create despair at the results uncovered. Only after the truth (and sometimes, despair) is revealed, can the real work begin. Honesty and an acceptable level of workplace intimacy are essential to the process.

2. Establish a Learning Climate
Identify, encourage and promote the positive and good practices which help the organization stay on its vision. Reduce the threat to the staff. Increase their resources to make changes. Continually discover and share what's working. Reward risk-taking with acknowledgments and celebrations. Allow for mistakes, celebrate the lessons learned and move on. Make this policy for both students and faculty. The questions are: Do you continually test your experience? Are you producing knowledge? Is it something your organization has not done before and values?

3. Build a Collective Vision
Do this through discussion, through reflection and through safe dialogue. Develop shared images of a successful organization. Include parents, the district goals, community needs, staff goals and your own kids. Map out the vision and post it where it's highly visible. Make it collective, huge, vivid and fun to look at. Develop the values and principles which will guide the organization on its path. Avoid forcing specific strategies at this time; let them emerge from the process.

4. Encourage Personal Mastery
There will be no organizational changes unless people change. That takes support to make it happen. Ostensibly, each member of an organization is practicing what is being preached, or it creates an uncomfortable dissonance. Support each member to create a personal vision, guiding life principles and both long and short-term personal goals. Provide source books from authors like Steven Covey, M. Scott Peck or

For brain-based learning to work school-wide, the approach must be for long-term, personal, systemic and organizational change— anything less is doomed to fail

Anthony Robbins. Provide videos on these topics and let staff share their personal quests with others during an in-house, in-service. Offer learn-to-learn skills for the faculty. Make sure that everyone knows how to learn successfully in their way. By being a great role model as a learner, your students will be more likely to become great learners and role models as well. If you believe it, live it.

5. Design and Promote Collaborative Learning

Through discussion, commitment and regular, purposeful reflection and meeting time, each learner absorbs and shares what is learned. It's a "share the wealth" mentality. Help others become resources for each other by making it easier on everyone to get what they need. The organization is now "sideways." It's not bottom-up, not top-down but is participatory at all levels. Does every teacher know the best ideas of most every other teacher?

Encourage all of the following: cooperation, shared ideas, strategies, learning plans, research, classroom supplies, guest speakers, videos and community support resources. Your question is, "Do you share the knowledge you gain with others, consistently?" At this step, it's finally appropriate to draw up your plans, action steps, and to create forms of support with on-going feedback.

6. Make It Easy to Learn

Make it fun! You can't force learning and changes upon a staff. You can, however, create a climate where learning is the "thing to do." You can make the school a place where creativity and change is easy to implement. You can provide low-cost resources in staff libraries, with guest speakers and other community resources. Offer choice in staff development. Role-model learning, make it easy and support it wherever it occurs. That will keep the process moving. Make staff development fun.

7. Feedback: How to Nourish the Dream

Discover what systems are in place that encourage the fulfillment of the collective vision and which ones are not. Understand the key relationships that make your organization a success. Create systems which make sense and make them simple. Ask the question, "Why?" over and over until you find out what investment the organization has in keeping a particular useless policy.

All the planning and "seed planting" in the world will produce nothing unless you nourish the dream. Create a fun and dramatic metaphor for the change. Discover what the key statistical indicators in your school are for quality of learning. Be satisfied with small, continuous

Share the wealth, make it fun, and nourish the dream

improvement. If you discover your key indicators were the wrong ones, find new indicators. "Kaizen" is a Japanese word that means "never ending improvement." Make this your 25-year theme. Create public scorecards so everybody knows how every team and the whole organization, is doing. Most importantly, learn from your in-house statistics and commit to improving them forever!

How do you know if your school is a learning organization? It's easy. Ask yourself: Does the staff act differently around management than around other staff? Does the staff act differently around "certain staff" than others? Are they afraid to speak their mind to colleagues or to management? Can they try out new ideas without any fear of repercussion? Do the members of the school feel generally satisfied in their work? Are discussions commonly held about educational practices or is it mostly about hurtful gossip or hopeless problems? These questions allow you to find out what kind of a learning climate exists.

In general, you'll find that your school is a learning organization when the following things are happening:

The number one thing that successful learning organizations do well is support people to embrace change

- The school's vision often emerges in discussion, artifacts and daily practices that are being used in the school.
- The staff feel that their work is meaningful and makes a difference.
- The staff seems much smarter when working together instead of dragging each other down or working alone.
- Staff members are encouraged to find out how others do their job so they know how individual changes influence the whole (systems thinking).
- Students, staff, management and others feel free to inquire about other's biases and assumptions. There are very few (if any) "sacred cows" (topics off limits for discussion). It's OK to admit mistakes.
- There's a great respect for the differences, the experience and concerns of others at the school. But that does not become an obstacle to change.
- Everyone in the organization is growing, stretching and becoming more of the person they want to be. The school is a good place to learn and grow!

Learning organizations will succeed well into the 21st century for many reasons. One of them is *not* that they will successfully know or predict or anticipate the future and prepare for it. Why would that *not* happen in a learning organization? It's simple. Even if we knew the future, we would: 1) not agree on how to interpret it; 2) have differing theories of how to deal with it; 3) have varying value systems that might conflict. What **would** happen in a learning institution is they would *learn their way into the future.* Educators, literally, learn **how** to succeed as needed. Where would they start? They would begin the steps to becoming a brain-based school. While many schools have found a formula that works, it always ends up being specific to the leadership, culture, vision, circumstances and resources of that school. Yet, there is always one good place to start the process.

Start From Within

Let's start the change process within ourselves

There's no better place to start than with ourselves. Learn this information, integrate it and make it yours. Read it, talk it over, try it out. You may want to attend a workshop on this material including a six-day training for becoming a brain-based facilitator which is described in the appendix.

✔ *Gather information...*Learn the basics of brain-based learning. Read about it and ask questions. This book is the beginning of your knowledge base. You may want to order *The Learning Brain* or *Brain-Based Learning & Teaching,* both mentioned in the Appendix or the Recommended Reading List. There are other resources recommended in the bibliography.

✔ *Make connections...*Use thematic mapping, greater content associations and learn how to learn the different skills of learning. Now learning will begin to make more sense, through more associations. Make mind maps, discuss these ideas. Find related ideas and share them, too. Integrate these ideas in your work and personal life. Unless you make the learning personal, it will lack potency and value.

✔ *Expand your learning and associations...*Relate it to self, community, and planet. Your content learning has now become related, "global" learning. It makes sense to you on a larger scale, encompassing both yourself, and the environment. This is often referred to as "natural knowledge." Form support groups, hold meetings, sponsor activities, write newsletters and get involved in brain-based networks.

✔ ***Become a local expert...*** Speak on this topic. Make sure you role model these principles. Speak at your school, in your district and the community. Write materials for the classroom that apply these important principles. It's a matter of re-contextualizing and using generalization. Your peers may now acknowledge you as an expert. Begin to develop a learning organization.

✔ ***New applications...*** Over time, and with reflection, you'll gain new insights and the ability to think "outside the box," with new themes, as a paradigm-creating pioneer. You'll discover novel and innovative applications for brain-based frameworks. Create new learning and systemic models based on current brain research. Let this material become a part of you. Start with implementing just one or two items, then keep adding. Use the ***"Self-Check Guidelines"*** on the next page (it is reproducible) as a reminder of the key brain-based strategies. Post it, tape it to a desk, or put each item on a 3 X 5 index card, then put them in a rotating stack. That way, each item that is on top can be integrated or evaluated over time, not as a crash "quick fix."

Prevention is the key to smooth change

An Ounce of Prevention

These are the areas that deserve consideration up front. An ounce of prevention here will insure you save a pound full of headaches later.

✔ ***Choice required.*** Staff must have choice in the process to make it work. Choice can come in the form of when, how much, who, materials, extent and degree of implementation, accountability, direction, and celebration.

✔ ***Frustration.*** Staff is likely to get frustrated without a "prescriptive, recipe-type" format of staff development. It's normal, it will change over time.

✔ ***Skills.*** Staff will need new skills (listening, leadership, creativity, teamwork, etc.). Without these skills, you'll experience a wide variety of problems. With them, teachers have a chance to make it work.

✔ ***Fear.*** Staff will experience fear in letting go of control & power and allowing students to make more choices in their learning.

✔ *Self-Check: Teacher's Brain-Based Guidelines*

Instructional Strategies
❏ Ability to get attention when appropriate
❏ Purposeful & productive activation of emotions
❏ Management & empowerment of learner states
❏ Strong learner choices offered
❏ Teacher role-models joy and love of learning
❏ Balance of novelty, rituals and challenge
❏ Use of natural memory (contextual, motor & sensory)
❏ More immediate & consistent learner feedback
❏ Emphasis on preventative and invisible discipline
❏ Use of a non-hostile non-threatening discipline system
❏ Makes learning safe, relevant & interesting
❏ Use of music, video, guest speakers & computers
❏ Appropriate use of nonverbals
❏ Understanding & use of learner-constructed meaning

The Learning Environment
❏ Create a secure, safe environment with an absence of threat
❏ Consistent use of collaborative learning (teams, partners, mixed groupings)
❏ Teacher-to-student & (student-to-student) quality, trusting relationships
❏ Room is physically comfortable, learners have choices
❏ Classroom is rich with posters, peripherals; it's real-life and multi-sensory
❏ Greater time flexibility on work projects

Use of Curriculum
❏ Use of integrated, multi-disciplinary thematic content
❏ Relies on more relevant, real-life learning
❏ Provides greater learner choice for topics
❏ Teacher invests longer time on fewer, more complex topics

Feedback, Assessment & Evaluation
❏ Emphasis on continuous daily feedback, de-emphasis on testing
❏ Demonstration of content mastery in 4-5 of the seven intelligences
❏ Learners can make an appropriate defense of their personal biases
❏ Students can show learning in context of the interdisciplinary relationships
❏ Learners demonstrate mastery of the process of learning as well as content
❏ Students give evidence of corresponding mental models learned
❏ Learners can show personal relevance or local, national or global relevance
❏ Specific "how-to" strategies are learned and demonstrated
❏ Teacher keeps logs or portfolios on student's observable behavior changes
❏ Learners have input & dialogue into the evaluation process

✔ **Time.** It will take longer than you think to switch over. Staff will need to create new planning time each week (1-2 hrs). Creating that time is critical to success.

✔ **Confusion.** Staff will experience confusion in changing over from a more "product-oriented" education to a more process-oriented one.

✔ *Feedback.* Staff will need far more feedback (better quality and more often) than ever before to understand and implement the principles.

✔ *Boredom.* Staff can become apathetic unless there are specific goals set, occasional infusion of fresh ideas, and celebration as part of the process.

Remember that brain-based learning is a continuous process

Suggested Time Line

How long would it take for you to implement a brain-based program? The answer is that you don't "implement" a brain-based program. Brain-based learning is a continuous process. As long as anyone is studying the brain, we can still learn from it and implement appropriate lessons. Realistically, it will take three years to get the majority of it firmly in place. However, it is not just a 3-year project. Why? Staff turnover, new insights, changes in student population and resources make this a dynamic strategy which needs continual attention.

This particular reform is the basis for all your other restructuring projects. It is compatible and complementary with most of the programs schools are already using. To start, go lightly unless the majority of your staff is already "sold" on the idea. In general, it's best to pre-expose staff to the idea well in advance. Discover any areas of resistance during this period and give them time to have those concerns addressed and dealt with.

What can you expect in this process? You can expect almost everything. Staff may be excited, resistant, overwhelmed, curious and burnt out. You'll encounter two forms of reform: surface level and genuine reform. If the process is easy and quick, it's likely that you're getting surface level reform. The key thing is to make the process sustainable. You do that with support, feedback, challenge, fun and novelty.

157

Pre-expose topic. Over a period of months, use post-its, magazine articles, video, books, & personal experience. Keep it low-key to stimulate interest.

First Year

✔ *Formal introduction*
Active presentation of key ideas. Initial skill-building.

✔ *Small discussion groups begin*
3-7 staff in each, low key. Trial of new ideas for instructional strategies, no threat, open expectations, no pressure on the degree of implementation.

✔ *Experimentation & support throughout the year*
Teachers get to try out what they want. Only requirement is to keep a journal and share personal experience with other teachers.

Second Year

✔ *Begin with extended 2-6 day institutes*
Curriculum planning, organizational changes begun. Instructional strategies enriched.

✔ *Experimentation becomes stronger*
Try feedback with discussion, curriculum planning, group work. Get the local media involved, newsletters, other schools, speakers.

✔ *Continued support*
Generate fresh ideas, invite guest speakers, and new points of view. Provide additional training in related areas. Plant the seeds for change in assessment and systems.

Third Year +

✔ *Continue the process*
Develop systems to keep the changes, as long as appropriate. Re-design assessment and the environment, curriculum, instructional strategies and the learning organization. Attend conferences, read new books, start discussion groups, talk about your success, write it up, and publish.

Reminders for the Change Process

1. The process requires new skills
Train the staff in teamwork, accountability, listening and support skills (the difference between talking *at* others vs. really communicating). Until each staff is individually and equally respected, the sharing and listening will continue in of the same power/status structures.

2. The change process works better with collegial input
(The difference between feeling isolated and being supported by others). Only in small process groups will the staff feel intellectually and emotionally safe to divulge their difficulties and concerns.

3. The change process is as personal as professional
(The difference between espoused theories vs. personal use strategies). The principles, theories and information will need to become part of each staff's own mental model of learning. The shifts to brain-based learning are so significant and dramatic; it takes time and honesty to really get at the personal meaning of them.

Discover, analyze, align, back it up, and commit

Take the Next Step

There are many, many ways to get started with a more brain-based school and community approach to learning. As you begin the process write to us and we can give you the names of other schools "in process" also. This network of support can make the difference between success and failure. Research suggests that all successful transformations had the following characteristics:

1. **Discover** – *"What else is out there?"* The staff searched near, far and wide for successes and solutions. They read, networked, called other schools, attended conferences, checked out books, bought newsletters and held discussion groups.

2. **Analyze** – *"What do we have so far?"* They analyzed and modified the solutions for their own needs & culture. Commit to building on existing strengths.

3. **Align** – *"Can we all agree on what we want?"* They had complete input and "buy-in" on the vision and the steps to make it happen... Develop a complete staff unity of purpose.

4. **Back it up** – *"If this is good, then let's make it policy"* Make your ideas into policy, not just another good idea. Willingly assume responsibility, but with corresponding amounts of authority to act on what is needed at the time.

5. **Commit** – *"If we believe in it, let's stick with it!"* Commit to staying with it until it works. No excuses. Emphasize the positives and celebrate the successes. Learn to communicate what isn't working and fix it. Take on reform as a permanent on-going process, not some one or two year gimmick to quiet critics. Quality is an endless process.

The quest for quality is an endless process

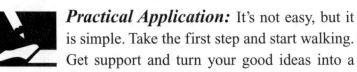 *Practical Application:* It's not easy, but it is simple. Take the first step and start walking. Get support and turn your good ideas into a movement. Learning can work for everyone. The dream begins with you taking action, right now.

How you can follow up: To get more information on brain-based learning, a free catalog of brain-based resources or to order multiple copies of this book for others at your school or district, please contact the publisher listed below. For further information, see page 162 in the appendix.

Turning Point, Box 2551
Del Mar, CA 92014, USA

Phone (619) 546-7555
Toll-Free (800) 325-4769
Fax (619) 546-7560

Appendix

The Author

Eric Jensen is a former teacher who has taught elementary, middle school, high school level students. He remains deeply committed to making a positive, significant, lasting difference in the way the world learns. He received his B.A. in English from San Diego State University and M.A. in Psychology from the University of California. He has taught as adjunct faculty at the University of California at San Diego, National University and the University of San Diego. He's listed in "Who's Who Worldwide" and is a former Outstanding Young Man of America selection.

Jensen was the co-founder of SuperCamp, the nation's first and largest brain-based learning program for teens. He authored the best-selling *Student Success Secrets, The Little Book of Big Motivation, Brain-Based Learning & Teaching, 30 Days to B's and A's, You Can Succeed, The Learning Brain* and *SuperTeaching.*

He was a key part of one of the largest (over 4,000 teachers trained) brain-based teacher training programs in the world. Trainers from AT & T, Disney, IBM, Digital, GTE, Hewlett-Packard, ICA, Motorola, Burroughs, Atlantic Bell, SAS and three branches of the military have used his methods. Jensen provides successful trainings for conferences, schools, organizations, and Fortune 500 corporations, and is an international speaker, writer and consultant.

Your Feedback to the Author

All feedback is welcomed. If you have any comments, corrections, additions or suggestions for the next printing of this book, please fax or write to the author at the address and phone number below. Also, if your school is currently in the change process, contact us, we can support your efforts.

For a speaker or trainer, contact the author: For brain-based training, conference speaking, consulting, corporate training, district or school in-services and workshops or for a *free* catalogue of Brain-Based Learning Products for Teaching and Training, call (800) 325-4769 or (619) 546-7555, fax (619) 546-7560 or mail your name and address to: **Turning Point**, P.O. Box 2551, Del Mar, CA 92014 USA

Distributor and Overseas Inquiries Welcome: If you distribute a catalogue, do workshops, or if you are a publisher overseas, your audience may be interested in learning more about these practical brain-based strategies. To offer a catalog and earn additional income, contact our publishing office for distributor price list. Call (619) 546-7555 or mail your name and address to: Turning Point, P.O. Box 2551, Del Mar, CA 92014 USA.

Partial Listing of Schools, Colleges & Universities Involved in the Brain-Based Movement

Cedar Rapids Schools, Cedar Rapids, IA • St. Mary's College, Millersville, WI • George Mason Univ. Fairfax, VA • Accelerated Academics Academy, Flint, MI • Rockhurst College, Kansas City, MO • Santa Monica Community College • Dry Creek Elementary, Rio Linda, CA • Portland Schools, OR • University of MA, Boston, MA • Univ. of Cincinnati • Univ. of Millersville, Millersville, PA • El Dorado County of Education, Placerville, CA • Gold Oak Union, Placerville, CA • Jefferson Parish, Marrero, LA • Minuteman Regional, Lexington, MA • La Mesa Dale Elementary School, La Mesa, CA • El Dorado High School, Las Vegas, NV • Mary Harrison School, Toledo, OH • Battle Ground, Battle Ground, WA • Fallbrook Union, Fallbrook, CA • Aurora University, Aurora, IL • Riverside Cty. office, Riverside, CA • Sylvester School, Hanover, CA • School District of Joplin, MO • Corpus Christi I.S.D. Corpus Christi, TX • School District #35, Langley, B.C. Canada • Rowe Junior High, Milwaukee, OR Yuma School District, Yuma, AZ • School District # 68, Nanaimo, B.C. Canada • Bonita Vista Middle School, Chula Vista, CA • Caesar Rodney School District, Camden DE • Long Beach Elementary schools, Long Beach, CA • Keller I.S.D., Keller, TX • Flint Community School, Flint, MI • Atwater Elem. S.D.Atwater, GA • W. Bloomfield S.D.W. Bloomfield, MI • Sobey Elem. School, Flint, MI • Hanford Adult School, Hanford, CA • School District # 64, Ganges B.C. Canada • Vancouver School, Vancouver, Canada Board #39-Staff Dev. Program Services •Spring Branch District, TX • Morrow Cty. S.D. #1 • Lexington, OR • Sam Boardman Elem. School • Dartmouth Pub. School, S. Dartmouth, MA • School Admin. #14, Epping, NH • Mecosta Osceola I.S.D., Big Rapids, MI • Ed. Cooperative, Wellesley, MA • Many San Diego County Schools, SD, CA • Hundreds more, far too numerous to mention, in the U.S., New Zealand, Denmark, Sweden and Australia.

Is your school in the process of becoming more brain-based?
Please write us so it can be included in our Neuro News newsletter. Thank you.

Glossary of Terms

ACTH... The most thoroughly studied and common neurotransmitter. It is abundant in the nervous system, particularly at the neuromuscular junctions.

Epinephrine... Under stress, fear or excitement, this hormone is released from your adrenal gland into your bloodstream. When it reaches your liver, it stimulates the release of glucose for rapid energy. Abrupt increases caused by anger can constrict heart vessels, requiring it to pump with higher pressure.

Amygdala... Located in the mid-brain, this almond-shaped complex may be the critical processing area for senses. It receives input from the visual, auditory areas and is involved in determining appropriate behavior. Stimulating this area can cause rage, fear and sexual feelings. Contains huge number of opiate receptor sites.

Axons... Each nerve cell can either get incoming information or send out information. These are the long fibers extending from the cell body (neurons) that carry the output (a nerve impulse) to another cell. Can be up to a meter long. Used often, axons build up a fatty white shield called myelin.

Brainstem... It links the spinal cord with the cerebral hemispheres. Often referred to as the reptilian brain in the triune model.

Broca's area... Part of the frontal lobe in the cerebrum. It converts thoughts into sounds and sends the message to the motor area. Impulses go first to Wernicke's area, then to Broca's area.

Cerebellum... A cauliflower-shaped appendage located below the occipital area and next to the brainstem. Almost an annex or add-on. It's responsible for balance, coordination, muscle movements, even speech.

Cerebral cortex... Also known as the neocortex. This is newspaper-sized, 1/4" thick, wrinkled and packed with brain cells (neurons).

Cerebrum... This is the largest part of the brain, composed of the left and right hemisphere. It has frontal, parietal, temporal and occipital lobes.

Cingulate gyrus... Part of the limbic system that lies directly above the corpus callosum. It mediates between the intellectual cortex and the emotional limbic.

Corpus callosum... A white matter bundle of nerve fibers which connect the left and right hemisphere. Located in the mid-brain area.

Dendrites... These are the strand-like fibers emanating from the cell body. Similar to spider webs or cracks in the wall, they are the receptor branches stimulated by incoming neurotransmitters.

Endorphin... A neurotransmitter similar to morphine; produced in the pituitary gland. Protects against excessive pain and is released with ACTH and enkephalins into the brain.

Enkephalin... A morphine like substance consisting of five amino acids. Released into the brain with ACTH and endorphins to combat pain.

Frontal lobes... One of four main areas of the cerebrum, the upper brain area. Controls voluntary movement on the opposite side of the body. In 99% of right handers and 60% of left handers, the left frontal lobe (our left hemisphere) is dominant. It deals with verbal expression, problem-solving, will-power and planning. Often referred to as prefrontal lobes. The other three areas of the cerebrum are the occipital, parietal and temporal.

Glia... These are one of two types of brain cells (the other is a neuron). These outnumber neurons ten to one, there may be up to 150 billion of them in the brain. They serve a nutrient and repair function and may form their own communication network. Short for neuroglia.

Hippocampus... Found deep in the temporal lobe, central to the mid-brain area. It's a seahorse-shaped organ responsible for learning, novelty and spatial, contextual memory. Receives sensory input, prioritizes it and establishes memory. Also has a role in emotions and sexuality.

Hypothalamus... Located in the bottom center of the midbrain area. Complex collection of cell groups that influences appetite, hormone secretion, digestion, circulation, emotions and sleep.

Lateralization... Refers to the activity of using one hemisphere more than another. The term "relative lateralization" is more accurate since we are usually using at least some of the left and right hemisphere at the same time.

Limbic system... A group of connected structures in the midbrain area. This area includes the hypothalamus, amygdala, hippocampus, cingulate gyrus and mammalian brain.

Medulla... Located in the brain stem, it channels information between the cerebral hemispheres and the spinal cord. It controls respiration, circulation, wakefulness, breathing and heart rate.

Myelin... A fatty white shield that coats and insulates axons. They can help make the cells (neurons) more efficient. Habits are probably a result of myelinated axons.

Neurons... One of two types of brain cells. We have about 10-15 billion of these. Receives stimulation from its branches known as dendrites. Communicates by firing a nerve impulse along an axon.

Neurotransmitters... Our brain's biochemical messengers. We have many types of them. These are usually the stimulus that excites a neighboring neuron.

Norepinephrine... Formerly known as adrenaline, this neurotransmitter is responsible for triggering our body's response to stress, threat, challenge and excitement.

Occipital lobe... Located in the rear of the cerebrum. One of the four major areas of the upper brain, this lobe processes our vision. The other three areas are parietal, frontal and temporal lobes.

Parietal lobe... The top of our upper brain. It's one of four major areas of the cerebrum. This area deals with reception of sensory information from the contralateral body side. It also plays a part in reading, writing and calculation. The other three lobes are the occipital, temporal and frontal.

Pineal gland... A small organ, located inside the blood-brain barrier that deals with the release of serotonin and its conversion into melatonin. It is affected by light and regulates our sleep-waking cycles.

Pons... Located near the top of the brain stem, above the medulla. It's an critical relay station for our sensory information.

Prefrontal lobes... Organizes and regulates our behavior. This area helps give us purpose, higher mental activities, and anticipation of the future

Reptilian brain... This is the lower portion of the brain composed of the upper spinal cord, medulla, pons and some say, the reticular formation. It sorts sensory information and regulates our survival functions like breathing and heart rate.

Reticular formation... A small area, at the top of the brain stem and bottom of the limbic area... It's the regulator responsible for attention, arousal, sleep/awake, consciousness.

Serotonin... A common neurotransmitter, most responsible for inducing deep relaxation and sleep.

Synapses... It's the junction point where two neurons communicate. Occurs when a presynaptic axon carrying an electrical impulse releases a neurotransmitter. That turns the reaction into a chemical one. That electrically stimulates a dendrite of the postsynaptic cell. The process of connections and growth is electrical to chemical to electrical.

Temporal lobes... Located on the side of the cerebrum (in the middle of our upper brain), it's an area believed responsible for hearing, language, learning, memory and emotion. The other three major cerebrum areas are the frontal, occipital and parietal lobes.

Thalamus... Located deep within the brain, it is a key sensory relay station. Its functions are involved in hearing, muscle movement, retrieving memories

Wernicke's area... The upper back edge of the left temporal lobe. Here the brain converts thoughts into language.

Index

Exciting 6-Day Workshop: Brain Based Learning

- **Six exciting days, $675**
- **For all levels of teachers, trainers & administrators**
- **Learn new teaching, training & staff development skills**
- **Practical applications of new brain research**
- **Great for staff who want to redesign their school**
- **Integrate brain-based approaches in all areas**
- **Learn over 100 specific and useful ideas**
- **Increase your market value and income**
- **Discover potent new ways to boost learning**
- **Boost your own self-confidence & self-esteem**
- **Make a bigger difference & feel good about it**

If you enjoyed this book, you may want to take the training that goes with it. Are you a teacher, trainer or administrator? Do you now, or would you like to make your living as a presenter? Would you like to master the art of using all these brain-based strategies? Would you like to be able to consistently get audience participation, engage meaning and motivate for lasting changes? You would? Good, then keep reading. You're about to learn why taking a 6-day brain-based training may be one the best things you can possibly do for yourself (and your audience).

- Upgrade your skills for the 21st century
- Boost attention, learning, recall & usage
- 100% satisfaction guaranteed

There's a surging tidal wave sweeping the country and some say, the world. It's not just a trend. It's a virtual explosion in neuroscience discoveries. In the last few years, maverick researchers have uncovered astonishing details about the brain and learning, and they're already being implemented in technology, medicine and business. Learn how to apply them now, and you'll possess rare, powerful and highly marketable 21st century skills that can transform the very foundations of the educational system. You will become more than a contributor, you'll become a "key player" to global learning transformation. *As we move towards the next century, you'll either be part of the new learning revolution or left behind wondering "What happened?"*

As a former classroom teacher, a world-wide staff developer and corporate trainer with over 15 years of successful brain-based training experience, I have successfully trained over 5,000 teens and 15,000 adults. I've been a key part of two of the largest brain-based programs in the world. This has been my passion for years and I love to share it. Wouldn't you want to tap into that kind of experience? I'll bet you would.

168

Would you like to know what we cover? I'll bet you're curious like me. Just for fun, read the course items below that you'd like to learn & experience:

- How to design and conduct a workshop or training based on the brain
- The 12 super-essentials to know about the brain
- Better curriculum strategies (with tons of examples)
- How this wave of the future will be impacting your work

If you could successfully do those things, would your work be easier, more effective? Of course. Yet, why take my word for it when you can get it straight from past course participants:

"Simply mind-boggling... learned more in 6 days than in twenty years in education" P. Kohlbacher, IL

"You've planted the seeds and the harvest will be a bumper crop!" P. Park, MA

"Never been to a course that gave me so many ideas that were so specific." K. Norman

"I wish I had learned this stuff in college... it should be a graduate requirement." J. Murphy

"One of the best workshops I've taken in 25 years in the field of education... and the most fun by a mile!" L. Miller, Supervisor of Instruction, DE

I could give you countless testimonials. But let's get back to the curriculum of the six-day San Diego course. You can also expect to learn the answers to these topics:

- How to get the whole staff to "buy into" this process
- What is the perfect learning and thinking diet
- How to translate information into "deeply felt" meaning
- How to build and maintain high-performance teams

Those are just some of the more powerful skills and ideas which you can expect to learn. What happens when you implement the results of this course? I can cite you example after example of how participants from my courses have gone on to become highly requested speakers, presenters and even experts in their field. Sometimes I smile when I see conferences with two, three and in one case *four* professional speakers, all trained by me. But please, don't get me wrong. The participants did all the hard work to get good. But I do have a knack for lighting a professional fire and opening up minds.

"Get ready for a mind explosion like you've never had before" S. Robertson, CA

"Your workshop positively and dramatically changed my teaching forever... I have so many parents coming to me and telling me what the difference I've made in their children's lives." I. Forber.

There are more; I'll save them for later. Since you're probably an insatiable learner like myself, you might be interested in what else is offered in this workshop:

- Ingenious rituals which boost learning and maintain optimal states
- How to specifically teach the brain as a learning organ
- Which types of music are best for learning and when to use them
- The 5 secrets to permanently eliminating discipline problems

You may be wondering how in the world can we do all of those things in just 6 short days. The answer is simple. Using the powerful strategies of accelerated learning, we'll be able to enhance absorption, speed up the pace and still absorb far more than you ever believed possible. This methodology, combined with the sizzling cutting-edge neuroscience discoveries will help you learn faster. These breakthroughs will help you discover:

- The real learning differences between males and females
- The 7 secrets to boost concentration and attention in learning
- How to guarantee that your audience will recall & use what they learn
- The 3 types of memory (& which one to reduce the use of dramatically)
- The most amazing new discoveries about the brain you **must** know

In addition, you'll learn through one of the all-time best methods ever: my role-modeling. The workshop is meticulously planned so that you get a real experience of **how** all these brain-based strategies actually work. To put it bluntly, I am one of the few that actually practice what I preach.

As you can tell, I'm not shy about asking you to enroll. Why should I be shy? It's the best investment you can make in yourself and your future. You've got a satisfaction or money back guarantee. After this workshop, the first paid presentation you make, will probably return your investment immediately. And your referral business will astonish you. By the way, are there any other reasons you might want to enroll? Of course!

- Network with "like-minded" people
- Gain new professional skills & confidence
- Discover the 50 best brain-based resources
- Get ready for the 21st century

Let's take care of the details. The course takes place at a beautiful location with relaxing scenery and great food nearby. The location and dates vary each year, so call for this year's location. You can walk from your hotel to the training, no rental car needed. We'll also provide a virtual supermarket of the best set of brain-based resources *anywhere* on this planet. This is going to be some kind of special event! You **are** planning on being a part of it, aren't you?

The tuition costs $675. Can you afford it? It just may be a case of "Can you afford *not* to register?" If you've read this far, you *know* it's for you. Get your school or district to pay for it. Put it on your credit card, use your savings or get a grant. It's a tax deduction. But move fast. You and I know, if you want anything badly enough, you'll find a way.

The demand for brain-based presenters is growing faster than the supply! This can be for your school, business or your next career. So, go for it. You've got a satisfaction or money back guarantee. The registration form is on the following page. Fill it out, copy, mail or fax it. today. While it's fresh in your mind, and there are still spaces left in this sock-hopping, idea-packed, transformational training, go ahead and register. Your future is important and this can positively and fundamentally alter its course. Do it now. You'll be glad you did. That's a promise....

Registration

✔ **YES!** *I'd like to register. Here's my $95 deposit on the $675 tuition.*
Tuition includes course workbook, certification, all special activities and supplies.
Remember...transportation to the event, meals and lodging are extra. Send me
confirmation, travel, lodging, course details and confirmation kit by first class mail.
Held several times each July in San Diego, California. June and August locations
usually include the East Coast, Midwest or Texas. Call for this year's exact dates and
locations. *(Prices and locations valid thru September 1997)*

Circle Payment Form: VISA/MC   wire transfer   check   purchase order
I understand the complete balance ($580) is due no later than 2 weeks prior to event.
Free! With my $95 deposit, send me the amazing, exclusive book "Brain Facts."
Credits: SDSU extension credits available for an additional fee.
Hotel: Call the hotel direct for reservations. We'll give you that information when you call.
We'll suggest an affordable hotel within walking distance. Register early, rooms go fast!

Name (print)

| School or Company Name | Role/Title |

Home Address   City

State & Zip Code   Country

Phone (include area code)   Fax (include area code)

VISA or Master card number   Expiration date

*Group Discounts: Group price for schools, businesses and other groups of three (3) or more. Details
available by phone or in registration kit. Sorry, no group discounts allowed on registration day
(the first day of the course)*

*Cancellation Policy: All monies paid are refundable except a $25 registration fee. To qualify, you must
contact us by phone, fax or letter prior to course start date.*

*Guarantee Policy: You can be assured of a first-class workshop. After completion of the six-day course,
if you don't feel you got your money's worth, you may request & receive a refund (minus the $95 materials
and registration fee). Refund requests honored up to, but not exceeding 90 days following the course.*

call: **1 (800) 325-4769 or (619) 546-7555**
fax: **1 (619) 546-7560**
mail: **TURNING POINT, Box 2551 Del Mar, CA 92014**

Brain-Based Learning & Teaching Video Staff Development

✔ Get others excited about learning   ✔ Save time & money

✔ Build enthusiasm & support   ✔ Cut learning time

✔ Reach large groups at a time   ✔ Make your job easier

For a staff of 50, this breakthrough $99 staff development program costs less than $2 a teacher. If you're hoping for miracles at your school, they may be closer than you think. As a top international consultant for the last 10 years, the travel schedule has been taking a toll on home and family time. So, although I still do some work, I'm cutting back. How does that affect you?

I'm on a mission to share difference-making principles of brain-based accelerated learning! And while I may not be able to do it in person, I sure can give you the best video training possible. I'm outraged by other school videos selling for $500-800. You *can* save a fortune and still get first-rate quality. Through the magic of video, I'll walk your staff through a meaningful one-hour or half-day in-service. The video covers all the key areas in this book:

- Physiology/Biology
- Timetables/Rhythms
- Memory & Recall
- Intelligence
- States/Attention
- Stress/Threats
- Emotions in Learning
- Strategies & Styles
- Different Learners
- Discipline Strategies
- Music/Environments
- Motivation & Rewards

See it in action! Enjoy state-of-the-art-virtual reality. Get specific classroom examples, graphics and colorful research-proven ideas. You get a lock-step "cookie-cutter" fail-safe video presentation, complete with step-by-step facilitator guide. It's guaranteed & risk-free. The topic is "Brain-based Accelerated Learning" and it is impacting education around the world. It can boost motivation, learning, attendance and help your staff consistently reach ALL of your learners. With spectacular special effects, the video highlights the key research in this book, making a persuasive and motivating case for the use of brain-based learning.

Use this video to provide a clear, concise and compelling case for why you do what you do. It uses state-of-the art virtual reality, classroom examples, graphics and interviews with administrators, teachers and trainers who use these strategies. Use it for staff development. Use it as an exciting tool for train-the-trainer programs.

How do you know this video will fit your needs? Four good reasons: 1) *It's based on this book.* If you like this book, you'll like the video. 2) *It's got a satisfaction, money-back guarantee.* 3) *It's got a fool-proof guidebook.* Keep your worries low and help make your presentation job easy. 4) *It's proven;* here's what others have said: *"Absolutely*

172

outstanding..couldn't take my eyes off it." Mary Francis, N.J. *"I can't say enough good things... all my expectations were met & exceeded...."* T. Johnson, Principal, NJ *"The whole course was so valuable & enlightening, I can't wait to start using it."* Staff Developer, Austin, TX. You can easily lower stress, save money, bring fresh ideas in and get motivated. Encourage and enthuse staff members with this exciting product. Next-day and 2-day delivery service available. Here's what to do...

How To Order:

✔ **YES!** *I'd like the $99 Budget Staff Development Package.*
Includes facilitator's Manual for conducting a terrific staff development session. Two exciting 38 min. color sessions which can be used as a 2-hour to full-day in-service.

Item #801 only $99

✔ **YES!** *I'd like the $375 Deluxe Staff Development Package.*
It's a budget-stretching $500 value: It's a fail-safe, lock-step staff-development kit in a box. You get the two-part, 76 min. video, a facilitator's guidebook, overheads, handouts, posters for the faculty lounge and two of the best "Brain-Based Learning" books ever written.

Item #802, well worth $375

Name (print)

School or Company Name   Role/Title

Shipping Address   City

State & Zip Code   Country

Phone (include area code)   Fax (include area code)

VISA or Master card number   Expiration date

Circle Payment Form: VISA/MC   wire transfer   check   purchase order

Video Format Requested: VHS   PAL

Shipping & Handling, U.S. Orders add $7.95. Fast 2-day and express overnight delivery available. Overseas orders add $35 for shipping (U.S. funds only). **Total Enclosed: $_____**

call: **1 (800) 325-4769 or (619) 546-7555**
fax: **1 (619) 546-7560**
mail: **TURNING POINT, Box 2551 Del Mar, CA 92014**

Follow-Up Resources & Networking Opportunities:

You may want to contact these organizations focused on "brain-based" learning:

- **Turning Point**
  Box 2551, Del Mar, CA 92014
  This is the author's organization. Call for a *free* catalog.
  (619) 546-7555, (800) 325-4769 or fax (619) 546-7560

  INTERNET contact: http://www.tpbrain.com

  Neuro News Newsletter
  Box 2551, Del Mar, CA 92014
  *The newsletter is quarterly and **free** to all product customers.*
  Contact the author for inservices/staff development.

- **ASCD's Brain-Based Learning Network, CARE**
  (attn: Dr. Joan Caulfield)
  Rockhurst College, 1100 Rockhurst Rd., Kansas City, MO 64110-2561
  newsletter quarterly, approx. $15 yr.

- **The Brain-Mind Bulletin**
  (213) 223-2500, approx. $45/yr.

Note: If you would like your organization listed here, please write to us with information about it so that we can include it in upcoming editions.

Start Here: Staff Interest Survey

To find out where your staff is at, make copies of this and give it to your staff. You might say, "Your opinions are valuable. Please be honest and check only one of the items below. The topic you are responding to is this: Regarding the implementation of a more brain-based approach at our school, how I feel is...." *(Check one)*

❒ "I'm 100% on board and ready, let's do it."

❒ "It's not great or perfect, but I like the concept enough to give it a chance."

❒ "I'm not sold on it, but..."
"I never complain, I'll do it."
"I complain about everything..."
"I'll do almost anything for a thrill!"

❒ "I don't like it, let's keep what we have. It's too much work, for too little return. I'm tired of all these reform scams, anyway. I'll kick and scream and who knows... I may even sabotage it. But as bad as that sounds, I'd be willing to give you some advice on how to really make things better at this school. I suggest...

Comments: _____

_____

_____

_____

_____

_____

Notes, Thoughts and Experiments

Idea I tried:_____

The results: _____

My conclusions: _____

Idea I tried:_____

The results: _____

My conclusions: _____

Idea I tried:_____

The results: _____

My conclusions: _____

Idea I tried:_____

The results: _____

My conclusions: _____

Idea I tried:_____

The results: _____

My conclusions: _____

Notes, Thoughts and Experiments

Idea I tried:_____

The results: _____

My conclusions: _____

Idea I tried:_____

The results: _____

My conclusions: _____

Idea I tried:_____

The results: _____

My conclusions: _____

Idea I tried:_____

The results: _____

My conclusions: _____

Idea I tried:_____

The results: _____

My conclusions: _____

Bibliography

Alkon, Daniel. *Memory's Voice* (1992). New York: Harper-Collins.

Allen, C. K. (1990). Encoding of Colors in Short-Term Memory. *Perceptual and Motor Skills* (71.1, 211-215).

Amabile, Teresa (1989). *Growing Up Creative.* New York: Crown Publishing.

Amabile, T. & Rovee-Collier, C. (1991, October). Contextual Variation and Memory Retrieval at Six Months. *Child Development,* 1155-66.

Ames, Carole. (1992). Achievement Goals and the Classroom Motivational Climate. *Student Perceptions in the Classroom.* (Ed. Dale Schunk and Judith Meece). Hillsdale, NJ: Erlbaum.

Ames, Carole. (1992). Classrooms: Goals, Structures, and Student Motivation. *Journal of Educational Psychology* 84, 261-71.

Ames, Carole. (1987).The Enhancement of Student Motivation. *Advances in Motivation and Achievement.* Eds. Maeher and Kleiber (Vol. 5, pgs.123-148). Greenwich, CT: JAI.

Anderson, R. C., & Pearson, P. D. (1984). A Schema-Theoretic View of Basic Processes in Reading Comprehension. *Handbook of Reading Research.* (Pearson, Ed.) New York, NY: Longman.

Annette, M. (1973). Handedness in Families. *Annals of Human Genetics* 37, 93-105.

Apacki, Carol. (1991). *Energize!* Granville, OH: Quest Books.

Armbruster, B. and Anderson, T. (1980). "The Effect of Mapping." *Center for the Study of Reading* 5th ed. Urbana, IL: University of Illinois.

Armstrong, Blake. (1991, June 12). "Studying and Television." *Bottom Line Personal.* Report of research at University of Wisconsin, 9.

Armstrong, Thomas. (1987). *In Their Own Way.* Los Angeles, CA: Jeremy Tarcher Publishing.

Asbjornsen A., Hugdahl, K., & Hynd, G. W. (1990). The Effects of Head and Eye Turns on the Right Ear Advantage in Dichotic Listening. *Brain and Language* 39.3, 447-58.

Backman L., Nilsson, L. G., & Nourp, R. K. (1993). Attentional Demands and Recall of Verbal and Color Information in Action Events. *Scandinavian Journal of Psychology* 34.3, 246-254.

Bandler, R. (1988). *Learning Strategies: Acquisition and Conviction.* (Videotape). Boulder, CO: NLP Comprehensive.

Bandura, A. (1986). *Social Foundations of Thought and Action: a social cognitive theory.* Englewood Cliffs, NJ: Prentice-Hall.

Barden, R. C., & Ford, M. E. (1990). *Optimal Performance in Golf.* Minneapolis, MN: Optimal Performance Systems.

Barkley R. (1988, September). *Attention-Deficit Hyperactivity Disorder.* (Lecture at conference) The Many Faces of Intelligence. Washington, D.C.

Barrett, Susan. (1992). *It's All in Your Head.* Minneapolis, MN: Free Spirit Publishing.

Baumeister, R. F. (1984). Choking Under Pressure: Self-Consciousness and Paradoxical Effects of Incentives on Skillful Performance. *Journal of Personality and Social Psychology* 46, 610-20.

Baumeister, R. F. (1992). Of humor, Music, Anger, Speed and Excuses: Reflections of an Editorial Team After One Year in Office. *Cardiovascular Research* 12, 1161-3.

Baumeister, R. F., Heatherton, T. F. & Tice, D. M. (1993). When Ego Threats Lead to Self-Regulation Failure: Negative Consequences of High Self-Esteem. *Journal of Personality and Social Psychology* 64.1, 141-56.

Becker, Robert. (1986). *Cross Currents.* Los Angeles, CA: Jeremy Tarcher, Inc.

Bennett, E.L., Diamond, M.C., Krech, D., & Rosenzweig, M. (1964). Chemical and Anatomical Plasticity of the Brain. *Science,* 146, 610-619.

Benton, D., & Roberts, G. (1988). Effect of Vitamin and Mineral Supplementation on Intelligence of a Sample of Schoolchildren. *The Lancet,* 140-143.

Bergin, D. (1989). Student Goals for Out-of-School-Learning Activities. Journal of *Adolescent Research* 4, 92-109.

Bergland, Michael. (1985). *The Fabric of Mind.* Ringwood, Vic.: Penguin.

Berliner, D. C. (1984). The Half-Full Glass: A Review of Research on Teaching. *Using What We Know About Teaching.* (Hosford, P.L., Ed.). Alexandria, VA: Association for Supervision and Curriculum Development.

Biggee, Al. (1982). *Learning Theories for Teachers* (4th ed.). New York, NY: Harper & Row.

Black J. E., et al. (1990, July). Learning Causes Synaptogenesis, Whereas Motor Activity Causes Angiogenesis, in Cerebral Cortex of Adult Rats. (Proc. of a conf. of the National Academy of Sciences). 87.14, 5568-72.

Black J. E. (1989). Effects of Complex Experience on Somatic Growth and Organ Development in Rats. *Developmental Psychobiology* 22.7, 727-52.

Blackman, et al. (1982). Cognitive Styles and Learning Disabilities. *Journal of Learning Disabilities* n2 15, 106-115.

Blakemore, Colin. (1977). *Mechanics of the Mind.* New York, NY: Cambridge University Press.

Blakemore, Colin. (1990). *The Mind Machine.* (with Richard Hutton & Martin Freeth). London, England: BBC Books.

Block R. A., et al. (1989). Unilateral Nostril Breathing Influences Lateralized Cognitive Performance. *Brain and Cognition* 9.2, 181-90.

Bloom, et al. (1988). *Brain, Mind and Behavior.* W. H. Freeman and Co.

Boller, K. & Rovee-Collier, C. (1992). Contextual Coding and Recoding of Infant's Memories. *Journal of Experimental Child Psychology* 53.1, 1-23.

Botella, J. & Eriksen, C. W. (1992). Filtering Versus Parallel Processing in RSVP Tasks. *Perception and Psychophysics* 51.4, 334-43.

Bourre, J. M., et al. (1993). Function of Polyunsaturated Fatty Acids in the Nervous System. 48.1, 5-15.

Bourre, J. M., et al. (1993). *Brainfood.* Translated from French. Boston, MA: Little, Brown & Co.

Bower, G. H. & Mann, T. (1992). Improving Recall by Recoding Interfering Material at the Time of Retrieval. *Journal of Experimental Psychology* 18.6, 1310-20.

Bower, G. H., Mann, T.D., & Morrow, G. (1990). Mental Models in Narrative Comprehension. *Science* 247.4938, 44-8.

Bracha, S. (1987). Circling Behavior in Right-handers. *Brain Research* 411, 231-235.

Braun, C. M. (1992). Estimation of Interhemispheric Dynamics from Simple Unimanual Reaction Time to Extrafoveal Stimuli. *Neuropsychological Review* 3.4, 321-65.

Breier, A. (1988). Noise and Helplessness. *American Journal of Psychiatry* 144, 1419-25.

Brewer, C. and D. Campbell. (1991). *Rhythms of Learning.* Tucson, AZ: Zephyr Press.

Bricker, William, McLoughlin & Caven. (1982). Exploration of Parental Teaching Style: Technical Note. *Perceptual & Motor Skills* n3 Pt. 2 55, 1174.

Brophy, J. (1981). Teacher Praise: A Functional Analysis. *Review of Educational Research* 51, 5-32.

Brophy, J. (1987). Socializing Student's Motivation to Learn. *Advances in Motivation and Achievement* (Maeher & Kleiber. Eds.) Vol. 3, pp. 181-210. Greenwich, CT: JAI.

Brown, J.S., & VanLehn, K. (1980). Repair Theory: A generative theory of bugs in procedural skills. *Cognitive Science* 4, 379-426.

Buckley, R. & Hawley, C. (1977). Hyperkenesis and Dye Sensitivity. *Journal of Orthomolecular Psychiatry* 2, 129-137.

Burton, L. A. & Levy, J. (1989). Sex Differences in the Lateralized Processing of Facial Emotion. *Brain and Cognition* 11.2, 210-28.

Birren, Faber. (1959). The Effects of Color on the Human Organism. *American Journal of Occupational Therapy.*

Butler, R. (1988). Enhancing and Undermining Intrinsic Motivation. *British Journal of Educational Psychology* 58, 1-14

Butler, R., & Nissan, M. (1986). Effects of No Feedback, Task-Related Comments, and Grades on Intrinsic Motivation and Performance. *Journal of Educational Psychology* 78, 210-216.

Buzan, Tony. (1993). *The Mind Map Book: Radiant Thinking.* London, England: BBC Books.

Caine, G., Caine, R.N., & Crowell, S. (1994). *Mindshifts.* Tuscon, AZ: Zephyr Press.

Caine, G., & Caine, R.N. (1990). Downshifting: A Hidden Condition That Frustrates Learning & Change *Instructional Leader* VI 3, 1-3, 12.

Caine, G., & Caine, R.N., Eds. (1993). Understanding a Brain-Based Approach to Learning and Teaching. *Educational Leadership* 48: 2,66-70.

Caine, G., & Caine, R.N., Eds. (1994). Making Connections: *Teaching and the Human Brain.* Menlo Park, CA: Addison-Wesley.

Calvin, William & Ojemann, George. (1994). *Conversations with Neil's Brain.* Reading, MA: Addison-Wesley Publishing Co.

Campbell, D. (1983). *Introduction to The Musical Brain.* St. Louis, MO: Magnamusic.

Campbell, D. (1992). *100 Ways to Improve Your Teaching Using Your Voice & Music.* Tucson: Zephyr Press.

Campbell, D. Ed. (1992). *Music and Miracles.* Wheaton, IL: Quest Books.

Carbo, M. (1980). An Analysis of the Relationship Between the Modality Preferences of Kindergartners and the Selected Reading Treatments as they Affect the Learning of a Basic Sight-Word Vocabulary. *Dissertation* St. John's University.

Carbo, M., Dunn, R., & Dunn, K. (1986). *Teaching Students to Read Through their Individual Learning Styles.* Englewood Cliffs, NJ: Prentice-Hall.

Cardinali, R. (1991). Computer Hazards: Real or Imaginary? *Health Care for Women International* 12.3, 351-8.

Carpenter, G. & Grossberg, S. (1993). Normal and Amnesic Learning, Recognition and Memory by a Model of Corticohippocampal Interactions. *Trends in Neuroscience* 16.4, 131-7.

Carper, Jean. (1993). *Food: Your Miracle Medicine.* New York, NY: Harper Collins Publishers.

Carruthers, S. & Young, A. (1980). Preference of Condition Concerning Time in Learning Environments of Rural versus Eighth Grade Students. *Learning Styles Network Newsletter* 1.2, 1.

Centerwall, B. S. (1992). Television and Violence: The Scale of the Problem and Where to go From Here. *Journal of the American Medical Association* 267.22, 3059-63.

Chapman, Carolyn. (1993). *If the Shoe Fits.* Palatine, IL: Skylight Publishing.

Cherry, C., Godwin, D., & Staples, J. (1989). Is The Left Brain Always Right? Sydney, Australia: Hawker & Brownlow.

Chi, M. (1985). Interactive Roles of Knowledge and Strategies in the Development of Organized Sorting and Recall. *Thinking and Learning Skills.* (Chipman, S.F., Segal, J.W., & Glaser, R.) Vol. 2. Hillsdale, NJ: Lawerence Erlbaum & Assoc.

Christianson, S. (1992). Emotional Stress and Eyewitness Memory: A Critical Review. *Psychological Bulletin* 112.2, 284-309.

Chugani, H. T. (1991). Imaging Human Brain Development with Positron Emission Tomography. *Journal of Nuclear Medicine* 32.1, 23-6.

Churchland, Paul. (1995) *Engine of Reason: Seat of the Soul.* Boston, MA: MIT Press.

Clark, D.L., Kreutzberg, J.R., & Chee, F.K.W. (1977). Vestibular Stimulation Influence on Motor Development on Infants. *Science* 196, 1228-1229.

Clynes, Manfred, Ed. (1982). *Music, Mind and Brain.* New York, NY: Plenum Press.

Clynes, Manfred, Ed. (1982). Neurobiologic Functions of Rhythm, Time, and Pulse in Music. *Music, Mind and Brain.* New York, NY: Plenum Press.

Cohen, E.G. (1990). Treating Status Problems in the Cooperative Classroom. *Cooperative Learning: Research and Theory.* (Sharan, S., Ed.) New York, NY: Praeger Press.

Condry, J., & Chambers, J. (1978). Intrinsic Motivation and the Process of Learning. [In *The Hidden Costs of Rewards: New Perspectives on the Psychology of Human Motivation.*] (Lepper, M.R., & Greene, D., Eds.) Hillsdale, NJ: Lawrence Erlbaum & Associates.

Connors, Keith. (1980). *Food Additives and Hyperactive Children.* New York, NY: Plenum Press.

Connors, Keith. (1989). *Feeding the Brain.* New York, NY: Plenum Press.

Cook, N.D. (1984). Callosal Inhibition: The Key to the Brain Code. *Behavioral Science* 29, 98-110.

Cook, N.D. (1984) The Transmission of Information in Natural Systems Journal of Theoretical Biology. 108, 349-367.

Corballis, M. (1983). *Human Laterality.* New York, NY: Academic Press.

Coren, S., & Halpern, D.F. (1991). Left-handedness: A Marker for Decreased Survival Fitness. *Psychological Bulletin* 109, 90-106.

Coren, S. & Porac, C. (1981). *Lateral Preferences in Human Behavior.* New York, NY: Springer-Verlag.

Cotton, M.M., & Evans, K. (1990). A Review of the Uses of Irlen (tinted) Lenses. *Australian and New Zealand Journal of Ophthalmology* 18.3, 307-12.

Covington, M.V. (1991). Motivation, Self-Worth, and the Myth of Intensification. (Paper presented at annual meeting of the American Psychological Association). San Francisco, CA.

Coward, Andrew. (1990). *Pattern Thinking.* New York, NY: Praeger Publishers.

Crick, Francis. (1994). *The Astonishing Hypothesis: The Scientific Search for the Soul.* New York, NY: Charles Scribner and Sons.

Csikszentmihalyi, M. & Isabella. (1990). *Flow: The Psychology of Optimal Experience.* New York, NY: Harper & Row.

Czeisler, C. A. (1986). Arousal Cycles Can Be Reset. *Science* 233, 667-71.

Cytowic, Richard. (1993) The Man Who Tasted Shapes. Time Warner New York.

Damasio, Antonio. (1994) *Descartes' Error.* New York, NY. Putnam & Sons.

Dansereau, D. F. (1985). Learning Strategy Research. *Thinking and Learning Skills.* (Chipman, S.F., Segal, J.W., & Glaser, R.) Vol 1. Hillsdale, NJ: Lawrence Erlbaum & Assoc.

Dartigues, Jean-Francois. (1994, February). Use It or Lose It. *Omni.* p. 34.

Davidson, R.J. (1992). Anterior Cerebral Asymmetry and the Nature of Emotion. *Brain and Cognition* 20.1, 125-51.

DeBello, T. (1985). A Critical Analysis of the Achievement and Attitude Effects of Administrative Assignments to Social Studies Writing Instruction Based on Identified, Eighth-Grade Students' Learning Style Preferences for Learning Alone, With Peers, or With Teachers. *Dissertation.* St. John's University.

DeBono, Edward. (1970). *Lateral Thinking.* New York, NY: Harper & Row.

Decety, J., & Ingvar, D.H. (1990). Brain Structures Participating in Mental Stimulation of Motor Behavior: A Neuropsychological Interpretation. *Acta Psychologica* 73.1, 113-34.

Deci, E. (1978). Application of Research on the Effects of Rewards. *The Hidden Costs of Rewards: New Perspectives on the Psychology of Human Motivation.* (Lepper & Greene, Eds.) Hillsdale, NJ: Lawrence Erlbaum & Assoc.

Deci, E., et al. (1982). Effects of Performance Standards on Teaching Styles: Behavior of Controlling Teachers. *Journal of Educational Psychology* 74, 852-59.

Deci, E. (1980). *The Psychology of Self-Determination.* Lexington, MA: DD Heath.

Deci, E. (1985, March). The Well-Tempered Classroom. *Psychology Today.* pp. 52-53.

Deci, E. and R. M. Ryan. (1985). *Intrinsic Motivation and Self-Determination in Human Behavior.* New York, NY: Plenum.

Deci, E., et al. (1992). Autonomy and Competence as Motivational Factors in Students with Learning Disabilities and Emotional Handicaps. *Journal of Learning Disabilities* 25, 457-71.

Deci, E., et al. (1991). Motivation and Education: The Self-Determination Perspective. *Educational Psychologist* 26, 325-46.

Dekaban, A. (1970). *The Neurology of Early Childhood.* Baltimore, MD: Williams and Wilkins.

Della Valle, J. (1984). An Experimental Investigation of the Relationship(s) Between Preference for Mobility and the Word Recognition Scores of Seventh Grade Students to Provide Supervisory and Administrative Guidelines for the Organization of Effective Instructional Environments. *Dissertation.* St.John's University.

Della Valle, J., et al. (1986). The Effects of Matching and Mismatching Student's Mobility Preferences on Recognition and Memory Tasks. *Journal of Educational Research* 79.5, 267-72.

Dennison, Paul, & Dennison, Gail. (1988). *Brain Gym.* (Teacher's Ed.) Ventura, CA: Edu-kinesthetics.

Dhority, Lynn. (1992). *The ACT Approach. The Use of Suggestion for Integrative Learning.* Philadelphia, PA: Gordon & Breach Science Publishers.

Diamond, Marian. (1988). *Enriching Heredity: The Impact of the Environment on the Brain.* New York, NY: Free Press.

Dienstbier, R. (1989). Periodic Adrenaline Arousal Boosts Health, Coping. *Brain-Mind Bulletin* 14.9A.

Dixon, N. (1981). *Preconscious Processing.* New York, NY: Wiley.

Doll, W.E.J. (1989). Complexity in the Classroom. *Educational Leadership* 47.1, 65-70.

Domino, G. (1970). Interactive Effects of Achievement Orientation and Teaching Style on Academic Achievement. *ACT Research Report* 39, 1-9.

Dossey, Larry. (1993) Healing Words. San Francisco, CA: Harper Collins Publishers

Douglass, C.B. (1979). Making Biology Easier to Understand. *American Biology Teacher* 41.5, 277-99.

Drucker, Peter. (1994, November). The Age of Social Transformation. *Atlantic Monthly,* 274,(5) pp. 53-80.

Dryden, Gordon & Vos, Jeannette. (1994). *The Learning Revolution.* Rolling Hills, CA: Jalmar Press.

Druckman, D. & Swets, J.A. (1988). *Enhancing Human Performance: Issues, Theories & Techniques.* Washington, D.C.: National Academy Press.

Dunn, R. & Dunn, K. (1978). *Teaching Students Through Their Individual Learning Styles: A Practical Approach.* Reston, VA: Reston Publishing Co.

Dunn, R. & Dunn, K. (1987). Dispelling Outmoded Beliefs About Student Learning. *Educational Leadership* 44.6, 55-61.

Dunn, Kenneth & Rita. (1992). *Bringing Out The Giftedness In Your Child,* New York, NY: John Wiley.

Dunn, R., et al. (1985). Light Up Their Lives: A Review of Research on the Effects of Lighting on Children's Achievement and Behavior. *The Reading Teacher* 38.9, 863-69.

Edelman, G. *Bright Air, Brilliant Fire.* (1992). New York, NY: Basic Books.

Efron, R. (1990). *The Decline and Fall of Hemispheric Specialization.* Hillsdale, NJ. Lawrence Erlbaum and Associates.

Ehret, C. (1981). From Report by the National Argonne Laboratory. Lemont, IL.

Ellison, Launa. (1993). *Seeing With Magic Glasses.* Great Ocean Publishers, Arlington, VA.

Emery, Charles. (1986, October). Exercise Keeps the Mind Young. *American Health.*

Engel, A. K., et al. (1992). Temporal Coding in the Visual Cortex: New Vistas on Integration in the Nervous System. *Trends in Neurosciences* 15.6, 218-26.

Epstein, H. (1974). Phrenoblysis: Special Brain and Mind Growth Periods. *Developmental Psychology* 7, 207-24.

Epstein, H. (1986). "Stages in Human Brain Development." Developmental Brain Research 30: 114-19.

Eysenck, Michael. (1994). *The Blackwell Dictionary of Cognitive Psychology.* Oxford.

Fabiani M., Karis, D., & Donchin, E. (1990). Effects of Mnemonic Strategy Manipulation in a Von Restorff Paradigm. *Electroencephalography and Clinical Neurophysiology* 75.2, 22-35.

Feingold, D. (1985). *Why Your Child is Hyperactive.* New York, NY: Random House.

Feldman, R.G. & White, R.F. (1992). Lead Neurotoxicity and Disorders in Learning. *Journal of Child Neurology*

Felix, Uschi. (1993).The Contribution of Background Music to the Enhancement of Learning in Suggestopedia: A Critical Review of the Literature. *Journal of the Society for Accelerative Learning and Teaching* 18.3-4, 277-303.

Feuerstein, Reuven, Klein, Pnina, Tannenbaum, Abraham. (1991). *Mediated Learning Experience.* London, UK: Freund Publishing House Ltd.

Fiske, S.T., & Taylor, S.E. (1984). *Social Cognition.* Reading, MA: Addison-Wesley.

Fitch, R.H., Brown, C.P. & Tallal, P. (1993). Left Hemisphere Specialization for Auditory Temporal Processing in Rats. *Annals of the New York Academy of Sciences* 682, 346-7.

Ford, Martin. (1992). *Motivating Humans.* Newbury Park, CA: Sage Publications.

Ford, R.N. (1969). *Motivation Through the Work Itself.* New York, NY: American Management Association.

Fox, N.A. (1991). If It's Not Left, It's Right. Electroencephalograph Asymmetry and the Development of Emotion. *American Psychologist* 46.8, 863-72.

Fox, N.A., Sexton, M. & Hebel, J.R. (1990). Prenatal Exposure to Tobacco: Effects on Physical Growth at Age Three. *International Journal of Epidemiology* 19.1, 66-71.

Frederiksen, N. (1984). Implications of Cognitive Theory for Instruction in Problem-Solving. *Review of Educational Research* 54, 363-407.

Freeley, M.E. (1984). An Experimental Investigation of the Relationships Among Teacher's Individual Time Preferences, Inservice Workshop Schedules, and Instructional Techniques and the Subsequent Implementation of Learning Style Strategies in Participant's Classroom. *Dissertation.* St.John's University.

Friedman, R. C., & Downey, J. (1993). Neurobiology and Sexual Orientation: Current Relationships. *Journal of Neuropsychiatry and Clinical Neurosciences* 5.2, 131-53.

Frijda, N.H. (1988). The Laws of Emotion. *American Psychologist* 43, 349-58.

Fuchs, J.L., Montemayor, M., & Greenough, W.T. (1990). Effect of Environmental Complexity on the Size of Superior Colliculus. *Behavioral and Neural Biology* 54.2, 198-203.

Gadow, K. D., & Sprafkin, J. (1989). Field Experiments of Television Violence With Children: Evidence for an Environmental Hazard? *Pediatrics* 83.3, 399-405.

Galin, D., & Ornstein, R. (1974). Individual Differences in Cognitive Style: Reflexive Eye Movements. *Neuropsychologia,* 12, 367-376.

Garai, J.E., & Scheinfield, A. (1968). Sex Differences in Mental and Behavioral Traits. *Genetic Psychology Monographs* 77, 169-229.

Gardner, Howard. (1985). *Frames of Mind.* New York, NY: Basic Books.

Gardner, Howard. (1993). *Multiple Intelligences: The Theory in Practice.* New York, NY: Basic Books.

Gazzaniga, M. (1992). *Nature's Mind.* New York, NY: Basic Books.

Geffen, G, J.L. Bradshaw and G. Wallace (1976) "Interhemispheric Effects on Reaction Time to Verbal and Nonverbal Visual Stimuli," Journal of Experimental Psychology 87 415-422.

Gelb, Michael. (1981). *Body Learning.* New York, NY: Delilah Books.

Gelb, Michael. (1988). *Present Yourself.* Rolling Hills, CA: Jalmar Press.

Glasser, William. (1981). *Stations of the Mind.* New York: Harper & Row.

Glasser, William. (1985). *Control Theory.* New York, NY: Harper Collins.

Gleik, J. (1987). *Making a New Science.* New York, NY: Viking.

Goldman, J., et al. (1986). Behavioral Effects of Sucrose on Preschool Children. *Journal of Abnormal Child Psychology* 14, 565-78.

Goleman, Daniel. (1995). *Emotional Intelligence:* Bantam Books, NY.

Gordon, H.W. (1978). Left Hemisphere Dominance for Rhythmic Elements in Dichotically Presented melodies. *Cortex* 14, 58-76.

Gouchie, C., & Kimura, D. (1990). The Relationship Between Testosterone and Cognitive Ability Patterns. *Research Bulletin* 690. University of Ontario, London, Canada.

Gratton, G., Coles, M. G., & Donchin, E. (1992). Optimizing the Use of Information: Strategic Control of Activation of Responses. *Journal of Experimental Psychology* 121.4, 480-506.

Green, K.P., et al. (1991). Integrating Speech Information Across Talkers, Gender and Sensory Modality: Female Faces and Male Voices in the McGurk Effect. *Perception and Psychophysics* 50.6, 524-36.

Greenough, W.T., & Anderson, B.J. (1991). Cerebellar Synaptic Plasticity: Relation to Learning Versus Neural Activity. *Annals of the New York Academy of Science* 627, 231-47.

Greenough, W.T., and B. Anderson. (1991). Cerebellar Synaptic Plasticity. *Annals of the New York Academy of Sciences* 627, 231-47.

Greenough, W.T., Withers, G. & Anderson, B. (1992). Experience-Dependent Synaptogenesis as a Plausible Memory Mechanism. *Learning and Memory: The Behavioral and Biological Substrates.* (Gormezano, I. & Wasserman, E., Eds.) Hillsdale, NJ: Erlbaum & Associates. pp. 209-29.

Grinder, Michael. (1989). *Righting the Educational Conveyor Belt.* Portland, OR: Metamorphous Press.

Grinder, Michael. (1995, revised). *Envoy.* Battle Ground, WA: Michael Grinder & Associates.

Grolnick, W.S. & Ryan, R.M. (1987). Autonomy in children's Learning: An Experimental and Individual Difference Investigation. *Journal of Personality and Social Psychology* 52, 890-898.

Grunwald, L., & Goldberg, J. (1993, July). Babies Are Smarter Than You Think. *Life Magazine,* 45-60.

Gur, R.E., Gur, R.C., & Harris, L.J. (1975). Cerebral Activation as Measured by Subject's Eye Movements. *Neuropsychologia,* 13, 35-44.

Hagan-Heimlich, J.E., and S.D. (1984). Pittelman. Classroom Applications of the Semantic Mapping Procedure in Reading and Writing. *Program Report* 84.4.

Halpern, D.F. (1990). Hand Preference and Life Span. (Unpublished manuscript).

Halpern, S. (1985). *Sound Health*. New York, NY: Harper & Row.

Hampden-Turner, Charles. (1981). *Maps of the Mind*. New York, NY: Macmillan Publishing.

Hampson, E. & Kimura, D. (1988). Reciprocal Effects of Hormonal Fluctuations on Human Motor and Perceptual Spatial Skills. *Behavioral Neuroscience* 102.3, 456-9.

Harmon, D.B. (1991). The Coordinated Classroom. Grand Rapids, MI: [In Liberman, Jacob, *Light: Medicine of The Future*] Santa Fe, NM.

Hannaford, Carla. (1995) Smart Moves. Great Ocean Publishing Co. Arlington, VA.

Harper, A.E., & Peters, J.C. (1989). Protein Intake, Brain Amino Acid and Serotonin Concentration and Protein Self-Selection. *Journal of Nutrition* 119.5, 677-89.

Harper, C., & Kril, J. (1990). Neuropathology of Alcoholism. *Alcohol and Alcoholism* 25.2-3, 207-16.

Harper, C., & Kril, J. (1991). If you drink your brain will shrink. *Alcohol and Alcoholism*. (Supplement) 1, 375-80.

Hart, Leslie. (1975). *How the Brain Works: A New Understanding of Human Learning*. New York, NY: Basic Books.

Hart, Leslie. (1983). *Human Brain and Human Learning*. Books for Educators City? .

Harter, S. (1978). Pleasure Derived form Challenge and the Effects of Receiving Grades on Children's Difficulty Level Choices. *Child Development*. 49, 788-799.

Harter, S. (1980). The Perceived Competence Scale for Children. *Child Development* 51, 218-35.

Harter, S. (1982). A Developmental Perspective on Some Parameters of Self-Regulation in Children. *Self-Management and Behavior Change: From Theory to Practice*. (Karoly, P., & Kanfer, F. H., Eds.) New York, NY: Pergammon Press.

Harth, Erich. (1995) *The Creative Loop*. Addison-Wesley, Reading, MA.

Hassler, M. (1991). Testosterone and Musical Talent. *Experimental and Clinical Endocrinology* 98.2, 89-98.

Hayne, H., Rovee-Collier, C., & Borza, M.A. (1991). Infant Memory for Place Information. *Memory and Cognition* 19.4, 378-86.

Haxbny, J.V., Grady, C.L. Horwitz, B., Ungerleider, L.G., Mishkin, M., Carlson, R.E., Herscovitch, P., Shapiro,. and Rapoport. S.I. (1991) "Dissociation of Object and Spatial Visual Processing Pathways in Human Extrastriate Cortex." Proceedings of the National Academy of Sciences, U.S.A. 88: 1621-1625.

Healer, Janet. (1977). Microwave Towers May Affect Brain. *Brain/Mind Bulletin* 2.14E.

Healy, Alice & Lyle Bourne. (1995) *Learning and Memory of Knowledge and Skills*. Thousand Oaks, CA. Sage Publications.

Healy, J. (1990). *Endangered Minds: Why Our Children Can't Think*. New York, NY: Simon and Schuster.

Healy, J. (1987). *Your Child's Growing Mind*. New York, NY: Doubleday.

Healy, J. (1993). Why Kids Can't Think. *Bottom Line Personal* 13.8, 1-3.

Herbert, Nick. (1993). *The Elemental Mind*. New York, NY. Dutton Books.

Hermann, D.J. & Hanwood, J.R. (1980). More evidence for the Existence of the Separate Semantic and Episodic Stores in Long-Term Memory. Journal of Experimental Psychology: Human Learning and Memory 6 & 5, 467-478.

Herrmann, Ned. *The Creative Brain*. Lake Lure, NC: Brain Books, 1988.

Herrnstein. (1994). A Bell-Shaped Curve. New York, NY: The Free Press.

Hirsch, A. (1993). Floral Odor Increases Learning Ability. Presentation at annual conference of American Academy of Neurological & Orthopedic Surgery. Contact: Allan Hirsch, Smell & Taste Treatment Foundation, Chicago, IL.

Hobson, J.A. (1989). *Sleep*. New York, NY: W.H. Freeman.

Hodges, H. (1985). An Analysis of the Relationships Among Preferences for a Formal/Informal Design, One Element of Learning Style, Academic Achievement, and Attitudes of Seventh and Eighth Grade Students in Remedial Mathematics Classes in a New York City Alternative Junior High school. *Dissertation*. St.John's University.

Hodges, Jeffrey. (1992). *Learn Faster Now*. Toowoomba, Queensland, Australia: Down Under Publications.

Hoffer, A., Walker, M. (1994). *Smart Nutrients*. Garden City Park, NY: Avery Publishing Group.

Hofman M.A., & Swaab, D.F. (1991). Sexual Dimorphism of the Human Brain. *Experimental and Clinical Endocrinology* 98.2, 161-70.

Hooper J., & Teresi, D. (1986). *The Three Pound Universe: The Brain, from Chemistry of the Mind to New Frontiers of the Soul*. New York, NY: Dell Publishing.

Hopfield, J., Feinstein, D., & Palmer, R. (1983, July). Unlearning Has a Stabilizing Effect in Collective Memories. *Nature*. pp. 158-59.

Horn, G. (1991). Learning, Memory and the Brain. *Indian Journal of Physiology and Pharmacology* 35.1, 3-9.

Horne J. (1989). Sleep Loss and Divergent Thinking Ability. *Sleep* 11.6, 528-36.

Horne J. (1992, October 15). Human Slow Wave Sleep: A Review and Appraisal of Recent Findings, with Implications for Sleep Functions and Psychiatric Illness. *Experientia* pp. 941-54.

Horowitz, L., & Sarkin, J.M. (1992). Video Display Terminal Operation: a Potential Risk in the Etiology and Maintenance of Tempromandidibular Disorders. *Cranio* 10.1, 43-50.

Houston, Jean. *The Possible Human: A Course in Enhancing Your Physical, Mantal and Creative Abilities.* Los Angeles, CA: Jeremy Tarcher, 1982.

Howard, Pierce. (1994). *Owners Manual for the Brain.* Leornian Press: Austin, Texas.

Huchinson, Michael. (1986). *Megabrain.* New York, NY: Beech Tree Books.

Huttenlocher, P.R. (1990). Morphometric Study of Human Cerebral Cortex Development. *Neuropsychologia* 28.6, 517-27.

Hynd, G.W. (1992). Neurological Aspects of Dyslexia: Comment on the Balance Model. *Journal of Learning Disabilities* 25.2, 110-2, 123.

Hynd, G.W., et al. (1991). Attention-Deficit Disorder Without Hyperactivity: A Distinct Behavioral and Cognitive Syndrome. *Journal of Child Neurology* 6, S37-43.

Hynd, G.W., et al. (1991). Corpus Callosum Morphology in Attention Deficit-Hyperactivity Disorder: Morphometric Analysis of MRI. *Journal of Learning Disabilities* 24.3, 141-6.

Iaccino, James. (1993). *Left Brain-Right Brain Differences: Inquiries, Evidence, and New Approaches.* Hillsdale, NJ: Lawrence Erlbaum & Associates.

Introini-Collision, I.B., Miyazaki, B. & McGaugh, J.L. (1991). Involvement of the Amygdala in the Memory-Enhancing Effects of Clenbuterol. *Psychopharmacology* 104.4, 541-4.

Isaacs, K.R., et al. (1992). Exercise and the Brain: Angiogenesis in the Adult Rat Cerebellum After Vigorous Physical Activity and Motor Skill Learning. *Journal of Cerebral Blood Flow and Metabolism* 12.1, 110-9.

Jacobs, B. Serotonin and Behavior: Emphasis on Motor Control. *Journal of Clinical Psychiatry* 52, 17-23. (Supplement).

Jacobs, B., Schall, M. & Scheibel, A.B. (1993). A Quantitative Dendritic Analysis of Wernicke's Area in Humans: Gender, Hemispheric and Environmental Factors. *Journal of Comparative Neurology* 327.1, 97-111.

Jacobs, W.J., & Nadel, L. (1985).Stress-Induced Recovery of Fears and Phobias. *Psychological Review* 92.4, 512-531.

James, T., Woodsmall, and Wyatt. (1988). *Timeline and the Basis of Personality.* Cupertino, CA: Meta Publications.

Jacques, E. Development of Intellectual Capability. *Essays on Intellect.* (Link, F.R., Ed.) Alexandria, VA: Association for Curriculum and Development.

Jauchem, J. (1991). Alleged Health Effects of Electromagnetic Fields: Misconceptions in the Scientific Literature. *Journal of Microwave Power and Electromagnetic Energy* 26.4, 189-95.

Jauchem, J., & Merritt, J.H. (1991). The Epidemiology of Exposure to Electromagnetic Fields: An Overview of the Recent Literature. *Journal of Clinical Epidemiology* 44.9, 895-906.

Jauchem, J., & Frei, M.R. (1992). Heart Rate and Blood Pressure Changes During Radio frequency Irradiation and Environmental Heating. *Comparative Biochemistry and Physiology* 101.1, 1-9.

Jenkins, D.J., et al. (1989). Nibbling Versus Gorging: Metabolic Advantages of Increased Meal Frequency. *New England Journal of Medicine* 321.14, PGS. 929-34.

Jensen, Eric. (1994). *The Learning Brain.* Del Mar, CA: Turning Point Publishing.

Jensen, Eric. (1995). *Brain-Based Learning & Teaching* Del Mar, CA: Turning Point Publishing.

Jensen, Eric. (1995). *SuperTeaching.* Del Mar, CA: Turning Point Publishing.

Jernigan, T.L., & Tallal, P. (1990). Late Childhood Changes in Brain Morphology Observable with MRI. *Developmental Medicine and Child Neurology* 32.5, 379-85.

Johnson, M. H., et al. (1991). Newborns' Preferential Tracking of Face-Like Stimuli and its Subsequent Decline. *Cognition* 40.1-2, 1-19.

Kagan, D. M. (1990). How Schools Alienate Students at Risk: A Model for Examining Proximal Classroom Variables. *Educational Psychologist* 25, 105-25.

Kage, M. (1991). The Effects of Evaluation on Intrinsic Motivation. (Paper presented at the meeting of the Japan Association of Educational Psychology). Joetsu Japan.

Kandel, M. & Kandel, E. (1994, May). Flights of Memory. *Discover Magazine,* 32-38.

Kandel, E. & Hawkins, R. (1992, September). The Biological Basis of Learning and Individuality. *Scientific American* pp. 79-86.

Kanter, R.M., Clark, D.L., Allen, L.C., & Chase, M.F. (1976). Effects of Vestibular Stimulation on Nystagmus Response and Motor Performance in the Developmentally Delayed Infant. *Physical Therapy,* 54:(4), 414-21.

Kaplan, R. (1983). Reader's Visual Fields Increase with Color Therapy. *Brain Mind Bulletin* 8.14F.

Karkowski, W., Marek, T., & Noworol, C. (1989). Stimulating Work Found to Boost Pain Perception. *Work and Stress* 2, 133-37.

Kavet, R., & Tell, R.A. (1991). VDT's: Field Levels, Epidemiology, and Laboratory Studies. *Health Physics* 61.1, 47-57.

Kenyon, Thomas. (1994). *Brain States.* Naples, FL: U.S. Publishing.

Kesner, R.P. (1983) "Mnemonic Functions of the Hippocampus: Correspondence between Animals and Humans" in Conditioning Representation of Neural Function, ed. C.D.Woody (New York: Plenum Press).

Khachaturian, Zaven. (1991). Mental Decline As We Grow Older. *Bottom Line Personal* 12.23, 9.

Khalsa, D., Ziegler, M., & Kennedy, B. (1986). Body Sides Switch Dominance. *Life Sciences* 38, 1203-14.

Kim, I.K. & Spelke, V. (1992). Infants' Sensitivity to Effects of Gravity on Visible Object Motion. *Journal of Experimental Psychology: Human Perception and Performance* 18.2, 385-93.

Kimura, D. (1985, November). Male Brain, Female Brain: The Hidden Difference. *Psychology Today.*

Kimura, D. (1986, October) How Different Are Male and Female Brains? *Orbit.*

Kimura, D. (1987). Are Men's and Women's Brains Really Different?" *Canadian Psychology* 28.2.

Kimura, D. (1989, November). Monthly Fluctuations in Sex Hormones Affect Women's Cognitive Skills. *Psychology Today* pp. 63-66.

Kimura, D., & Hampson, E. (1990, April). Neural and Hormonal Mechanisms Mediating Sex Differences in Cognition. *Research Bulletin* 689. Dept. of Psych. University of Ontario, London, Canada.

Kimura, D. (1992, September). Sex Differences in the Brain. *Scientific American* pp. 119-25.

King, Jeff. (1991). Comparing Alpha Induction Differences Between Two Music Samples. Abstract from the Center for Research on Learning and Cognition, University of North Texas, TX.

Klein & Armitage. (1979). Brainwave Cycle Fluctuations. *Science* 204, 1326-28.

Kline, Peter. (1990). *Everyday Genius: Restoring Your Children's Natural Joy of Learning - And Yours, Too.* Arlington, VA: Great Ocean Publishers.

Kline, Peter & Martel, Lawrence. (1992). *School Success: The Inside Story.* Arlington, VA: Great Ocean Publishers.

Kline, Peter & Saunders, Bernard. (1993). *Ten Steps to a Learning Organization.* Arlington, VA: Great Ocean Publishers.

Klivington, Kenneth, Ed. (1989). *The Science of Mind.* Cambridge, MA: MIT Press.

Klutky, N. (1990). Sex Differences in Memory Performance for Odors, on Sequences and Colors. *Zeitscrift fur Experimentelle und Angewandte Psychologie* 37.3, 437-46.

Kohn, Alfie. (1987). *No Contest: The Case Against Competition.* New York, NY: Houghton-Mifflin.

Kohn, A. (1993, September). Choices for Children: Why and How to Let Students Decide. *Phi Delta Kappan,* 8-20

Kohn, A. (1994) Punished by Rewards. Houghton-Mifflin. Boston, MA

Kohn, A. (1994, October). Grading: the Issue Is Not How But Why. *Educational Leadership* Volume 52, 2, 38-41.

Kopera, H. (1980). Female Hormones and Brain Function. *Hormones and the Brain.* (de Wied & Van Keep, Eds.) Lancaster, England: MTP Press. pp. 189-203.

Kosmarskaya, E.N. (1963). The Influence of Peripheral Stimuli on Development of Nerve Cells. [In The Development of the Brain and its Disturbance by Harmful Factors, Klosovski, B.N., Ed.] New York, NY: Macmillan Publishing.

Kohn, Alfie. (1993). *Punished by Rewards.* New York, NY: Houghton Mifflin.

Kosslyn, Steven. (1988) Wet Mind. Simon & Schuster. New York, NY.

Kotulak, Ronald. Unraveling Hidden Mysteries of the Brain. (1993, 11-16 April).*Chicago Tribune.*

Krashen, Steven. (1982). *Principles and Practice in Second Language Acquisition,* New York, NY: Pergamon Press.

Krashen, S. & Terrell, T. (1983). *The Natural Approach.* San Francisco, CA: Alemany Press.

Krimsky, J.S. (1982). A Comparative Analysis of the Effects of Matching and Mismatching Fourth Grade Students With Their Learning Styles Preferences for the Environmental Element of Light and Their Subsequent Reading Speed and Accuracy Scores. *Dissertation.* St. John's University.

Kroon, D. (1985). An Experimental Investigation of the Effects on Academic Achievement and the Resultant Administrative Implications of Instruction Congruent and Incongruent with Secondary Industrial Arts Student's Learning Style Perceptual Preferences. Dissertation. St. John's University.

Lakoff, G., & Johnson, M. (1980). *Metaphors We Live By.* Chicago, IL: University of Chicago Press.

Land, R.G. (1993). The Video Violence Debate. *Hospital and Community Psychiatry* 44.4, 347-51.

Lashley, K.S. (1950). "In Search of the Engram." in Symposium for the Society of Experimental Biology, No.4 (London: Cambridge University Press.

Lavabre, Marcel. (1990). *Aromatherapy Workbook.* Rochester, VT: Healing Arts Press.

Lavond, D.G., Kim, J.J. & Thompson, R. F. (1993). Mammalian Brain Substrates of Aversive Classical Conditioning. *Annual Review of Psychology* 44, 317-42.

LeDoux, J., & Hirst, W. (1986). Attention. Mind and Brain: Dialogues in Cognitive Neuroscience. New York, NY: Cambridge. pp. 105-85.

LeDoux, J.E. (1989) "Cognitive-emotional Interactions in the Brain," Cognition and Emotion: 3 pgs.267-89.

Leff, H. & Nevin, A. (1994). *Turning Learning Inside Out.* Tucson, AZ: Zephyr Press.

Lenneberg, E.H. (1967). Biological Foundations of Language. New York: Wiley & Sons.

Lepper, M.R. (1981). Intrinsic and Extrinsic Motivation in Children: Detrimental Effects of Superfluous Social Controls. [W.A. Collins, Ed.] Aspects of the Development of Competence: The Minnesota Symposium on Child Psychology. Vol 14. Hillsdale, NJ: Lawrence Erlbaum. pp. 155-214.

Levine, S.C., Jordan, N.C., & Huttenlocher, J. (1992). Development of Calculation Abilities in Young Children. *Journal of Experimental Child Psychology* 53.1, Ú72-103.

Levinson, H. (1991). Why Johnny Can't Pay Attention. *Bottom Line Personal* 12.20, 11.

Levinthal, C. (1988). *Messengers of Paradise: Opiates and the Brain.* New York, NY: Doubleday.

Levy, J. (1983). Research Synthesis on Right and Left Hemispheres: We Think With Both Sides of the Brain. *Educational Leadership* 40.4, 66-71.

Levy, J. (1985, May). Right Brain, Left Brain: Fact and Fiction. *Psychology Today.* p. 38.

Lewicki, P., Hill, T., & Czyzewska, M. (1992). Nonconscious Acquisition of Information. *American Psychologist* 47.6, 796-801.

Lieberman, H.R., Wurtman, J.J., & Teicher, M.H. (1989). Circadian Rhythms in Healthy Young and Elderly Humans. *Neurobiology of Aging* 10.3, 259-65.

Lingerman, H. (1983). *The Healing Energies of Music.* Wheaton, IL: Theosophical Publishing House.

Livingstone, M., et al. (1991, September). Physiological and Anatomical Evidence for a Magnocellular Defect in Developmental Dyslexia. *Proceedings of the National Academy of Science* 88, 9743-7947.

Lloyd, Linda. (1990). *Classroom Magic.* Portland, OR: Metamorphous Press.

Locke, E.A. & Latham, G.P. (1990). Work Motivation and Satisfaction: Light at the End of the Tunnel. *Psychological Science* 1, 240-46.

Lozanov, Georgi. (1979). *Suggestology and Outlines of Suggestopedia.* New York, NY: Gordon & Breach.

Lozanov, Georgi. (1991). On Some Problems of the Anatomy, Physiology and Biochemistry of Cerebral Activities in the Global-Artistic Approach in Modern Suggestopedagogic Training. *The Journal of the Society for Accelerative Learning and Teaching* 16.2, 101-16.

Luiten, J., Ames, W., & Ackerson, G. (1980). A Meta-Analysis of the Effects of Advance Organizers on Learning and Retention. *American Educational Research Journal* 17, 211-18.

Michaud, Ellen. (1991). Boost Your Brain Power. Rodal Press, Emmaus, PA.

MacLean, Paul. (1978). A Mind of Three Minds: Educating the Triune Brain. *77th Yearbook of the National Society for the Study of Education.* Chicago, IL: University of Chicago Press. pp. 308-42.

MacLean, Paul. (1990). *The Triune Brain in Education.* New York, NY: Plenum Press.

MacMurren, H. (1985). A Comparative Study of the Effects of Matching and Mismatching Sixth Grade Students With Their Learning Style Preferences for the Physical Element of Intake and Their Subsequent Reading Speed and Accuracy Scores. *Dissertation.* St. John's University.

Mager, R.F., & McCann, J. (1963). *Learner-Controlled Instruction.* Palo Alto, CA: Varian Press.

Maguire, J. (1990). *Care and Feeding of the Brain.* New York, NY: Doubleday.

Malloy, John. (1975). *Dress for Success.* New York, NY: Warner Books.

Malone, T., & Lepper, M. (1987). Making Learning Fun: A Semanticomy of Intrinsic Motivations for Learning. *Aptitude, Learning and Instruction III: Cognitive and Affective Process Analyses.* (Snow & Farr, Eds.) Hillsdale, NJ: Lawrence Erlbaum & Assoc. pp. 223-53.

Mandler, G. (1983). The Nature of Emotions. *States of Mind.* (Miller. J., Ed.) New York, NY: Pantheon Books.

Mandell, A., (1980). Toward a Psychology of Transcendence: God in the Brain. [In Davidson, J.M. & Davidson, R.J., Eds.] *Psychology of Consciousness.* New York, NY: Plenum Press.

Mark, Vernon. (1989). *Brain Power.* Boston, MA: Houghton-Mifflin.

Marzolla, Jean & Lloyd, Janice. (1972). *Learning Through Play.* New York, NY: Harper & Row.

Martin, R.C. (1993). Short-Term Memory and Sentence Processing: Evidence from Neuropsychology. *Memory and Cognition* 21.2 , 176-83.

Marzano, Robert. (1992). *A Different Kind of Classroom.* Alexandria, VA: ASCD.

McCarthy, B. (1990). Using the 4MAT System to Bring Learning Styles to Schools. *Educational Leadership* 48.2, 31-37.

McCarthy, Michael. (1991). *Mastering the Information Age.* Los Angeles, CA: Jeremy Tarcher.

McGaugh J.L. (1989). Dissociating Learning and Performance: Drug and Hormone Enhancement of Memory Storage. *Brain Research Bulletin* 23.4-5, 339-45.

McGaugh J.L., et al. (1990). Involvement of the Amygdaloid Complex in Neuromodulatory Influences on Memory Storage. *Neuroscience and Biobehavioral Reviews* 14.4, 425-31.

McGee, M. (1979). Human Spatial Abilities: Psychometric Studies and Environmental, Genetic, Hormonal and Neurological Influences. *Psychological Bulletin* 86.5, 889-918.

McGuiness, D. (1976). Sex Differences in Organisation, Perception and Cognition. *Exploring Sex Differences.* (Lloyd, B., & Archer, J.) London, England: Academic Press. pp. 123-55.

McGuiness, D. (1985). *When Children Don't Learn.* New York, NY: Basic Books.

McNamara, R.K., & Skelton, R.W. (1993). The Neuropharmacological and Neurochemical Basis of Place Learning in the Morris Water Maze. *Brain Research Reviews.* 18.1, 33-49.

Meese, J.L., Wigfield, A., & Eccles, J.S. (1990). Predictors of Math Anxiety and its Influence on Young Adolescents' Course Enrollment Intentions and Performance in Mathematics. *Journal of Educational Psychology* 82, 60-70.

Meleges, F.T., & Hamburg, D.A. (1976). Psychological Effects of Hormonal Changes in Women. *Human Sexuality in Four Perspectives.* (Beach, F.A., Ed.) Baltimore, MD: Johns Hopkins University Press. pp. 269-95.

Messant, P.K. (1976). Female Hormones and Behavior. *Exploring Sex Differences.* (Lloyd, B. & Archer, J.) London, England: Academic Press. pp. 183-211.

Michaud, E., & Wild, R. (1991). *Boost Your Brain Power.* Emmaus, PA: Rodale Press.

Milich, R., & Pelham, W.E. (1986). The Effects of Sugar Ingestion on the Classroom and Playgroup Behavior. *Journal of Consulting & Clinical Psychology* 54, 1-5.

Mills, R.C. (1987, April). Relationship Between School Motivational Climate, Teacher Attitudes, Student Mental Health, School Failure and Health Damaging Behavior. (Paper at Annual Conference of the American Educational Research Association). Washington, D.C.

Mills, L. & Rollman, G.B. (1980). Hemispheric Asymmetry for Auditory Perception of Temporal Order. *Neuropsychologia,* 18, 41-47.

Minsky, Marvin. (1986) *The Society of Mind.* Touchstone/Simon & Schuster, New York.

Mitler, Merrill, Carskadon, M., Czeisler, C., Dement, W., Dinges, D., & Graeber, R. Curtis. (1988). Catastrophes, Sleep and Public Policy: Consensus Report. *Association of Professional Sleep Societies, Committee on Catastrophes, Sleep, and Public Policy, Sleep* 2 (1), 100-109. New York, NY: Raven Press.

Miura, I.T. (1987). A Multivariate Study of School-Aged Children's Computer Interest and Use. (Ford, M.E., & Ford, D.H.) *Humans As Self-Constructing Living Systems: Putting the Framework to Work.* Hillsdale, NJ: Lawrence Erlbaum & Assoc. pp. 177-97.

Miyamoto, R.T., et al. (1989). Comparison of Sensory Aids in Deaf Children. *Annals of Otology, Rhinology and Larynology* 142 (Supplement) pp. 2-7.

Miyamoto, R.T., et al. (1991). Comparison of Speech Perception Abilities in Deaf Children With Hearing Aids or Cochlear Implants. *Otolaryngology and Head and Neck Surgery* 104.1, 42-6.

Miyamoto, R.T., et al. (1992). Longitudinal Evaluation of Communication Skills of Children With Single or Multichannel Cochlear Implants. *American Journal of Otology* 13.3, 215-22.

Moeller, A.J. & Reschke, C. (1993). A Second Look at Grading and Classroom Performance. *Modern Language Journal* 77, 163-169.

Moir, Anne, & Jessel, D. (1991). *Brainsex.* New York, NY: Dell.

Morgan, Brian, & Morgan, Roberta. (1987). *Brainfood.* Los Angeles, CA: Price, Stern, Sloan.

Morgan, M., & Granger. (1989). Electric and Magnetic Fields from 60 Hertz Electric Power: What Do We Know About Possible Health Risks? *Dept. of Engineering and Public Policy.* Pittsburg, PA: Carnegie Mellon University.

Morgane, P.J., et al. (1993). Prenatal Malnutrition and Development of the Brain. *Neuroscience and Biobehavioral Reviews* 17.1, 91-128.

Murphy, M. & Donovan, S. (1988). *The Physical and Psychological Effects of Meditation.* San Rafael, CA: Esalen Institute.

Murrain, P.G. (1983). Administrative Determinations Concerning Facilities Utilization and Instructional Grouping: An Analysis of the Relationship(s) Between Selected Thermal Environments and Preferences for Temperature, an Element of Learning Style. *Dissertation.* St. John's University.

Nadel, L. (1990). Varieties of Spatial Cognition. Psychobiological Considerations. *Annals of the New York Academy of Sciences* 608, 613-26.

Nadel, L., Wilmer, J. & Kurz, E. M. (1984). Cognitive Maps and Environmental Context. *Context and Learning.* (Balsam and Tomi. Eds.) Hillsdale, NJ: Lawrence Erlbaum & Assoc.

Nadler, J.V., et al. (1990). Kindling, Prenatal Exposure to Ethanol and Postnatal Development Selectively Alter Responses to Hippocampal Pyramidal Cells to NMDA. *Advances in Experimental Medicine and Biology* 268, 407-17.

Nakamura, K. (1993). A Theory of Cerebral Learning Regulated by the Reward System. *Biological Cybernetics* 68.6, 491-8.

Needleman, H.L., et al. (1979). Deficits in Psychologic and Classroom Performance of Children with Elevated Dentine Lead Levels. *New England Journal of Medicine* 300, 689-695.

Neisser, Ulric & Harsch, Nicole. (1992). Phantom Flashbulbs: False recollections of hearing the news about Challenger. [In *Affect and Accuracy in Recall: Studies of "flashbulb" memories*] Cambridge University (Winograd, E. & Neisser, U., Eds.)

Nelig, A., Daval, J.L., & Debry, G. (1992). Caffeine and the Central Nervous System: Mechanisms of Action, Biochemical, Metabolic and Poststimulant Effects. *Brain Research Reviews* 17.2, 139-70.

Neve, C.D., Hart, L., & Thomas, E. (1986, October). Huge Learning Jumps Show Potency of Brain-Based Instruction. *Phi Delta Kappan* pp. 143-8.

Nisbett, R.E. & Ross, L.D. (1980). *Human Inference: Strategies and Shortcomings of Social Judgment.* Englewood Cliffs, NJ: Prentice-Hall.

Nummela, R., & Rosengren, T. (1986). What's Happening in Student's Brain's May Redefine Teaching. *Educational Leadership* 43.8, 49-53.

Nummela, R., & Rosengren, T. The Brain's Routes and Maps: Vital Connections in Learning. *NAASP Bulletin 72:* 83-86.

Oakhill, J. (1988). Time of Day Affects Aspects of Memory. *Applied Cognitive Psychology* 2, 203-12.

Obler, L.K. & Fein, D. (1988). *The Exceptional Brain.* New York, NY: Guilford.

O'Keefe, J., & Nadel, L. (1978). *The Hippocampus as a Cognitive Map.* Oxford, England: Clarendon Press.

Olds, James. (1992). Mapping the Mind onto the Brain. *The Neurosciences: Paths of Discovery.* (Worden, F., Swazey, J., & Adelman, G., Eds.) Boston, MA: Birkhauser.

Olney, J. (1982). The Toxic Effects of Glutamate and Related Compounds in the Retina and the Brain. *Retina* 2.4, 341-59.

Orlock, Carol. (1993). *Inner Time.* New York, NY: Birch Lane Press, Carol Publishing.

Ornstein, Robert. (1984). *The Amazing Brain.* Boston, MA: Houghton-Mifflin.

Ornstein, Robert. (1986). *Multimind.* Boston, MA: Houghton-Mifflin.

Ornstein, Robert. (1991). *The Evolution of Consciousness.* New York, NY: Simon & Schuster.

Ornstein, Robert & Sobel, D. (1987). *The Healing Brain and How It Keeps Us Healthy.* New York, NY: Simon & Schuster.

Ornstein, Robert, & Thompson, Richard. (1986). *The Amazing Brain.* Boston, MA: Houghton-Mifflin.

Osberger, M.J., Maso, M., & Sam, L.K. (1993). Speech Intelligibility with Cochlear Implants, Tactile Aids or Hearing Aids. *Journal of Speech and Hearing Research* 36.1 186-203.

Ostrander, Sheila & Schroeder, Lynn. (1991). *SuperMemory.* New York, NY: Carroll & Graf Publishers.

Paris, S.G., et al. (1991). Developmental Perspective of Standardized Achievement Testing. *Educational Researcher* 20, 12-20.

Parker, Kenneth. (1982). Effects of subliminal symbiotic stimulation on academic performance: Further evidence on the adaptation-enhancing effects of oneness fantasies. Journal of Counseling Psychology, Vol. 29 (1).

Pearce, Joseph Chilton. (1992) *Evolution's End.* San Francisco. Harper Collins.

Pelton, Ross. (1989). *Mind Food & Smart Pills.* New York, NY: Bantam Doubleday.

Petty, R.E., & Cacioppo, J.T. (1984). Motivational Factors in Consumer Response Advertisement. (Green, Beatty, & Arkin, Eds.) *Human Motivation: Physiological, Behavioral and Social Approaches.* Boston, MA: Allyn & Bacon. pp. 418-454.

Pfurtscheller, G. & Berghold, A. (1989). Patterns of Cortical Activation During Planning of Voluntary Movement. *Electroencephalography and Clinical Neurophysiology* 72, 250-58.

Pintrich, P.R., & Garcia, T. (1991). Student Goal Orientation and Self-Regulation in the College Classroom. *Advances in Motivation and Achievement.* (Maeher & Pintrich, Eds.) Vol. 7. Greenwich, CT: JAI. pp. 371-402.

Pizzo, J. (1981). An Investigation of the Relationships Between Selected Acoustic Environments and Sound, an Element of Learning Style, as They Affect Sixth Grade Students' Reading Achievement and Attitudes. *Dissertation.* St. John's University.

Popper, K.R. (1972). *Objective Knowledge.* Oxford, England: Oxford University Press.

Prasad, A.N., & Prasad, C. (1991). Iron Deficiency; Non-Hematological Manifestations. *Progress in Food and Nutritional Science* 15.4, 255-83.

Pribram, K.H. and McGuiness, D. (1975). "Arousal, Activation and Effort in the Control of Attention." Psychological Review 82: 116-149.

Price, G. (1980). Which Learning Style Elements are Stable and Which End to Change? *Learning Styles Network Newsletter* 4.2, 38-40.

Prigogine, I., & Stengers, I. (1984). *Order Out of Chaos.* New York, NY: Bantam.

Prince, Francine & Harold. (1987). *Feed Your Kids Bright.* New York, NY: Simon and Schuster.

Prinz, R.J., Roberts, W.A., & Hantman, E. (1980). Sugar Consumption and Hyperactive Behavior in Children. *Journal of Consulting and Clinical Psychology.* 48, 760-69.

Pulvirenti, L. (1992). Neural Plasticity and Memory: Towards an Integrated View. *Functional Neurology* 7.6, 49-57.

Redfield, D.L. & Rousseau, E.W. (1981). A Meta-Analysis of Experimental Research on Teacher Questioning Behavior. *Review of Educational Research.* 51.2, 237-45.

Restak, R. (1988). *The Brain.* New York, NY: Warner Books.

Restak, R. (1988). *The Mind.* New York, NY: Bantam Books.

Restak, R. (1991). *The Brain Has a Mind of its Own.* New York, NY: Harmony Books, .

Restak, R. (1994). *Receptors.* New York, NY: Bantam Books.

Restak, R. (1994). *The Modular Brain.* Charles Scribner's Sons. New York, NY.

Rice, R. (1975). The Effects of Tactile-Kinesthetic Stimulation on the Subsequent Development of Premature Infants. (Unpublished doctoral dissertation) University of Texas at Austin. *Dissertation Abstracts* 35(5): 2148B.

Robin, D.E., & Shortridge, R.T., (1979). Lateralization of Tumors of the Nasal Cavity and Paranasal Sinuses and its Relation to Etiology. *Lancet* 8118, 695-696.

Roederer, Juan. (1981). Physical and Neuropsychological Foundations of Music. *Music, Mind and Brain.* (Clynes, Manfred, Ed.) New York, NY: Plenum Press.

Roland, P., et. al. (1990). Functional Anatomy of Storage, Recall and Recognition of a Visual Pattern in Man. *Neuroreport: An International Journal for the Rapid Communication of Research in Neuroscience* 1.1, 53-6.

Rose, Colin. (1986). *Accelerated Learning.* New York, NY: Dell Publishing.

Rose, F., Davey, M., & Attree, E. (1993). How Does Environmental Enrichment Aid Performance Following Cortical Injury in the Rat? *Neuroreport: An International Journal for the Rapid Communication of Research in Neuroscience* 4.2, 163-6.

Rose, Steven. (1992). *The Making of Memory.* New York, NY. Anchor/Doubleday.

Rosenberg, B.A., (1980). Mental Task Instruction and Optokinetic Nystagmus to the Left and Right. *Journal of Experimental Psychology: Human Perception and Performance,* 6, 459-472.

Rosenfield, I. (1988). *The Invention of Memory.* New York, NY: Basic Books.

Rosenfield, M., & Gilmartin, B. (1990). Effect of Target Proximity on the Open-Loop Accommodative Response. *Optometry and Vision Science* 67.2, 74-9.

Rosenfield, M., & Gilmartin, B., & Ciuffreda, K.J. (1991). Effect of Surround Propinquity on the Open-Loop Accommodative Response. *Investigative Ophthalmology and Visual Science* 32.1, 142-7.

Rosenthal, R. & Jacobsen, L. (1968). *Pygmalion in the Classroom.* New York, NY: Rinehart & Winston.

Rosenzweig, M.R., Love, W. & Bennett, E.L. (1968). Effects of a Few Hours a Day of Enriched Experience on Brain Chemistry and Brain Weights. *Physiology and Behavior* 3:819-825.

Rosenzweig, M.R., Krech, D., Bennett, E.L.,. & Diamond, M.C. (1962). Effects of Environmental Complexity and Training on Brain Chemistry and Anatomy. *Journal of Comparative Physiological Psychology* 55(4): 429-437.

Ross, E.D. (1984). Right Hemisphere's Role in Language, Affective Behavior and Emotion. *Trends in Neuroscience* 7, 342-345.

Rossi, A.S., & Rossi, P.E. (1980). Body Time and Social Time: Mood Patterns by Cycle Phase and Day of the Week. *The Psychobiology of Sex Differences and Sex Roles.* (Parsons, J.E., Ed.) London, England: Hemisphere. pp. 269-301.

Rossi, A.S., & Rossi, P.E. (1986). Hemispheric Dominance Switches.

Rossi, E.L. & Nimmons, D. (1991). The 20-Minute Break: Using the New Science of Ultradian Rhythms. Los Angeles: Tarcher.

Rovee-Collier, C., et al. (1993). Infants' Eyewitness Testimony: Effects of Postevent Information on a Prior Memory Representation. *Memory and Cognition* 21.2, 267-79.

Rozanski, Alan. (1988, April 21). Mental Stress and the Induction of Silent Ischmia in Patients with Coronary Artery Disease. *New England Journal of Medicine* Vol. 318, 16. pp.1005-12.

Rush, D., Stein, Z., & Susser, M. (1980). Prenatal Nutritional Supplementation. *Pediatrics* 65, 683-97.

Ryan, R.M., Connell, J.P., & Deci, E.L. (1985). A Motivational Analysis of Self-Determination and Self-Regulation in Education. *Research on Motivation in Education.* (Ames, C. & Ames, R., Eds.) Vol.2. Orlando, FL: Academic Press. pp. 13-51.

Ryan, R.M., & Stiller, J. (1991). The Social Contexts of Internalization: Parent and Teacher Influences on Autonomy, Motivation, and Learning. *Advances in Motivation and Achievement.* (Maeher, M.L., & Pintrich, R., Eds.) Vol. 7. Greenwich, CT: JAI. pp. 115-49.

Salthouse, T. (1986). A Cognitive Theory of Aging. Berlin, Germany: Springer-Verlag.

Samples, Bob. (1987). *Open Mind/Whole Mind.* Rolling Hills, CA: Jalmar Press.

Santostefano, S. (1986). Cognitive Controls, Metaphors and Contexts. An Approach to Cognition and Emotion. *Thought and Emotions: Developmental Perspectives.* (Bearson, D.J. & Zimilies, H., Eds.) Hillsdale, NJ: Erlbaum & Associates.

Scartelli. (1984). *Journal of Music Therapy* 21, 67-78.

Schacter, D.L. (1992). Understanding Implicit Memory. *American Psychologist* 47.4, 559-69.

Schatz, C.J. (1990). Impulse Activity and the Patterning of Connections During CNS Development. *Neuron* 5.6, 745-56.

Schatz, C.J. (1992, September) The Developing Brain. *Scientific American*. pp. 60-7.

Schatz, C.J. (1992, October). Dividing Up the Neocortex. *Science* 9, 237-8.

Scheibel, Arnold. (1994, November 1). You Can Continuously Improve Your Mind and Your Memory. *Bottom Line Personal* (15) 21, pgs..9-10.

Schiffler, Ludger. (1992). *Suggestopedic Methods and Applications*. Philadelphia, PA: Gordon & Breach.

Schneider, M.L., & Coe, C.L. (1993). Repeated Social Stress During Pregnancy Impairs Neuromotor Development of Primate Infant. *Journal of Developmental and Behavioral Pediatrics* 14.2, 81-7.

Schneider, W. (1993). Varieties of Working Memory As Seen in Biology and in Connectionist/Control Architectures. *Memory and Cognition* 21.2, 184-92.

Scholz, J. (1990). Cultural Expressions Affecting Patient Care. *Dimensions in Oncology Nursing* 4.1, 16-26.

Schunk, D.H. (1990). Goal Setting and Self-Efficacy During Self-Regulated Learning. *Educational Psychologist* 25.1, 71-86.

Schwartz, J & Tallal, P. (1980). Rate of Acoustic Change May Underlie Hemispheric Specialization for Speech Perception. *Science* 207, 1380-1381.

Segal, J., Chipman, S., & Glaser, R. (1985). *Thinking and Learning Skills.* Vol. I. Hillsdale, NJ: Lawrence Erlbaum & Associates.

Seligman, M.E.P, (1987) "Learned Helplessness in Children: A Longitudinal Study of Depression, Achievement and Explanatory Style" *Journal of Personality and Social Psychology* 51: 435-42.

Seligman, Martin. (1992). *Learned Optimism.* New York, NY: Pocket Books.

Senge, Peter. (1992). *The Fifth Discipline.* New York, NY: Random House.

Senge, P., Kleiner, A., Roberts, C., Ross, R. & Smith, B. (1994). *The Fifth Discipline Fieldbook.* New York, NY: Currency/Doubleday.

Shea, T.C. (1983). An Investigation of the Relationship Among Preferences for the Learning Style Element of Design, Selected Instructional Environments, and Reading Achievement of Ninth Grade Students to Improve Administrative Determinations Concerning Effective Educational Facilities. *Dissertation.*

Shields, P.J., & Rovee-Collier, C. (1992). Long-Term Memory for Context Specific Category Information at Six Months. *Child Development* 63.2, 245-59.

Shipman, V. & Shipman, F. (1983). Cognitive Styles: Some Conceptual, Methodological, and Applied Issues. (Gordon, E.W, Ed.) *Human Diversity and Pedagogy.* Westport, CT: Mediax.

Silver, E.A., & Marshall, S.P., (1990). Mathematical and Scientific Problem Solving: Findings, Issues, and Instructional Implications. [In *Dimensions of Thinking and Cognitive Instruction* (Jones, B.J., & Idol, L., Eds.) Hillsdale, NJ: Lawrence Erlbaum & Assoc.

Silverman, K., & Griffiths, R.R. (1992). Low-Dose Caffeine Discrimination and Self-Reported Mood Effects in Normal Volunteers. *Journal of the Experimental Analysis of Behavior* 57.1, 91-107.

Silverman, K., et. al. (1992). Withdrawal Syndrome After the Double-Blind Cessation of Caffeine Consumption. *New England Journal of Medicine* 327.16, 1109-14.

Silverman, L.H. A Comprehensive Report of Studies Using the Subliminal Psychodynamic Activation Method. *Psychological Research Bulletin.* Lund University 20.3, 22.

Silverstein, Alvin, & Silverstein, Virginia. (1986). *The World of the Brain.* New York, NY: Morrow Jr. Books.

Singer, J. (1977). *Ongoing Thought: The Normative Baseline for Alternative States of Consciousness.* (Zinberg, N.E.,Ed.) New York, NY: Free Press.

Singer, W. (1993). Synchronization of Cortical Activity and its Putative Role in Information Processing and Learning. *Annual Review of Physiology* 55, 349-74.

Sirevaag, A.M., & Greenough, W.T. (1991). Plasticity of GFAP-Immunoreactive Astrocyte Size and Number in Visual Cortex of Rats Reared in Complex Environments. *Brain Research* 540.1-2, 273-8.

Smith, A.P., Kendrick, A.M., & Maben. (1992). Effects of Caffeine on Performance and Mood in the Late Morning and After Lunch. *Neuropsychobiology* 26.4, 198-204.

Smith, B.D., Davidson, R.A., & Green, R.L. (1993). Effects of Caffeine and Gender on Physiology and Performance: Further Tests on a Biobehavioral Model. *Physiology and Behavior* 54.3, 415-22.

Soloveichik, Simon. (1979, May). Odd Way to Teach, But It Works. *Soviet Life Magazine.*

Sperry, R. (1968). Hemisphere Disconnection and Unity in Conscious Awareness. *American Psychologist* 23, 723-33.

Spielberger, C.D., Ed. (1972). *Anxiety: Current Trends in Theory and Research* Vol. 1 & 2. New York NY: Academic Press.

Squire, L. (1992). Memory and the Hippocampus: A Synthesis from Findings with Rats, Monkeys and Humans. *Psychological Review* 99.2, 195-231.

Sternberg, Robert. Beyond I.Q.: *A Triarchical Theory of Human Intelligence.*

Sternberg, R., & Kolligan, J. Jr., Eds. (1990). *Competence Considered.* New Haven, CT: Yale University Press.

Sternberg, Robert & Wagner, Richard. (1994). *Mind in Context.* New York, NY: Cambridge University Press.
    Stone, C.L. (1983). A Meta-Analysis of Advance Organizer Studies. *Journal of Experimental Education* 54, 194-9.

Strasburger, V.C. (1992). Children, Adolescents and Television. *Pediatrics in Review* 13.4, 144-51.

Sullivan, R.M., McGaugh, J.L. & Leon, M. (1991). Norepinephrine-Induced Plasticity and One-Trial Olfactory Learning in Neonatal Rats. *Brain Research* 60.2, 219-28.

Sutter, Alice. (1991, January). VDT Noise Causes Stress. *Issues in Human Resources.*

Swabb, D.F., Gooren, L.J. & Hofman, M.A. (1992). Gender and Sexual Orientation in Relation to Hypothalamic Structures. *Hormone Research* 38 Supplement 2, 51-61.

Swanson, James. (1980). Contact: Research Institute, HSC, Toronto, Ontario, Canada. M5G 1X8.

Sylwester, Robert. (1993, December - 1994, January). What the Biology of the Brain Tells Us About Learning. *Educational Leadership.* pp. 46-51.

Sylwester, R. & Cho, J. (1993 January). What Brain Research Says About Paying Attention. *Educational Leadership.* pp. 71-5.

Sylwester, Robert. (1994, October). How Emotions Affect Learning. *Educational Leadership* Volume 52, 2, 60-65.

Sylwester, R. (1995) *A Celebration of Neurons.* ASCD. Alexandria, VA.

Tallal, P. (1991). Hormonal Influences in Developmental Learning Disabilities. *Psychoneuroendocrinology* 16.1-3, 203-11.

Tallal, P., Ross, R., & Curtiss, S. (1989). Unexpected Sex-Ratios in Families of Language/Learning-Impaired Children. *Neuropsychologia* 27.7, 987-98.

Tallal, P., Miller, S., & Fitch, R.H. (1993). Neurobiological Basis for Speech: a Case for the Preeminence of Temporal Processing. *Annals of the New York Academy of Sciences* 682, 27-47.

Taylor, E. (1988). *Subliminal Learning.* Salt Lake City, UT: Just Another Reality Publishing.

Taylor, H.L., & Orlansky, J. (1993). The Effects of Wearing Protective Chemical Warfare Combat Clothing on Human Performance. *Aviation Space and Environmental Medicine* 64.2, A1-41.

Thal, D.J., & Tobias, S. (1992). Communicative Gestures in Children with Delayed Onset of Oral Expressive Vocabulary. *Journal of Speech and Hearing Research* 35.6, 1281-9.

Thal, D.J., & Tobias, S., & Morrison, D. (1991). Language and Gesture in Late Talkers: A 1-Year Follow-Up. *Journal of Speech and Hearing Research* 34.3, 604-12.

Thayer, R. (1986). Time of Day Affects Energy Levels. *Brain-Mind Bulletin* 12, 3D.

Thayer, R. (1989). *The Biopsychology of Mood and Arousal.* New York, NY: Oxford University Press.

Thompson, Richard. (1993) The Brain. W.H. Freeman and Company. New York.

Tonge, B.J. (1990). The Impact of Television on Children and Clinical Practice. *Australian and New Zealand Journal of Psychiatry* 24.4, 552-60.

Torrance, P. & Ball, O. (1978). Intensive Approach Alters Learning Styles in Gifted. *Journal of Creative Behavior* 12, 248-52.

Trautman, P. (1979). An Investigation of the Relationship Between Selected Instructional Techniques and Identified Cognitive Style. *Dissertation.* St. John's University.

Treisman, A. & Gormican, S. (1988). Feature Analysis in Early Vision: Evidence from Search Asymmetries. *Psychological Review* 95, 15-48.

Trevarthen, Colin. (1972). Brain Bisymmetry and the Role of the Corpus Callosum in Behavior and Conscious Experience. [In *Cerebral Interhemispheric Relations*] Bratislavia, Czechoslovakia: Publishing House of the Slovak Academy of Sciences.

Trevarthen, Colin. (1990). Growth and Education of the Hemispheres. *Brain Circuits and Functions of the Mind: Essays in Honor of Roger W. Sperry.* (Trevarthen, Colwyn, Ed.) New York, NY: Cambridge University Press.

Tryphonas, H., & Trites, R. (1979). Food Allergy in Children with Hyperactivity. *Annals of Allergy* 42, 22-7.

Uhl, F., et al. (1990). Cerebral Correlates of Imagining Colors, Faces and a Map - Negative Cortical DC Potentials. *Neuropsychologia* 28.1, 81-93.

Unger, Georges. (1976). Biochemistry of Intelligence. *Research Communications in Psychology, Psychiatry & Behavior* 1.5-6, 597-606.

Urban, M.J. (1992). Auditory Subliminal Stimulation: A Re-examination. *Perceptual and Motor Skills* 74.2, 515-41.

U.S. Department of Education. (1986). *What Works.* Washington, DC.

Van Dyke, D.C., & Fox, A.A. (1990). Fetal Drug Exposure and its Possible Implications for Learning in the Pre-School and School-Age Population. *Journal of Learning Disabilities* 23.3, 160-3.

Vasta, R., & Sarmiento, R.F. (1979). Liberal Grading Improves Evaluations But Not Performance. *Journal of Educational Psychology* 71, 207-211.

Verlee Williams, Linda. (1983). *Teaching for the Two-Sided Mind.* New York, NY: Simon & Schuster/Touchstone.

Vincent, J-D. (1990). *The Biology of Emotions.* Cambridge, MA: Basil Blackwell.

Virostko, J. (1983). An Analysis of the Relationships Among Academic Achievement in Mathematics and Reading, Assigned Instructional Schedules, and the Learning Style Time Preferences of Third, Fourth, Fifth and Sixth Grade Students. *Dissertation.* St. John's University.

Vygotsky, L.S. (1985). *Thought and Language.* Cambridge, MA: MIT Press.

Walker, Morton. (1991). *The Power of Color.* Avery Publishing, Garden City   Park, NY.

Wallace, C. S., et al. (1992). Increases in Dendritic Length in Occipital Cortex After 4 Days of Differential Housing in Weanling Rats. *Behavioral and Neural Biology* 58.1, 64-8.

Ward, C., & Jaley, Jan. (1993). *Learning to Learn.* New Zealand: A&H Print Consultants.

Webb, D., & Webb, T. (1990). *Accelerated Learning with Music.* Norcross, GA: Accelerated Learning Systems.

Webster, J.S., et al. (1992). A Scoring Method that is Sensitive to Right-Hemispheric Dysfunction. *Journal of Clinical and Experimental Neuropsychology* 14.2, 222-38.

Weil, M.O., & Murphy, J. (1982). Instructional Processes. *Encyclopedia of Educational Research.* (Mitzel, H.E., Ed.) New York, NY: The Free Press. pp. 892-893.

Weinstein, C.E., & R.E. Mayer. (1986). The Teaching of Learning Strategies. *Handbook of Research on Teaching.* (Wittrock, M.C. Ed.) 3rd edition. New York, NY: Macmillan Publishing. pp. 315-27.

Wenger, Win. (1992). *Beyond Teaching & Learning.* Singapore. Project Renaissance.

Wentzel, K.R. (1989). Adolescent Classroom Goals, Standards for Performance, and Academic Achievement: An Interactionist Perspective. *Journal of Educational Psychology* 81, 131-42.

Wheatley, Margaret. (1994) Leadership and the New Science. Berret-Koehler, San Francisco, CA.

White, R.T. (1980). An Investigation of the Relationship Between Selected Instructional Methods and Selected Elements of Emotional Learning Style Upon Student Achievement in Seventh-Grade Social Studies. *Unpublished Dissertation.* St John's University.

Whitleson, S. (1985). The Brain Connection: the Corpus Callosum is Larger in Left-Handers. *Science* 229, 665-8.

Whitleson, S. Sex Differences in the Neurology of Cognition: Social, Educational and Clinical Implications. *Le Fait Femenin.*

Wilson, D.A., Willnre, J., Kurz, E.M., & Nadel, L. (1986). Early Handling Increases Hippocampal Long-Term Potentiation in Young Rats. Behavioral Brain Research, 21, 223-227.

Willis, Christopher. (1993) *The Runaway Brain.* Basic Books, New York NY.

Wittrock, M.C., Ed. (1977). *The Human Brain.* Englewood Cliffs, NJ: Prentice-Hall.

Wlodkowski, R. (1985). *Enhancing Adult Motivation to Learn.* San Francisco, CA: Jossey-Bass Publishers.

Wolfe, Patricia & Sorgen, Marny. (1990). *Mind, Memory & Learning.* Fairfax, CA: Self-Published.

Wolman, B., Ed. (1973). *Handbook of General Psychology.* Englewood Cliffs, NJ: Prentice-Hall.

Wree, Andrea. (1989). Sexes Differ in Brain Degeneration. *Anatomy and Embryology* 160, 105-19.

Wurtman, J. *Managing Your Mind & Mood Through Food.* New York, NY: Harper/Collins, 1986.

Wurtman, J. (1988). *Dietary Phenylalanine and Brain Function.* Boston, MA: Birkhauser. p. 374.

Wurtman, R.J. (1990). Carbohydrate Craving. *Drugs* Supplement 39.3, 49-52.

Wurtman, R.J., & Ritter-Walker, E. (1988). *Dietary Phenylanine and Brain Function.* Boston: Birkhauser.

Wurtman, R.J., Ritter-Walker, E., & Wurtman, J.J. (1989, January). Carbohydrates and Depression. *Scientific American,* 68-75.

Wurtman, R.J., et al. (1989). Effect of Nutrient Intake on Premenstrual Depression. *American Journal of Obstretrics and Gynecology* 161.5, 1228-34.

Wynn, K. (1990). Children's Understanding of Counting. *Cognition* 36.2, 155-93.

Wynn, K. (1992, August). Addition and Subtraction by Human Infants. *Nature* 27, 749-50.

Yeap, L.L. (1989). Hemisphericity and Student Achievement. *International Journal of Neuroscience* 48, 225-32.

Zalewski, L.J., Sink, & Yachimowicz, D.J. (1992). Using Cerebral Dominance for Education Programs. *Journal of General Psychology* 119.1, 45-57.